High Performance Through
Business Process Management

Mathias Kirchmer

High Performance Through Business Process Management

Strategy Execution in a Digital World

Third Edition

Dr. Mathias Kirchmer
Managing Director and Co-CEO
BPM-D
475 Timberline Trail
West Chester, PA 19382
USA
mathias.kirchmer@bpm-d.com

Affiliated Faculty
Organizational Dynamics
School of Arts and Sciences
University of Pennsylvania
3440 Market Street, Suite 100
Philadelphia, PA 19104
USA

ISBN 978-3-319-51258-7   ISBN 978-3-319-51259-4   (eBook)
DOI 10.1007/978-3-319-51259-4

Library of Congress Control Number: 2017935007

© Springer International Publishing AG 2009, 2011, 2017
This work is subject to copyright. All rights are reserved by the Publisher, whether the whole or part of the material is concerned, specifically the rights of translation, reprinting, reuse of illustrations, recitation, broadcasting, reproduction on microfilms or in any other physical way, and transmission or information storage and retrieval, electronic adaptation, computer software, or by similar or dissimilar methodology now known or hereafter developed.
The use of general descriptive names, registered names, trademarks, service marks, etc. in this publication does not imply, even in the absence of a specific statement, that such names are exempt from the relevant protective laws and regulations and therefore free for general use.
The publisher, the authors and the editors are safe to assume that the advice and information in this book are believed to be true and accurate at the date of publication. Neither the publisher nor the authors or the editors give a warranty, express or implied, with respect to the material contained herein or for any errors or omissions that may have been made. The publisher remains neutral with regard to jurisdictional claims in published maps and institutional affiliations.

Printed on acid-free paper

This Springer imprint is published by Springer Nature
The registered company is Springer International Publishing AG
The registered company address is: Gewerbestrasse 11, 6330 Cham, Switzerland

Foreword to Third Edition

Business process management (BPM) is the cornerstone of running a business effectively and efficiently for growth, income, and customer satisfaction. Only when we understand how the business runs end to end can we optimize the processes and systems to enable customer satisfaction and innovation, both igniting growth for the organization.

BPM addresses the product or general solution cycle from inception to completion. It provides the framework to align all activities of an organization and focus them on the market. Recent studies show that there is a huge opportunity for improvement in the integration and alignment of an organization's departments. In other words, the main improvement potential is between the verticals of a company rather than inside the verticals. A great approach to BPM, such as value-driven BPM, unlocks significant value by providing insights into the areas of an organization most critical to work on.

Business process management explains the business information flows throughout the enterprise. It is like the spinal cord of the body. Yet very few businesses adopt this holistic management approach well enough to realize its full potential. Typical challenges are as follows: the organizational structure that drives the work in functions, not in processes, missing alignment of the BPM-Discipline to the overall business goals and the business strategy, insufficient consideration of the vision of the company or absence of vision, missing or wrong metrics to measure the BPM success, and non-supportive leadership behavior.

With the mobile and digital revolutions an urgent need has emerged for a business to understand and improve its processes. As we move to a society with 3X5" screen interaction for commerce, communication, and instant collaboration, a clear view of the simplicity of business processes is paramount for tomorrow's companies to succeed. Our customers have escalating expectations—they are more knowledgeable and demanding. Our competition is intense and very diverse. Technology, markets, societies, politics, and economies are changing at a rapid pace. BPM is the enterprise's mechanism to deal with this current and future change. Value-driven BPM shows you HOW TO DO THIS? It provides the techniques and methods to optimize your business and enable high performance in this environment of change.

One of the biggest challenges has been to translate and transfer the business strategy into operational execution. Value-driven BPM links business strategies to processes and supports fast execution at low risk. This is essential for a high-performance organization. Value-driven BPM enables the monitoring and control of the processes by providing a powerful outcome-driven governance model for the enterprise.

When improving a business, the key challenge is often to identify and define the business problem. Continuous improvement is the capability of an organization to do both: *Improve* processes and *manage* the resulting change successfully. If there is a maturity gap between an enterprise's ability to improve processes and its ability to manage change, the sustainability of any improvement made is questionable. A value-driven BPM-Discipline can be a great way to select the appropriate areas for a focused improvement, as well as provide the required change management methods to sustain those improvements.

Mathias' extensive knowledge and experience comes through every section of this elegantly written book. His discussion of a jazz band illustrates the key theme of a true BPM deployment. Business people need to behave the same way jazz musicians do: they constantly change roles and have the freedom to improvise while keeping the harmony and direction of the band. A great value-driven BPM deployment cannot only bring operational improvements but also innovation for business growth and market leadership.

It was a pleasure for me to write this foreword. I expect that this new edition of Mathias' book will enable great success for all readers. A high-performing strategy execution capability is key for the survival and growth of today's businesses in a rapidly changing world. I am counting on value-driven BPM to be a beacon of light in such an endeavor.

Embark on your adventure.

Vice President, Process Excellence & Innovation Verizon Basking Ridge, NJ USA December 2016	Sisir Padhy

Foreword to Second Edition

Economic volatility, increasing globalization, rising complexity, and growing interconnectivity have forced businesses to make major changes to their operations in recent years. This trend is likely to continue with change being the new normal and business agility being an absolute imperative to achieving high performance in the future.

At the same time, advances in technology such as cloud computing and service-oriented architectures are creating more flexible and configured application environments that can deliver tremendous value if used in the proper way.

Pragmatic business value-led approaches to business process management are increasingly seen as key enablers in creating transparency of the business environment, managing the complexity of a diverse technology portfolio, and creating the agile link between business strategy and its execution.

Mathias Kirchmer has an exceptional academic background in the understanding of process-centricity and the methods and tools to support it. By joining the Accenture BPM team, he has mastered the pragmatic business application of these approaches to drive real value. He has also had numerous opportunities to apply this process management know-how in a number of large global clients. It is this experience that has been added to the revised version of this book.

Managing Director – Business Process
Management Accenture
London, UK
July 2011

Peter H. Franz

Foreword

Globalization, speed, and fierce competition are some of the key attributes of the business environment that modern enterprises face each day. Companies must act fast and develop new business models in order to be successful. Innovation and agility are no longer optional, but a crucial capability for companies to survive in the long term.

Business processes are the critical link between strategy and execution. Business process management enables agility within an organization by turning ideas into action. It helps with the development and implementation of new business models across an organization. This book demonstrates how proven practices, like the use of the ARIS framework, can be successfully combined with new process management developments to achieve the best business value for an enterprise. SOA and Web 2.0 are important hot topics, just like process governance, people change management, reference models, emergent processes, and global inter-enterprise processes. This book combines real-life examples with the newest research findings.

For many years, Mathias Kirchmer worked at the company I founded: IDS Scheer, a leading provider of solutions for business process excellence. His practical experience with numerous companies and the findings of his innovation initiatives are reflected in this book.

Founder of IDS Scheer August-Wilhelm Scheer
Saarbruecken, Germany
May 2008

Preface

Business process management (BPM) has continued to evolve at pace over the last years, influenced through an all-present digitalization and the struggle of many organizations to deliver on their business strategies. BPM has become a value-driven management discipline for strategy execution. My business partner, Peter Franz, and I have reflected that trend in our last book about value-driven BPM and a series of white papers published by the company we co-founded, BPM-D. In this third edition of my "high-performance" book, I reflect these developments in the title and the content of the different chapters. The book is a complement to our various publications already available. It discusses specific aspects and usage scenarios of the BPM-Discipline, such as process innovation, internationalization, inter-enterprise processes, the management of emergence, or process management in mid-market companies—all in the context of our digital world.

This third edition includes significant updates in almost all chapters. I have, for example, revised or adjusted over 40 figures. New practice experience from interesting client projects and the latest academic findings have been included. The influence of digitalization is discussed in almost all chapters; I have also added a case study that makes many of the discussed topics more tangible.

However, I have kept the initial structure of the book. Each chapter can still be read either in the context of the entire book or as stand-alone article. At the end of each chapter, I highlight the major findings in a "Bottom Line" to give the reader the opportunity to get a quick overview of the content. Each bullet point of the Bottom Line refers to a section in the chapter.

I would like to thank the clients I have been fortunate enough to work with for the many inspiring discussions and initiatives. Special thanks to the people who endorsed this third edition: Sisir Padhi, VP Process Excellence & Innovation of Verizon; Ronan Loaec, CIO North America of Groupe Savencia; Jim Romine, President of the Research Institute for Fragrance Materials (RIFM); Deb Boykin, Director of Business Process Management at Pfizer; and Pat Paladina, Senior Strategy Manager at Telus. Big thanks also to my colleagues at BPM-D: my partner and Co-CEO, Peter Franz, who provided valuable input to basically every chapter,

Alexander Lotter, Erin Marranca, Matt Natale, Rakesh Gusain, Iain Watford, Dixit Jain, and all the other team members. Thank you to my students at the University of Pennsylvania, Widener University, Philadelphia University, and the Universidad de Chile. I am proud to work with such talented people. Thanks also to my academic colleagues. I want to specially mention here Yvonne Antonucci, Alan Barstow, Larry Starr, Natalie Nixon, and Sigifredo Laengle. Thanks to my friends Trevor Naidoo, with whom I have been working for many years, and Martin Braun, who is always ready to provide intelligent and pragmatic input. A big thank you to my long-year teacher, mentor, and friend, August-Wilhelm Scheer, for the many interesting and enlightening discussions.

Most special thanks to my wife Monica for her understanding and support!

West Chester, USA
December 2016

Mathias Kirchmer

Contents

1	**Business Process Management: What Is It and Why Do You Need It?**..	1
	1.1 What Is a Business Process?...........................	3
	1.2 What Is BPM?.......................................	8
	1.3 What Is Value-Driven BPM?...........................	10
	1.4 Value-Driven Business Process Management Applied to the Process Life Cycle...................................	14
	1.5 The Process Factory: A Core Component of Value-Driven BPM...	16
	1.6 Running the Process Factory...........................	18
	1.7 The Bottom Line.....................................	25
	References..	27
2	**Innovation: Enabled by Process Management**.................	29
	2.1 What Has Innovation to Do with Business Processes?........	30
	2.2 Some More Thoughts About Innovation and Processes.......	33
	2.3 What Is the Business Process of Innovation?...............	37
	2.4 How Does BPM Enable Innovation Systematically?.........	40
	2.5 Examples for Innovation Through Appropriate Process Management?..	43
	2.6 The Bottom Line.....................................	44
	References..	45
3	**Digital Technologies for Process Execution**....................	47
	3.1 The "Traditional" Path to Process Execution: Enterprise Resource Planning (ERP) and More......................	48
	3.2 New Flexibility in Process Execution: Service-Oriented Architecture (SOA)....................................	53
	3.3 The Next Generation of Process Execution: The Power of Digitalization..	57

4 People Enablement for Process Execution ... 67
- 4.1 What Is Business Process Change Management? ... 68
- 4.2 How Do You Provide Information and Communication? ... 73
- 4.3 How Do You Provide Process Training? ... 76
- 4.4 Digitizing the Process of Change Management ... 78
- 4.5 The Bottom Line ... 79
- References ... 80

5 Business Process Governance ... 81
- 5.1 Business Process Governance: What Is It and Why Do You Need It? ... 82
- 5.2 How Do You Establish Business Process Governance? ... 88
- 5.3 What Does It Mean to Sustain Process Governance? ... 95
- 5.4 The Bottom Line ... 99
- References ... 100

6 Reference Models: Accelerators and More ... 103
- 6.1 What Are Reference Models and Why Should You Use Them? ... 104
- 6.2 How to Obtain Reference Models and How to Evaluate Them? ... 108
- 6.3 How Do You Apply Reference Models? ... 114
- 6.4 The Bottom Line ... 116
- References ... 117

7 Managing Inter-enterprise Processes ... 119
- 7.1 Why Is the Management of Inter-enterprise Processes So Important? ... 120
- 7.2 What Is Special with the Design and Implementation of Inter-enterprise Processes? ... 124
- 7.3 What Is Special with the Execution and Controlling of Inter-enterprise Processes? ... 130
- 7.4 Bottom Line ... 132
- References ... 133

8 Managing Emergent Processes in a Digital World ... 135
- 8.1 What Are Emergent Processes and Why Are They Managed Differently? ... 137
- 8.2 How Can One Manage Emergent Processes? ... 139
- 8.3 What Tools Support the Management of Emergent Processes? ... 145
- 8.4 The Bottom Line ... 147
- References ... 148

(3.4 Bottom Line ... 63; References ... 64)

9	**Globalization Requires Value-Driven BPM**	151
	9.1 Some Personal Impressions	153
	9.2 Globalization Changes Processes	157
	9.3 How Can Value-Driven BPM Help?	163
	9.4 The Bottom Line	166
	References	167
10	**Small and Medium Enterprises Need Value-Driven BPM**	169
	10.1 Definition and Characteristics of SMEs	170
	10.2 Why Do Small and Medium Enterprises Need BPM?	173
	10.3 How Do SME Characteristics Impact Business Process Management?	175
	10.4 Examples for Mid-market Business Process Management Offerings	177
	10.5 What Does It All Mean for Value-Driven BPM in the Mid-market?	180
	10.6 The Bottom Line	181
	References	181
11	**What Has Jazz to Do with BPM?**	183
	11.1 Teamwork with Continuously Changing Roles	185
	11.2 Find the Right Degree of Freedom	187
	11.3 Use a Common Language	188
	11.4 Continuous Innovation	189
	11.5 Having Fun Is Important, Too	191
	11.6 The Bottom Line	193
	References	193
12	**The Discipline of Value-Driven BPM in Practice: A Case Example**	195
	12.1 Company and Situation Faced	195
	12.2 BPM Actions Taken	196
	12.3 Business Results Achieved	201
	12.4 Some Lessons Learned	203
	12.5 The Bottom Line	204
	References	205

Epilogue: Business Process Management Is Becoming Popular in the Digital World ... 207

Appraisals to the Previous Editions ... 211

Bibliography ... 213

Abbreviations

A/P	Accounts payable
A/R	Accounts receivable
ARIS	Architecture of integrated information systems
ASP	Application service provider
B2B	Business-to-business
BAM	Business activity monitoring
Blog	Web log
BPEL	Business process execution language
BPG	Business process governance
BPM	Business process management
BPMN	Business process modeling notation
BPM-D	Business process management discipline
BSC	Balanced scorecard
CBT	Computer-based training
CD	Compact disk
CIO	Chief information officer
CPI	Continuous process improvement
CPO	Chief process officer
CRM	Customer relationship management
DMN	Decision modeling notation
DoDAF	Department of Defense Architecture Framework
EA	Enterprise architecture
EAI	Enterprise application integration
e-business	Electronic business
EPC	Event-driven process chain
ERP	Enterprise resource planning
EDI	Electronic data interchange
EPI	Electronic process interchange
HR	Human resources
IT	Information technology
KM	Knowledge management

KPI	Key performance indicator
M&A	Merger and acquisition
m-Business	Mobile business
MDM	Master data management
MRP	Materials requirement planning
PC	Personal computer
PDA	Personal digital assistant
R&D	Research and development
RFID	Radio frequency identification
RM	Reference models
RPV	Resources, process, values
SaaS	Software as a service
SCM	Supply chain management
SCOR	Supply chain operations reference model
SME	Small and medium enterprise
SOA	Service-oriented architecture
SOX	Sarbanes-Oxley
SCOR	Supply chain operations reference model
vBPM	Value-driven business process management
VRM	Value reference model
VCE	Value chain evolution
WWW	World Wide Web

Chapter 1
Business Process Management: What Is It and Why Do You Need It?

Today, businesses need to master the volatile business environment with its opportunities and threats to ensure short-term success and long-term survival. The agile transformation, improvement, and adjustment of business processes are no longer an option but mandatory for sustainable business success. Therefore, business process management (BPM) has become an important topic for most organizations—even if they sometimes call it something different.

That has not always been the case—although the concept has been around for over 20 years as publications from the "founders of modern BPM," August-Wilhelm Scheer and Michael Hammer, show [1, 2]. When I first moved from Germany to the United States in 1995, I expected that every company would be discussing business processes and BPM. Familiar as I was with the process management books of Scheer [1] and Hammer [2], I was certain that BPM was a hot topic in US business, just as it was in Germany; however, this expectation proved to be an illusion.

I still remember the first time I met the executives on a vice president level of an American manufacturing company. I was so excited to discuss how BPM could help them overcome some of their challenges and enable higher performance. They looked at me and said: "Please implement this enterprise resource planning (ERP) software system. Don't waste our time or money with your ideas about this business process stuff. We don't know anything about BPM, we don't want it, and we don't need it. So, please discuss those topics with your academic friends, and let's get back to real business here." At that point, I realized it would not be easy to position the topic and value of BPM, and it would take quite a bit of "missionary" work before business process management would become mainstream.

This situation only began to change around the year 2000 with the advent of the e-business hype, followed about 10 years later by discussions regarding "digitalization." Suddenly, companies and departments within those companies were forced to talk to each other about how to best organize their collaboration. They had to discuss business processes. It soon became clear that the concept of "process" and BPM is extremely useful and that it can be applied across and within an

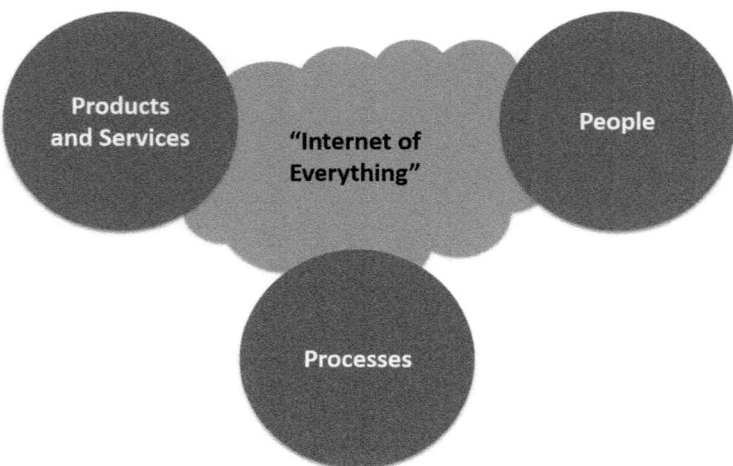

Fig. 1.1 Definition of digitalization

organization to drive high performance. In parallel, the development of methods, tools, and technologies facilitated process-oriented approaches, which also helped to push BPM to the forefront. In the last years, especially with the start of digitalization initiatives and the volatile business environment, BPM has really become an exciting and mainstream topic in the United States and around the world. Digitalization is about new business models through the integration of physical objects, especially products, people, and processes based on the "Internet of everything" as shown in Fig. 1.1 [3, 4]. Everything talks to everything. In order to get value from this, the interaction has to happen in the context of a business process, ultimately providing value for the client and improve the competitive position of a company. Businesses normally have a solid management discipline around products, a product management discipline, a solid approach to people management, e.g., through human resources or customer and supplier relationship management, as well as a discipline handling the Internet and related information technologies, for example, the information technology (IT) department. However, the management discipline focused on managing processes often still needs to be developed or moved to the next level. This leads to the current traction of the BPM topic and the interest in establishing and applying this new management discipline.

Many business people talk about business processes or the integration across functional units. However, when you participate in more in-depth discussions, it also becomes clear that many people are unsure what a business process is and what BPM really means. Consequently, many organizations face great challenges in finding the right approach to it. They find it challenging using process orientation and culture as a management paradigm that really moves an enterprise forward and produces value—quickly and at low risk. Therefore, this first chapter introduces the basic definitions of business process and BPM and presents value-driven BPM (vBPM), a specific outcome-driven approach to BPM. The discipline of vBPM focuses on business outcomes, not just methods and tools.

In the following chapters, we will discuss various important aspects of BPM and show how they relate to vBPM. The goal is to give an overview of important topics and trends in the field of BPM, focusing on the value they provide to organizations as in the pursuit of high performance through strategy execution in our digital world.

1.1 What Is a Business Process?

Let us examine a situation that occurred at a company in the machinery industry. I was engaged to support an enterprise-wide process improvement initiative. At the beginning of the project, the head of the sales department received an award from the company president because he was able to reduce the sales cycle time from 10 days to less than 5. That meant an incoming order was forwarded to the manufacturing department in less than a week. This seemed to be a great success. However, when we later discussed this "improvement" with the head of production, the downside became clear. He explained that he had to organize a team of people collecting the information that had formerly been included in the order sheets coming from the sales department. But because his team did not have close contact with the customer and the engineering department, this collection took a lot of time, often up to 2 weeks.

This means, if you look at the reorganization from a customer's point of view, it took up to a week longer to get the desired product. The customer does not care if sales activities are fast or slow, he only cares about the total time he has to wait for the product he ordered. The organizational change in the sales department had a negative impact on this customer experience. A truly business process-oriented approach would have led to real improvements.

The term "process" is used in many different ways. Hence it is important to define what we mean when we talk about a business process. A business process is a set of functions in a specific sequence that finally deliver value for an internal or external customer. Its start is also clearly defined by an external event [1, 2, 5–7]. This definition is visualized in Fig. 1.2.

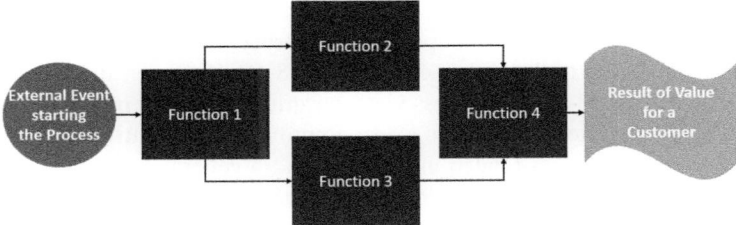

Fig. 1.2 Definition of the term "business process"

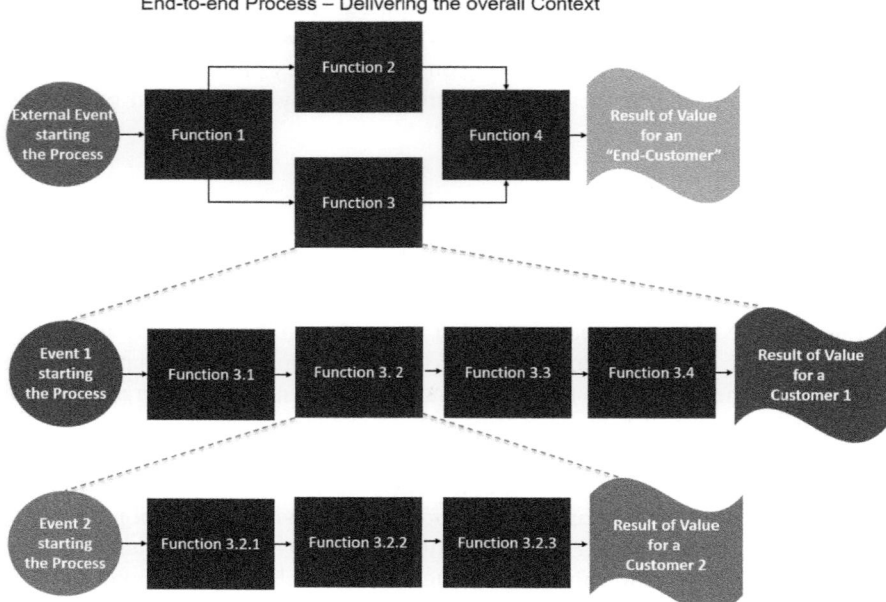

Fig. 1.3 Hierarchical decomposition of a business process

This means every process is a defined subset of functions of an overall organization. Each business process can be assigned a responsible person, who is generally called the "process owner." Because the process delivers a value for a customer, its performance can always be measured on the basis of this value: the impact on the customer and the related market. The result of a process-led management approach is a customer-focused organization because the customer basically sets the indicators and metrics by which the process performance is targeted, produced, and measured. A process-oriented organization can react quickly to the market since trends are reflected in changing customer requests and expectations that lead to appropriate process adjustments.

Every function in a process can again be interpreted as a process by itself, a so-called subprocess. This subprocess is triggered by the previous subprocess (or the overall starting event) and delivers a result of value for the next subprocess or the final customer and his processes, if it is the last subprocess of an end-to-end process. Such a hierarchical decomposition of a process allows increasingly higher detail of examination of the end-to-end process [8, 9]. However, the key is to start initiatives with an end-to-end process view, ensuring an overall process orientation to set the appropriate context for every improvement initiative focused on a subprocess. Every process-related initiative must, in general, have a positive or at least neutral impact on the overall result of value of the end-to-end process. The decomposition of a process is shown in Fig. 1.3.

1.1 What Is a Business Process?

I have often been asked how much one can detail the description of a business process so that it still adds value. This answer is relatively simple: A business process can be decomposed as long as the resulting functions still make sense from a business point of view. The subprocess "handle sales order" may be described in detail using functions, such as "enter sales order," "check availability of products," or "reserve products for customer order." This is the highest level of detail that still makes business sense. Decomposing, for example, the function "enter sales order" further, would result in activities such as "enter name," "enter address," etc. These functions are not relevant from a business point of view.

The aforementioned machinery company did not improve the entire business process from the point the customer order arrives, the start of the process, until the product is delivered to the client, hence the end of the process with result of value for the customer. They only improved one function of the end-to-end process, hence one subprocess: sales. This led to overall lower performance of the entire business process. Such situations can be avoided through "real" process orientation, working in an end-to-end business process context—even when only a subprocess is in project scope.

Consequence of such a process orientation is an integrated view of an organization. In a process-oriented organization, people always wonder how their work affects that of others—and at the end, of course, the customer. Employees do not just execute an activity, but they contribute to the overall process and its deliverables of value.

Many organizations struggle achieving such a company-wide process orientation. The main reason is that the process itself is not a tangible object. There are no processes lying in a warehouse. We first have to make them tangible. To achieve this, we must examine in more detail what the components of a process are and how they can be described so that the business process becomes tangible and can be managed.

I was at an analyst conference once that featured a presentation claiming that there was a shift from "electronic data interchange" (EDI) to "electronic process interchange" (EPI). Everyone was excited about the new idea—until someone asked a simple question: "What is in this case really exchanged between the companies?" What does "process interchange" mean? Let's look at a pragmatic but academically sound answer to that question and examine the components of a process.

August-Wilhelm Scheer has done leading work in that field. He has developed an approach to process architecting and modeling that has become widely used in practice [5, 6]. It provides a way to describe even complex processes easily without missing important aspects. This approach is called "architecture of integrated information systems" (ARIS). It explains that a business process can be described from five different points of view, answering all relevant questions regarding the process:

- Organization view: Who (people, departments, enterprises, etc.) is involved in the process?

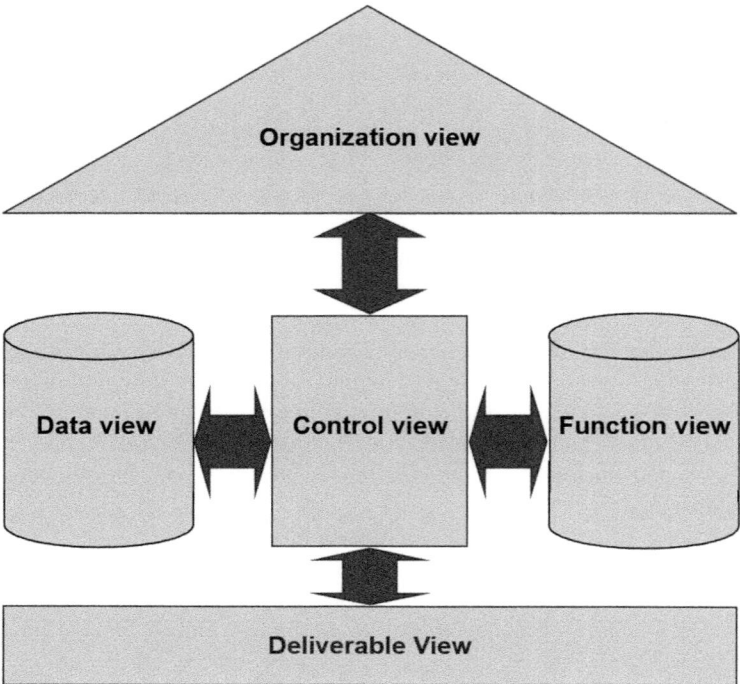

Fig. 1.4 Architecture of integrated information systems by August-Wilhelm Scheer (ARIS, Scheer [5, 6])

- Function view: What functions are carried out within the process?
- Data view: What data or information is needed or produced in the process?
- Deliverable view: What are the deliverables of the process, why do I need it?
- Control view: How do all those views fit together that means who is doing what by means of which data to produce which deliverables and in which logical sequence are the functions carried out?

The ARIS Architecture is shown in Fig. 1.4.

The terms "function" and "activity" are used synonymously in this book. The most important element of ARIS is the control view. It shows how two or more aspects of a process fit together, e.g., who is responsible or accountable for a specific function or which function uses certain data. The resulting integrated view of various aspects of a business process is the key for the successful management of those processes. ARIS helps make processes "tangible" by defining how to describe them. It enables the active management of business processes. This is the basis to make BPM a real management discipline.

Coming back to our question about EPI, we can now describe what could be exchanged between companies: There may be a shift of organizational units from

1.1 What Is a Business Process?

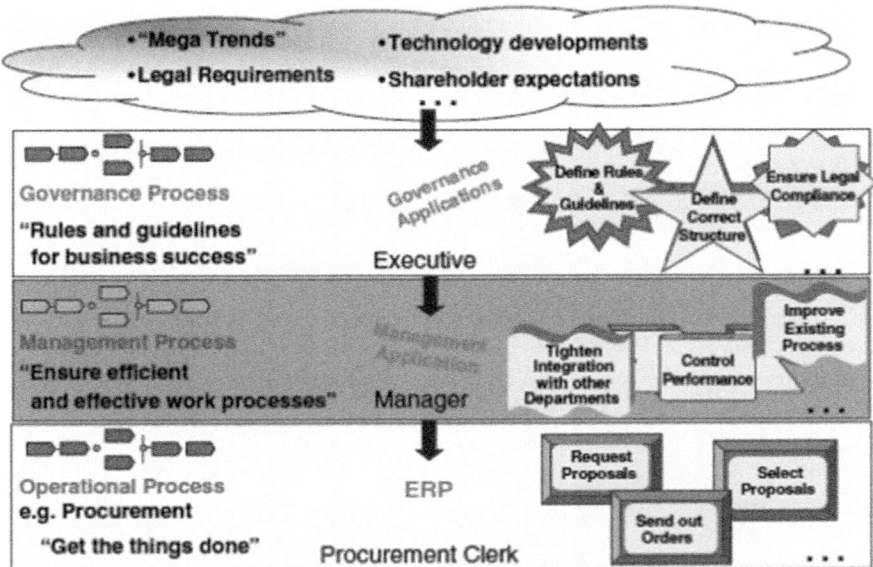

Fig. 1.5 Types of business processes

one organization to the other, a reallocation of functions or deliverables, an exchange of data, or a change of control activities between the companies.

If you can answer the "ARIS questions" shown above, then a business process is sufficiently described so that the description can be used to drive real business process improvement. The description of processes is mostly done through graphical methods [6], ensuring the greatest efficiency and effectiveness.

Examples of business processes include the "sales order-to-delivery" process from the point of time a customer order enters an enterprise until the required products are delivered, a "maintenance order-to-equipment ready" process from the point of time the maintenance order is created until the equipment is maintained and ready for use, or a "hire-to-retire" process from the point of time the hiring request is submitted until the employee is on board or even until this employee retires from the company.

These examples are operational processes. In other words, their focus is on the execution of the operational tasks of a company. Every organization also needs management processes, which ensure the appropriate performance of the operational processes. Examples include the evaluation of employee performance or the process of managing a company's information technology (IT) support. Last, but not least, organizations need governance processes to ensure compliance with overall rules and guidelines. Those processes enforce, for example, compliance with legal regulations, general "megatrends," technology developments, or shareholder expectations. The three types of process are illustrated in Fig. 1.5.

This classification reminds us to "manage" all business processes of an organization through an appropriate process management approach—not just operational ones. There are many additional ways of classifying processes, e.g., in core and supporting processes. Although these classifications may be relevant for certain BPM aspects, we will not discuss them further in this book to avoid getting sidetracked.

To identify the processes of an organization, one can either use existing industry best-practice models or apply a more analytic approach. Industry best-practice models, also called reference models, can be used in the context of a specific company [1, 10]. In other words, the models serve as a sort of checklist to determine the processes of an enterprise. The use of reference models will be discussed in more detail later.

Another possibility is the analytic identification of processes, using the relevant objects with which a process interacts, especially the products and services of an organization or the targeted markets and channels used [7, 11]. After identification of all market offerings, one defines which processes it takes to sell and deliver those offerings, as well as to manage and govern the organization.

Now we know what a business process is and how it can be described, but what does it mean to manage it? What is BPM all about?

1.2 What Is BPM?

The term BPM is used in many different ways in literature and practice. A BPM software vendor may tell you "Just buy our BPM process execution engine and you have process management in place." The Six Sigma expert may tell you just to use this process improvement approach and then you make BPM happen. And there are many more such definitions in use—all of them having one thing in common: they stress one small aspect of BPM. A broader useful definition that has been accepted more widely was published by Melenowsky [12] for The Gartner Group. According to this definition, BPM is a management discipline that provides governance for a process-oriented organization with the goal of agility and operational performance. Therefore, it uses methods, policies, metrics, management practices, and software tools to manage and continuously improve an organization's business processes. It also requires a general "process thinking," as explained at the beginning of this chapter. This definition is consistent with an even broader and academically well-researched way of explaining what BPM is. Swenson and von Rosing define BPM as follows: BPM is "a discipline involving any combination of modeling, automation, execution, control, measurement and optimization of business activity flows in applicable combinations to support enterprise goals, spanning organizational and system boundaries, and involving employees, customers and partners, within and beyond enterprise boundaries" [13].

Approaches like the "agile organization," the "real-time enterprise," or similar concepts are nothing other than the result of the consequent use of BPM. BPM is the

1.2 What Is BPM?

enabler of the next-generation enterprise because it links all activities of an organization to its clients and their fast-changing requirements.

This means BPM is more than just the improvement of a single process. It is more than a single project or program. Such a focused initiative may be the entry point into BPM, but no more. Also, BPM is not just about technology. There are more and more vendors in today's market that develop and deliver BPM software. However, that is also only a part of a holistic BPM approach, a building block for process-related infrastructure. The systematic management of business processes can lead to standardized processes, e.g., in various sales subsidiaries of an enterprise, the same process is carried out the same way. But BPM does not mean standardization for the sake of standardization. Organizations should standardize when it makes sense for process performance. It also does not necessarily mean the implementation of great changes in an organization. On the contrary, a BPM approach can be used to adjust the size of a change to fit the needs and capabilities of an enterprise—to meet its goals.

Naturally, the goal of BPM, used in a value-driven way, is to manage business processes in a way that enables the overall company to achieve high performance. Accenture, a major consulting company, has developed research that has shown high performance has several building blocks [14]:

- Market focus and position.
- Recognition of the value of market leadership but not pursuing scale for scale's sake.
- Distinctive capabilities.
- Company is different from their peers.
- High-performance anatomy.
- Number of mindsets that are observable in decisions and actions, including aspects like innovation and agility, performance measuring, strategic value of IT, people development, and leadership.

These building blocks can be influenced by an appropriate approach to BPM, as the definition above shows. According to Spanyi [8], BPM delivers three crucial outcomes for an organization:

- Clarity on strategic direction and related actions
- Alignment of an organization's resources
- Increased discipline in daily operations

It is important that BPM focuses on cross functional end-to-end processes, as defined before, which always touch internal or external customers with their "result of value" at the end of the process. It is not just the management and improvement of isolated subprocesses. Those need to be examined in the context of the overall end-to-end business process.

In general, the BPM approach is structured according to the life cycle of business processes [1, 2, 5–8, 10–12]. It can be organized as a process itself: the process of process management [15, 16]. One can roughly distinguish between the activities necessary to build a business process, the build-time activities, such as the design and implementation of a process, and the tasks focused on the ongoing process, the run-time activities. As run-time activities, we generally consider the execution of the process which can be manual through people, automated, or a mixture of both, as well as the monitoring and continuous management of business processes, including the measurement of key performance indicators (KPIs).

All phases of the business process life cycle can be supported by appropriate software systems. In most cases, this is a precondition for an efficient and effective BPM-Discipline. Because of the fact that the phases are integrated, the supporting software should also be integrated, thus entire software suites are required to reach the full potential of process management, not just single tools to support some of the activities. Those suites support all BPM-related activities, hence the entire "process of process management."

This shows the importance of digitalization for BPM: the process of process management itself becomes more and more digital, and the BPM-Discipline helps to digitalize other processes as required through an appropriate life cycle management.

What does it take to get most value out of such a BPM-Discipline? What do successful process management organizations do differently? The answers to those questions are provided by "value-driven business process management" (vBPM) what we are going to discuss now.

1.3 What Is Value-Driven BPM?

My colleague and partner, Peter Franz, and I have been working in the field of process management for over 20 years. We noticed that in the last years several many characteristics of process management have fundamentally changed. Over a long time the typical BPM practitioner was the person sitting in a room working on the development of new modeling methods, a repository, or an automation engine—without thinking too much about the business itself. This is very different now. BPM methods and tools have achieved a maturity level that allows process practitioners to focus on outcomes, the achievement of business value, using existing BPM components instead of inventing new ones.

It becomes clear that BPM is not just an improvement approach but an ongoing management discipline, as the aforementioned definitions also point out. For many processes it is not enough to fix them once and leave them then alone for several years. More and more processes require permanent adjustments to new and changing market conditions or even major transformations. Organizations need to establish the required process management capabilities to maintain and improve their competitive positioning. BPM has become a "C-Level" topic, seen more and more as an approach for fast- and low-risk strategy execution—leveraging the opportunities of our digital world. We came to the conclusion that the existing BPM definitions address those key trends but don't stress them enough. Therefore, we decided to define value-driven BPM (vBPM) in our book *Value-driven Business*

1.3 What Is Value-Driven BPM?

Process Management—The Value-Switch for Lasting Competitive Advantage as the management discipline that transfers strategy into people and technology-based execution—at pace with certainty [17]. This definition is consistent with definitions discussed before, but it stresses the importance of BPM as "discipline for strategy execution"—leveraging the opportunities of our digital world. This is what organizations need. According to research conducted by The Gartner Group [18], only 13 % of businesses meet their yearly strategic goals; hence 87% fail to do so. This is the big issue BPM can address and vBPM focuses on.

The definition of vBPM is short and with that practical to use—and it doesn't contain the term "process" which simplifies it and avoids misunderstandings when people don't exactly know what a business process is. Defining BPM as "strategy execution" stresses its importance for the overall performance of an organization. It brings people and opportunities of a digital world together and uses a cross functional end-to-end enterprise-wide approach to execute strategy systematically. vBPM stresses an outcome-oriented view on process management contrary to the traditional method and tool-focused approach to BPM. It emphasizes that its goals are directly linked to the strategy of an organization and are therefore company specific.

The overall characteristics of vBPM, especially the link of process to strategy, are discussed in detail in the previously introduced book about value-driven BPM. "High Performance through BPM" shows selected areas of operational application of vBPM in an organization.

vBPM applies the newest methods, approaches, tools, and related digital technologies and uses them in a consistent business-outcome-driven manner. vBPM targets the transfer of strategy into operational performance and value-driven execution. It selects the appropriate BPM components for a specific company context and points them to the right targets to achieve best value. This includes the systematic use of digitalization opportunities for the different business processes.

From a high-level point of view, vBPM delivers two things:

1. Enable smart decisions regarding strategy execution—in other words, high-quality decisions made in a timely manner.
2. Ensure the fast execution of the actions resulting from those decisions.

vBPM not only clarifies strategic direction, aligns resources, and increases discipline but also provides quality information in the required time frame to support the right decisions on all levels of an organization. vBPM delivers the infrastructure necessary to enable the fast execution of resulting tasks and if necessary their correction. This is essential for a successful organization in today's business environment of continuous change and agile improvement approaches.

vBPM is the critical link between an organization's strategy and operational execution activities. It makes the right things happen—quickly and at low risk. It delivers the necessary transparency over an organization. This transparency enables the mitigation of trade-offs between other key values an enterprise needs to realize using BPM. Empirical studies have shown that BPM enables through the

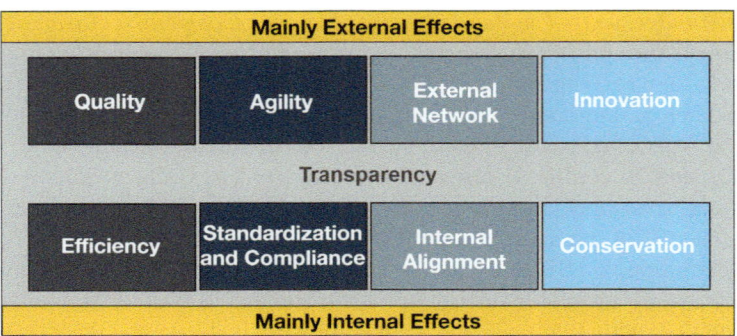

Fig. 1.6 The Value Framework—values vBPM delivers

appropriate transparency the realization of the following four "value pairs" [16, 17, 19] for an organization:

- Quality and efficiency
- Agility and standardization/compliance
- External integration into organizational networks and internal alignment
- Innovation and conservation of successful practices

The values vBPM enables are shown in Fig. 1.6. This "Value Framework" [16, 20] describes the impact vBPM delivers on a high level. The Value Framework is a good starting point of executive discussions about BPM. Top executives are in general not interested in detailed information about the "mechanics" behind process management but in outcomes that impact the performance of their organization [21]. In practice, these values are detailed in a specific enterprise context.

vBPM ensures the desired results at the lowest cost level, reflecting management's desire to get "more for less" [22]. Only the economically feasible approach is relevant in practice. Therefore, vBPM requires the use of available standards and best practices wherever possible, based on an approach known as "open BPM" [23]. This "open" approach leads to high flexibility around the process life cycle because it is easy to switch from one tool or approach to another one when this creates additional business benefits. This is achieved in a cost-efficient way by using available standards to support the BPM activities, instead of creating methods and tools from scratch on a case-by-case basis.

The BPM-Discipline (BPM-D) Framework, defining value-driven BPM, is shown in Fig. 1.7 [16, 17]. It positions the BPM-Discipline (BPM-D) as the owner of the process life cycle and with that the owner of the "process of process management" [20] which works on the life cycle. It has been developed on the basis of Scheer's ARIS Three Level Framework for Process Excellence [24, 25], a widely used general approach for business process life cycle management. Value-driven BPM underlines BPM's role as driver of strategy execution and reflected business outcomes, which determines the entire process of process management for vBPM.

1.3 What Is Value-Driven BPM?

Fig. 1.7 BPM-Discipline Framework—defining value-driven BPM (vBPM)

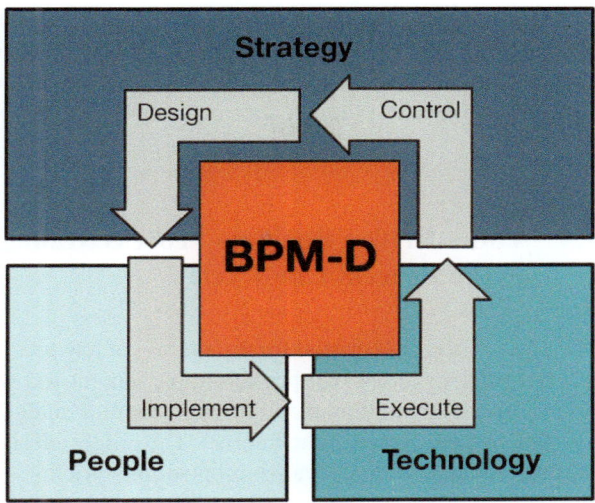

The patent-pending BPM-D Framework with its subcomponents such as the Value Framework has been developed and successfully applied by the company Peter Franz, and I founded and named after it: BPM-D [26]. There are hundreds of reference models and job aids behind this top-level structure to support the setup and application of a value-driven BPM-Discipline. The BPM-D Framework is not just academically sound but has been proven in practice in many organizations around the world. The BPM-D reference model aspect is discussed a further in Chap. 6. We use the overall framework in this book to position different aspects of value-driven BPM.

The discipline of value-driven BPM links the overall business strategy to processes by identifying the main strategic value drivers and the impact various processes have on these value drivers [27]. The result is the segmentation of processes into high-impact and commodity processes. A company only competes with about 15–20% of its processes. These are the high-impact processes. Those processes require detailed optimization and best process innovation leveraging the opportunities digitalization provides. Commodity processes need to function on industry average; hence the key improvement approach is the alignment with industry or functional standards.

High-impact processes and commodity processes are designed and implemented using an appropriate combination of people and technology to have the desired impact of the strategic value drivers. The execution is guided through appropriate performance indicators related to the value drivers. The KPIs are measured to control the performance of a process and trigger a revision and adjustment of the design or a complete new process transformation when required. In order to keep processes on track and launch the appropriate improvements, the right process governance needs to be in place. This is discussed in Chap. 5.

Let's now see how the discipline of value-driven BPM addresses the different phases of the process life cycle. This is important because it helps understand the different activities of the process of process management of vBPM and their impact on strategy execution though appropriate process improvement initiatives.

1.4 Value-Driven Business Process Management Applied to the Process Life Cycle

The process design is crucial for the success of any process-related initiative since it determines the success of a process improvement and with that of the discipline of vBPM. It identifies digitalization opportunities integrating physical objects and people using the power of the Internet. The process design reflects a new or adjusted business model with its value proposition, pricing, and target customers. The approach of a "process factory" is used to develop the process design as efficiently and effectively as possible. This "process factory" concept is discussed in Sect. 1.4. Such a process factory is necessary to ensure a quick move from strategy to the implementation and execution phase while still having sufficient time to focus on process innovations and important strategic improvements of high-impact processes. The process design is produced using techniques like simulation, activity-based costing, or creativity methods in combination with available process modeling methods. In the design phase, business processes must be specified in detailed and consistent descriptions that include all information necessary to drive the process implementation and execution. In other words, the created knowledge assets must include all relevant information about the processes to be executed successfully to realize the strategy of the organization. The result is a process blueprint consisting of business process models that form the enterprise's process knowledge assets and drive the following phases of the business process life cycle.

On the basis of these process models, all physical and information-processing activities are implemented within an enterprise and across organizational boundaries. This can happen in different pilot projects that allow the adjustment of the design based on the findings during the pilot. The results are intra- and inter-enterprise processes, ready for execution. The implementation can be done based on digital technology to support the following automated execution or manual execution through people. Generally, it is a mixture of both. Some parts of a process may even need to be executed in teams, e.g., brainstorming activities in a research department [28]. This implementation phase includes digitalization activities with the technology and software configuration or development, as well as the people change management, consisting of information, communication, and training [29]. Here you prepare to realize the value from your process design, to make strategy happen. For the implementation phase, it is important to have the process blueprint in a format that enables a time-efficient implementation, so that the execution and with that the value creation can start quickly. This is achieved through the aforementioned process factory. During the implementation phase of the process life cycle, the organization goes through a transformation process to achieve the business strategy reflected in appropriate value drivers and resulting in the targeted competitive advantage.

During the process execution phase, processes are executed on the basis of the implemented technology and people resources. The use of different digital technologies will be discussed in Chap. 3. The software systems can be standard application packages, such as enterprise resource planning (ERP), supply chain management (SCM), or customer relationship management (CRM) systems that primarily support "common-practice" processes. Alternatively, processes can be executed on the basis of more flexible application and organization approaches, such as next-generation business process automation systems based on a service-oriented architecture (SOA) or the use of social media, cloud solutions, cyber-physical systems, omni-channel approaches, mass customization, or other concepts enabled through digital technologies [3]. These aspects will be described further in Chap. 3. The people-based execution may be supported by continuous learning and talent management initiatives, e.g., through computer-based training approaches or regular face-to-face training initiatives. These people aspects of the process execution will be discussed in Chap. 4. The execution delivers on a day-to-day basis on the business strategy with its targeted outcomes.

The executed processes, also referred to as process instances, are measured and controlled in the process control phase of the life cycle. If there are negative differences observed between the actual values and the planned values of KPIs, appropriate corrective actions must be taken. Either a "continuous process improvement" (CPI) is initiated through the process design phase which means the design is improved to meet the defined goals and passed on to implementation and then to execution of the process or the situation is resolved on a strategic level if the business environment has changed significantly. This means new value drivers and related KPIs are defined. This control phase of the process life cycle management overlaps with the execution phase. In this control phase, process performance improvement methodologies, such as Six Sigma [9, 30], Lean, or combinations of such approaches [31], can be applied—if suitable in the specific context [16, 32]. This phase delivers necessary information about the execution to ensure smart decisions, based on process KPIs [33]. It enables a continuous focus on value and helps to drive the success of the strategy execution. Also newer tool-based approaches like "process mining" to discover instances of as-is processes can be useful in this control phase [34].

An organization can establish a BPM-Discipline and begin a BPM improvement initiative at any of the phases of the process life cycle. Of course, the typical entry point is the process segmentation and identification of high-impact processes, followed by the analysis and design of processes. However, there are more and more organizations starting with the monitoring and controlling of existing processes, which leads to revised process design and supports process segmentation. The process-oriented implementation of digital solutions can also serve as a starting point. The decision about the starting point for vBPM initiatives should be based on the company-specific situation: the current needs and budgeted initiatives, the political situation, the staffing situation, and similar aspects.

In many cases, companies select a two-step approach and begin with a pilot initiative focused on one or two processes. On the basis of the results, the entire value-driven BPM-Discipline can be rolled out. Whatever starting point is chosen, it is important to envision the entire value-driven BPM-Discipline [20] as guideline for the process management journey, so that every initiative becomes a building block of a successful enterprise-wide management discipline for strategy execution in a digital world.

Digitalization is also very relevant for BPM itself, as explained before. The data volume to be handled and vBPM's specific demand for speed and high-quality information make this aspect even more important. The necessary integration and consistency of process-related knowledge, especially the business process models, cannot be achieved manually.

A core component of value-driven BPM as a management discipline is the aforementioned process factory. It is used to support the design phase of the process life cycle and helps to organize the link between design, implementation, and execution. The process factory creates and manages most of the "master data" in form of information models required by a value-driven BPM-Discipline. Therefore it is worth to have a more detailed look at this topic. Let's discuss this core component of vBPM.

1.5 The Process Factory: A Core Component of Value-Driven BPM

vBPM moves strategy into operational execution through people and technology, fast and at low risk. The success of vBPM greatly depends on the efficient and value-driven design of processes. This requires an effective and fast management of process knowledge in the form of information models, especially business process models.

Many organizations still rely in the design phase on traditional manual approaches: walls full of "post-it" notes, lengthy discussions, and at the end tons of informal or semiformal write-ups describing future processes. The implementation, execution, and control of this process design are time-consuming since it takes a while to read all information. In addition there is a high risk of inconsistencies between the design intent and the implemented process because of missing or unclear process descriptions. The next initiative involving the same processes starts again from scratch since the created process knowledge is not in an easily reusable format.

The process factory uses the opportunities of our digital world to come to a faster and more effective process design that creates reusable process assets so that each process-related initiative benefits from the previous one. Process models, for

1.5 The Process Factory: A Core Component of Value-Driven BPM

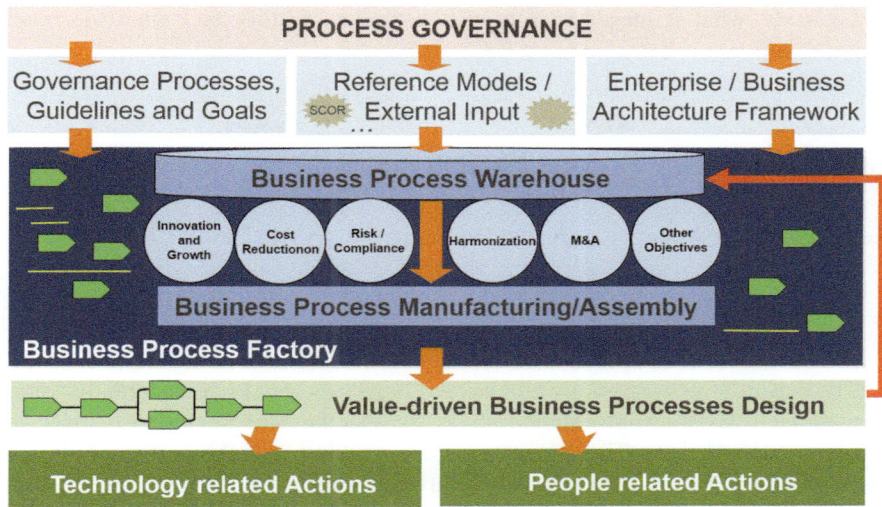

Fig. 1.8 The business process factory

example, can first be used to teach people how the process works, and then that can be the basis for improvement projects and later on for the requirements definition of required software and testing of the developed solutions. Using formal information models also leads to a consistent fast to understand process design.

A digital process factory eliminates the rework and double work of traditional approaches. It helps digitize the process of process management—or at least important components of it. I like using the term "factory" in this context to stress the move toward a more systematic and technology supported design approach.

The approach of the process factory is shown in Fig. 1.8. It is based on the storage of the information models related to a business process in a "process warehouse," the process repository, and the use of those models or parts of them to "manufacture" and "assemble" new information models, describing new or modified processes. Hence, the process warehouse contains the "process components," the raw material that is transformed in the manufacturing and assembly unit. New information models are stored again in the warehouse so that they can be reused as input for future assembling and manufacturing activities.

Business process-related information models need to be developed and modified frequently to support agility and, with that, a continuous innovation or improvement of the described processes. The process factory is the environment that enables productivity and performance of the management of information models related to business processes [35]. These models include process models but also other information models, like organization models, data models, value trees, application architecture models, or decision models. The process factory is the critical link between the strategic decision and the fast operative realization and execution of related actions.

Let's see what it means to run such a process factory and what the main activities are.

1.6 Running the Process Factory

Key activities of the process "manufacturing and assembly" are the following:

- Design of new or improved processes
- Analysis of processes
- Support of the implementation, execution, and control of processes

The design of new or improved business processes should, in general, not start from scratch. Existing information about the specific process has to be used to accelerate the design. The process factory enables a highly efficient design approach. Best practices, for example, are available in the form of reference models which will be discussed in Chap. 6. These reference models can be automatically loaded into the process warehouse. They are delivered, e.g., by industry organizations, consulting, or software companies [7]. More and more companies also produce their own internal reference models that they use to transport learning from one unit of the organization to others. The assembly of process uses the content of the warehouse to produce the desired process design efficiently. Missing components are manufactured on demand and added to the warehouse—ready for further use. Hence, we have a design approach the combines the systematic use of existing knowledge and experience with the introduction of new innovative process components.

Objectives derived from the enterprise strategy guide the production of processes and make sure that the end product has the appropriate characteristics. These strategic business objectives can be compared to the quality guidelines of a real factory. Examples for such objectives are innovation and growth, cost reduction, risk and compliance management, harmonization and standardization of processes, or the post-merger and acquisition (M&A) integration. Every manufacturing and assembly step has to maintain or improve the performance level of a process in regard to those objectives. The final products have to meet the quality requirements, hence enable the achievement of the defined KPIs.

For straight forward "commodity processes," this step is in most cases relatively simple, since existing process reference models reflecting common practices may be used with only minor modifications. This leads to significant efficiency gains compared to a traditional process design approach.

The more important a process is to achieve competitive advantage, the higher its impact on the company strategy is and the more sophisticated is the process manufacturing and assembling. You may apply process improvement techniques like Six Sigma to come up with reliable process designs or combine the modeling with creative techniques to come up with innovative ideas—using the process factory as effective infrastructure. "Design thinking" is in this context becoming

1.6 Running the Process Factory

more and more important: you examine the processes from a client's point of view, transfer findings from completely different fields, define processes on different maturity levels to enable a rapid prototyping, and develop the story around the process to drive the design activities forward [36]. This is especially important for the design of client facing processes in form of "customer journey mapping" initiatives. The process factory delivers the transparency and flexibility necessary to apply such creative approaches fast and effectively.

The enterprise-specific models must be consistent and reflect the desired future business processes, as far as they can be predefined. Emergent processes, for example, may only be partly defined at the beginning as explained in Chap. 8. Each mistake in the process design can lead to costly consequences in the following implementation and execution phase. Therefore, the simulation of processes using the developed information models in the process factory, the development and comparison of various scenarios, the implementation of small pilots, and a thorough analysis of the designed processes are extremely important and a core component of the process factory.

In a future "visionary scenario," those information models may be used to create "virtual worlds," which are digital environments that allow the user to experience the process before execution, to "live" the process. They offer the opportunity to experience a process change idea before it is rolled out in an organization. The result allows the user to make better educated decisions on process transformations and create the basis for upcoming change management activities [37]. The process factory becomes a high-performance "video game" using the power and opportunities of our digital world.

Here are some general guidelines for the process design [38, 39] that can be applied in the process manufacturing and assembly—as supporting "operating procedures":

- Work in an end-to-end process context—think of impacts outside subprocesses in scope.
- Simple is better.
- Identify the appropriate quality of process outcomes; not everything needs to be perfect.
- Parallelize activities as far as possible, even if you have to reorder working steps.
- Move work to clients without upsetting them.
- Take over process work from clients and position this as new additional service.
- Identify the right degree of centralization of activities.
- Work should be done by whomever is best suited for it, at the most appropriate time, at the best location.
- Subsume information processing work into the real work that produces that information.
- Place the decision point in the process where the work is performed and build control into the process; be proactive.
- Create efficiency through early decisions and agility through late decisions.
- Integrate and compress tasks.

- Capture information once, at the source.
- Use the best available data.
- Eliminate non-value-adding activities.
- Perform activities only when value exceeds cost.
- Align different process components organization, function, data, deliverables, and control.
- Identify the right automation level: Automate only where it really provides additional benefits.
- Use as few people as possible to execute a process.

It has also to be mentioned that the definition of environmental goals for business processes will have an increasing importance due to new and expected legal regulations. Results are so-called green processes, such as the "green supply chain." Jim Sinur, a well-known BPM expert, even talks about "green BPM" [40].

The analysis of information models, especially process models, is also conducted through process production. The business content of the models plays the key role. In most cases, the semantic content cannot be analyzed sufficiently in an automated way. Manual manufacturing and assembly activities are required—supported through reports and other tools of the process factory. The analysis can be guided through the ARIS Architecture presented at the beginning of this chapter. Improvement potentials of processes are discovered by applying the structure provided by ARIS to the process models. This leads to a straightforward rapid improvement approach as we discuss it in the case study in Chap. 12. The following questions are typically asked during such an analysis:

- Organization:
  - Are there too many organizational units involved in the process, causing it to become inefficient?
  - Are the right organizational units involved?
  - Should additional organizational units be involved (e.g., external units such as customers, suppliers, etc.)?
  - Which external organizational units (e.g., from customers) should be included?
  - Are the responsibilities and accountabilities of the different organizational units clearly defined and understood?
  - Are appropriate roles defined?
  - Do we have the right degree of centralization and decentralization? Is there an opportunity for efficiency gains through a "shared services" organization?

- Functions:
  - Are some of the functions redundant?
  - Is the execution quality of the functions sufficient?
  - Are the functions executed efficiently?
  - Do we need additional functions (e.g., to ensure quality or minimize risk)?
  - Have we minimized the number of variations of the same function?

1.6 Running the Process Factory

- Are there any opportunities for "mass customization," e.g., individualize products through the appropriate process?
- Is there an opportunity to add self-leaning components to the process?
- Can we outsource parts of the process?

- Data:
  - Is the data quality sufficient (master data, customer order data, etc.)?
  - Is there redundant data (leading to inconsistencies)?
  - Do we need to adjust the data structure to include relevant information?
  - Do we need additional data, e.g., from external sources?
  - Do we handle data that is not really needed in the processes?

- Deliverables:
  - Is the quality sufficient?
  - Do we really need all deliverables?
  - Can we reduce the complexity without negative impact on the value for clients?
  - Do we have to add deliverables?
  - Shall we individualize deliverables?
  - Shall we replace physical products through services or information?
  - Do we have to add components to our products (e.g., services to our physical products)?

- Control:
  - Can we execute sequential functions parallel?
  - Does the process logic make sense or should we change the sequence of functions?
  - Do we need to centralize or decentralize activities, e.g., establish shared service centers?
  - Should we change organizational responsibilities or accountabilities?
  - Should we change data responsibilities or accountabilities?
  - Is the final responsibility for the deliverables defined?

- Technology
  - Is the degree of IT support appropriate?
  - Is the functionality sufficient?
  - Is the integration sufficient?
  - Does technology support deliver the necessary flexibility?
  - Is the total cost of ownership of technology support acceptable?
  - Can we leverage the Internet to increase performance? Is the "Internet of things" relevant for the specific process?
  - Can we transfer any of the physical objects involved in the process into information to facilitate a more efficient and effective handling?
  - How do we best integrate physical objects, people, and processes using the Internet of things?

– Is there an opportunity to leverage social media?
– Shall we leverage cloud-based applications?

Those questions can be answered based on the semantic content of the process and related information models. In most cases, no sophisticated quantitative approaches or complex algorithms are required. Only if further information is necessary, simple simulation and animation of processes using the models in the process factory can help to identify bottlenecks or other improvement potentials.

Whether or not a process design should be changed due to revealed improvement potentials depends on the process goals. For example, if a process has pure quality goals, it may not be worthwhile to invest in eliminating weak points solely related to cycle times.

A detailed analysis of an as-is process may not be necessary if a fundamental transformation is planned that will not take detailed aspects of existing processes into account or if you just intend to introduce an industry standard, e.g., using reference models as a starting point. You can then just focus on the to-be design in your process production.

A higher level process analysis begins with the analysis of relevant products. The term "product" is used here in a wide sense, including physical products, services, information products, rights, etc. [11]. The simplification, change, elimination, or addition of products has significant impact on the definition and design of end-to-end processes. For example, a company producing engineered-to-order locomotives may need just one core process starting with the complex sales and engineering of the locomotive, ending with the delivery of this locomotive. If this company also sells its standardized motors that are produced, but not engineered to order, a second core process is necessary. Then the company may decide to also sell its engineering capabilities as a service on the market, leading to another set of processes. Consequently, the structure of the products drives the process design and is, therefore, the entry point to high-impact process improvement. It is of highest importance to reduce the complexity of products as much as possible and keep just that degree of complexity customers are really willing to pay for [41].

Product analysis is fairly straightforward in the field of physical products, such as a car. These products are generally already documented in a structured way, in the form of bills of material. This is an excellent basis for a change of product structure to support simplification or create synergies with other products. In service industries, for example, banks, the "products" are usually not as well described. For this reason, it is often more challenging to change and simplify them. Therefore, a specific approach, called "service engineering," was developed, targeting a more systematic analysis and design of service products [42].

The definition and simplification but also innovation of products can be enabled through special information models, the "product models." These models describe key aspects of an offering in a semiformal way [11]. The product models are also stored in the process warehouse and modified in the process manufacturing and assembly leveraging the efficiency tools available in the factory. Product models are part of the process-related information.

1.6 Running the Process Factory

The results of the manufacturing and assembly in the process factory are the to-be models showing the blueprint of the organization. Those information models are used to drive appropriate technology and people-based implementation actions and guide execution, as well as control activities. Hence, indirectly the process factory influences the entire life cycle of the process. A good business process design drives technology and people into the right direction, resulting in strategy execution and high performance for the organization as a whole. Digitalization of many of the implementation, execution, and control activities allows the reuse of the digital process design information. The model hierarchy can be loaded into digital requirements definition tools, testing tools, or process monitoring environments to structure and guide the related implementation actions in a process-oriented way, another step toward the systematic strategy execution.

The process warehouse is the basis of a well-performing process factory. Therefore, "warehouse management" is very important. Many businesses make the mistake by trying to get as much information into the process warehouse as possible. They don't want to lose time or spend money in thinking about structure and organization of the warehouse. This is a big mistake that costs a lot of money later on because the factory does not work properly: process components cannot be found, they are not structured for reuse or use in a specific context, they are not in a format that people can easily understand, etc. It is absolutely key to plan the warehouse thoroughly.

Let's discuss a value-driven approach to the process warehouse, focusing on the desired outcomes of the process factory. This process warehouse approach consists of five steps [17]:

1. Identify the usage scenarios: How do you want to get value out of your process warehouse? What do you use the models for, e.g., improvement, training, collaboration with partners, or software development?
2. Define the content to be captured to support the usage scenarios: What do you need to store in the warehouse, such as process models, organizational models, technology models, decision models, or other information models?
3. Define the format for the different models required to capture the content: Which modeling approach do you use, for example, value chain diagrams (VCD), event-driven process chains (EPC), business process modeling notation (BPMN), decision modeling notation (DMN), and entity relationship diagrams (ERM), to name just a few? What level of detail is required? Which overall "architecture" do you use so that you can easily find and access the models?
4. Design the process warehouse governance: Who plans, fills, accesses, etc. the warehouse?
5. Select the necessary tool support: What technology tools are necessary to manage the warehouse? Does this technology support the process manufacturing and assembly appropriately? Is it "open" and, hence, can easily be integrated with implementation, execution, and control tools?

The value-driven design of the process warehouse is visualized in Fig. 1.9.

Fig. 1.9 Value-driven design of the process warehouse

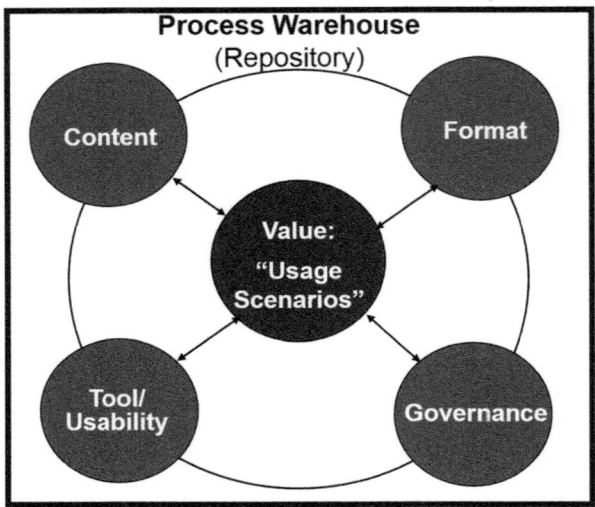

The reuse of information models and related approaches in the process factory makes them to real business process assets. It makes every new process initiative more productive than preceding ones, ultimately leading to the continuous improvement of the process of process management. Every reuse increases the delivered value. I have client statements that the process factory approach with all the components discussed above led to a reduction of design time for business processes of over 50 % compared to a traditional design while maintaining or even increasing quality.

Process governance, which will be discussed in detail in Chap. 5, delivers more guiding parameters for the process factory: the kind of reference models to be used, other external input required, e.g., reflecting the capabilities of a certain ERP system, guidelines about company-wide responsibilities and accountabilities, and inputs regarding existing architecture frameworks to be used to structure the process warehouse.

The physical realization of the process factory can occur through the use of process modeling and repository applications [43] as part of the value-driven BPM-Discipline. The integration of some of those environments into implementation, execution, and control software systems is key as explained before. For example, the ARIS Platform, software built based on the earlier discussed ARIS Architecture [44], and Signavio [45] are integrated into process automation environments, such as SAP NetWeaver, Oracle BPM, webMethods, or solutions from other process execution software vendors [23, 44–46]. This enables the seamless handover of the process models and their reuse in the digital execution environments to at least partially automate the software configuration or development.

The same process models can also be transferred automatically into people-friendly formats to support change management activities, hence people-based process execution. First modeling and repository tools are able to load traditional manual process documents into the process factory. Drawings of simple process flows on whiteboards or flip charts are digitized through the photo made by a simple digital camera. The software tools interpret those pictures and transform them into information model components that can be stored in the process repository—the warehouse [44].

The discipline of value-driven BPM, with its process factory, is a management discipline that enables the use of BPM methods, tools, knowledge, and approaches in a business value-driven manner to support the most appropriate performance of an organization, based on its overall strategy. It allows for smart decisions and fast execution of the resulting actions at the lowest possible cost level. vBPM is the critical link between strategy and execution, enabling systematic strategy execution in a digital world.

In the following chapters of this book, specific aspects of value-driven BPM will be discussed. New BPM developments and trends, as well as their impact on vBPM, are presented. The goal is to highlight key aspects and provide know-how on topics not already discussed in numerous other BPM-related books. At the beginning of each chapter it is explained how its content fits into the BPM-D Framework we discussed earlier.

In Chap. 2, we examine the relation between process management and innovation—a relation that is often misunderstood. In the following two chapters, digital technology and people-related aspects of value-driven BPM are highlighted. Once those topics are clarified, the process governance for vBPM is discussed followed by a presentation of the concept of "reference models." Inter-enterprise processes and emergent processes require special management approaches. It is shown how the discipline of value-driven BPM approaches those processes. After that follows a discussion of the impact of globalization on vBPM. Chapter 10 provides information about the specific situation of small and medium enterprises. This is followed by a chapter showing what Jazz has to do with BPM. At the end we discuss a case study illustrating many of the topics discussed before. In the epilog, you will have the opportunity to find out more about process management and pop art. I hope you enjoy the reading and find it helpful.

1.7 The Bottom Line

- A business process is a set of functions in a specific sequence that ultimately delivers value for an internal or external client. Its start is defined by an external event (Sect. 1.1).
- Every process is a clearly defined subset of an overall organization that can be managed by a "process owner" (Sect. 1.1).
- Since a business process delivers value for a customer, its performance can always be measured based on the impact on this value. The result is a customer-oriented and market-driven organization (Sect. 1.1).

- Key views on a business process to understand and describe it are the organization, function, data, deliverable, and control views (Sect. 1.1).
- BPM is a management discipline that provides governance for a process-oriented organization with the goal of systematic strategy execution in a digital world (Sect. 1.2).
- BPM uses methods, policies, metrics, management practices, and software tools to manage and continuously improve an organization's business processes or transform it to move to the next performance level (Sect. 1.2).
- BPM links strategy and operational execution of an organization (Sect. 1.2).
- The key outcomes of BPM are clear strategic direction, alignment of resources, and increased discipline in daily operations (Sect. 1.2).
- BPM is a process in and of itself. It can be supported by appropriate software systems to make the discipline of BPM efficient and effective (Sect. 1.2).
- Value-driven BPM (vBPM) takes the elements of a general BPM approach and uses them in a consistent value-driven way to enable high performance for the organization as a whole (Sect. 1.3).
- The discipline of value-driven BPM targets the transfer of strategy into operational performance delivering systematic strategy execution in a digital world (Sect. 1.3).
- Typical values delivered by vBPM are transparency which enables the mitigation of trade-offs between other values: quality and efficiency, agility and standardization/compliance, external integration and internal alignment, and innovation and conservation (Sect. 1.3).
- Value-driven BPM supports smart decisions (timely, high quality) and fast execution of the resulting actions at the lowest possible cost level (Sect. 1.3).
- Value-driven BPM begins with the link of business strategy to processes which is the basis for value-driven process life cycle management. It manages IT-related aspects, as well as people aspects in an integrated value-driven manner (Sect. 1.3).
- Value-driven BPM makes every phase of the process life cycle part of a systematic strategy execution. This includes the design, implementation, execution, and control of processes (Sect. 1.4).
- Value-driven BPM is dependent on an efficient and effective management of process knowledge in the form of information models. This is supported by the approach of the process factory (Sect. 1.5).
- The process factory includes the process warehouse and the process manufacturing/assembly. The process warehouse is a repository that enables the efficient reuse of process knowledge assets. It is an important aspect to ensure vBPM's overall efficiency and effectiveness (Sect. 1.5).
- The improvement of processes is based on the achievement of strategic business goals. The first step is generally an analysis of offerings and their structure because they drive the process identification (Sect. 1.6).
- There exist various guidelines and best practices to support the analysis and design of business processes within the process factory (Sect. 1.6).

- The process factory requires a value-driven management of a process modeling and repository environment (Sect. 1.6).

References

1. Scheer, A.-W.: Business Process Engineering—Reference Models of Industrial Enterprises, 2nd edn. Springer, Berlin (1994)
2. Hammer, M., Champy, J.: Reengineering the Corporation. Harper Collins, New York (1993)
3. Scheer, A.-W.: Industry 4.0: From Vision to Implementation. Whitepaper Number 5, August-Wilhelm Scheer Institute for Digital Products and Processes, Scheer GMBH, Saarbruecken, Germany, May 2015
4. McDonald, M. P.: Digital Strategy Does Not Equal IT Strategy, Harvard Business Review, November 19, 2012
5. Scheer, A.-W.: ARIS—Business Process Frameworks, 2nd edn. Springer, Berlin (1998)
6. Scheer, A.-W.: ARIS—Business Process Modeling, 2nd edn. Springer, Berlin (1998)
7. Kirchmer, M.: Business Process Oriented Implementation of Standard Software—How to Achieve Competitive Advantage Efficiently and Effectively, 2nd edn. Springer, Berlin (1999)
8. Spanyi, A.: Business Process Management is a Team Sport—Play It to Win! Anclote Press, Tampa (2003)
9. Harmon, P.: Business Process Change Management—A Manager's Guide to Improving, Redesigning, and Automating Processes. Morgan Kaufmann, San Francisco (2003)
10. Porter, M.: Competitive Strategies: Techniques for Analyzing Industries and Competitors. Free Press, New York (1998) (Originally published in 1980)
11. Kirchmer, M.: Market- and product-oriented definition of business processes. In: Elzina, D.J., Gulledge, T.R., Lee, C.-Y. (eds.) Business Engineering, pp. 131–144. Kluwer, Norwell (1999)
12. Melenowsky, M.J.: Business process management as a discipline. Gartner Research, 08/2006
13. Swenson, K.D., von Rosing, M.: Phase 4: What is BPM? In: von Rosing, M., Scheer, A.-W., von Scheel, H. (eds.) The complete Business Process Handbook—Body of Knowledge from Process Modeling to BPM, vol. 1, p. 79–88. Amsterdam, Boston (2015)
14. Cheese, P., Thomas, R.J., Craig, E.: The Talent Powered Organization—Strategies for Globalization, Talent Management and High Performance. Kogan Page, London/Philadelphia (2008)
15. Kirchmer, M.: The Process of Process Management: Delivering Sustainable Business Value Through BPM. Accenture Point of View Document, Philadelphia (2011)
16. Kirchmer, M.: The Process of Process Management—Mastering the New Normal in a Digital World. In: Business Modeling and Software Development (BMSD) Proceedings (July 2015)
17. Franz, P., Kirchmer, M.: Value-driven business Process Management—The Value-Switch for Lasting Competitive Advantage. McGraw-Hill, New York (2012)
18. Cantara, M.: Start up your Business Process Competency Center. In: Documentation of the Gartner Business Process Management Summit, National Harbor (2015)
19. Franz, P., Kirchmer, M., Rosemann, M.: Value driven Business process Management—Which values matter for BPM. Accenture, Queensland University of Technology (QUT) White Paper, London, Philadelphia, Brisbane (2011)
20. Kirchmer, M., Franz, P.: The Process of Process Management—Strategy Execution in a Digital World. BPM-D Whitepaper, Philadelphia, London (2015)
21. Kirchmer, M.: Competitive advantage is an era of change: 11 Typical situations where Business Process Management delivers Value. Accenture Point of View Document. Philadelphia (2011)
22. Spanyi, A.: More for Less—The Power of Process Management. Meghan-Kiffer Press, Tampa (2006)

23. Kirchmer, M.: Knowledge communication empowers SOA for business agility. In: The 11th World Multi-Conference on Systemics, Cybernetics and Informatics, Proceedings, vol. III, pp. 301–307. Orlando, 8–11 July 2007
24. Jost, W., Scheer, A.-W.: Business process management: a core task for any company organization. In: Scheer, A.-W., Abolhassan, F., Jost, W., Kirchmer, M. (eds.) Business Process Excellence—ARIS in Practice, pp. 33–43. Springer, Berlin (2002)
25. Kirchmer, M., Scheer, A.-W.: Business process automation—combining best and next practices. In: Scheer, A.-W., Abolhassan, F., Jost, W., Kirchmer, M. (eds.) Business Process Automation—ARIS in Practice, pp. 1–15. Springer, Berlin (2004)
26. See: www.bpm-d.com, 2016
27. Kirchmer, M., Franz, P.: Targeting Value in a Digital World. BPM-D Whitepaper, Philadelphia, London 2014
28. Harmon, P.: A new type of activity. In: Business Process Trends (ed.) Newsletter 5(19) (2007)
29. Kirchmer, M., Scheer, A.-W.: Change management—key for business process excellence. In: Scheer, A.-W., Abolhassan, F., Jost, W., Kirchmer, M. (eds.) Business Process Change Management—ARIS in Practice, pp. 1–14. Springer, Berlin (2003)
30. Snee, R., Hoerl, R.: Leading Six Sigma—A Step-by-Step Guide Based on Experience with GE and Other Six Sigma Companies. Prentice-Hall, Upper Saddle River (2003)
31. George, M.L.: Lean Six Sigma for Service—Conquer Complexity and Achieve Major Cost Reductions in Less Than a Year. McGraw-Hill, New York (2003)
32. Kirchmer, M., Franz, P., Lotterer, A.: The BPM-Discipline—Getting more value out of Six Sigma and Traditional Process Improvement. BPM-D Whitepaper, Philadelphia, London (2015)
33. Kaplan, R., Norton, D.: The Balanced Scorecard—Translating Strategy into Action. Harvard Business School Press, Boston (1996)
34. Kirchmer, M., Gutierrez, F., Laengle, S.: Process Mining for Organizational Agility. Industrial Management. January/February 2010
35. Kirchmer, M., Brown, G., Heinzel, H.: Using SCOR and other reference models for e-business process networks. In: Scheer, A.-W., Abolhassan, E., Jost, W., Kirchmer, M. (eds.) Business Process Excellence—ARIS in Practice, pp. 45–64. Springer, Berlin (2002)
36. Nixon, N.: Viewing Ascension Health from a Design Thinking Perspective. Journal of Organization Design (2013)
37. Greenbaum, J.: SimEnterprise: the video gamer's guide to SAP's business-process revolution. In SAP NetWeaver Magazine, vol. 2 (2006)
38. Hammer, M.: Don't automate, obliterate. In: Harvard Business Review, pp. 104–112 (July/August 1990)
39. Kirchmer, M.: The Discipline of Value-driven Business Process Management. BPM-D Executive Education Documentation (3 Days). Philadelphia (2015)
40. Sinur, J.: It's time to consider green BPM. In: Global360 (ed.): Jim Sinur's BPM, www.global360.com (2007)
41. George, M.L., Wilson, S.A.: Conquering Complexity in Your Business—How Wal-Mart, Toyota and Other Top Companies Are Breaking Through the Ceiling on Profits and Growth. McGraw-Hill, New York (2004)
42. Bullinger, H.-J., Scheer, A.-W.: Service Engineering—Entwicklung und Gestaltung innovativer Dienstleistungen. In: Bullinger, H.-J., Scheer, A.-W. (eds.) Service Engineering—Entwicklung und Gestaltung innovativer Dienstleistungen. Springer, Berlin/Heidelberg (2003)
43. Blechard, M.: Magic quadrant for business process analysis tools, 2 H07-1 H08. In: The Gartner Group (ed.) Research Publication G00148777, 6/8/07
44. See: www.softwareag.com, 2015
45. See: www.signavio.com, 2016
46. Newman, D.: BPM & SOA: real world stories of business success. In: IQPC (ed.) Proceedings of the Business Process Management Summit, Las Vegas (2007)

Chapter 2
Innovation: Enabled by Process Management

Today's business environment is constantly changing—new opportunities and challenges arise every day—often driven through increased digitalization. Achieving and sustaining high performance has become more and more difficult. New competitors emerge from all around the world empowered through the "Internet of things," while others disappear. A company becomes a member of many enterprise networks, resulting in more changes and additional competitive situations. Fingar, a well-known BPM expert, introduces "extreme competition" as a result of different market forces, like knowledge as business capital, the Internet, "jumbo transportation," billions of new "capitalists," as well as the new dimension of information technology and digitalization [1].

To master the resulting challenges, innovation—especially business process innovation—has become a core focus area for successful organizations. To ensure long-term survival, an enterprise must make innovation part of its day-to-day business. Only then can enterprises attain desired revenue and profit targets—and with that high performance.

Two major forms of innovation can be distinguished: business model innovation and technology innovation. Both require the change of existing or the development of new business processes. Business process innovation is a major success factor for the next-generation enterprise and often necessary to benefit from opportunities in a digital world. Companies need to create an environment that encourages and enables process innovation. Business process management (BPM) becomes the driver of innovation initiatives. The discipline of value-driven BPM moves to the center of an organization's innovation initiatives.

Value-driven BPM applies the philosophy of "open BPM" to connect various components of the BPM-Discipline seamlessly. This concept delivers a business process infrastructure that provides optimal agility at the lowest cost level through the use of business and technology standards. Open BPM enables an agile BPM-Discipline and, in turn, the efficient and effective management of business process innovation [2]. Innovation opportunities can be identified and easily tried out leveraging new open components within an existing BPM-Discipline

Fig. 2.1 Focus of innovation through vBPM

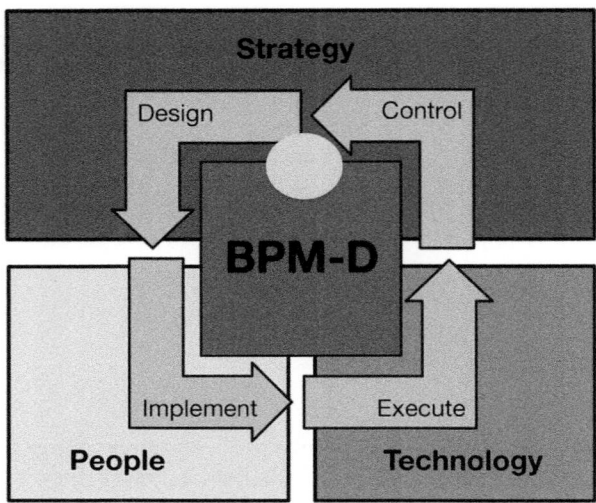

infrastructure. This enables the use of innovation techniques like design thinking and the agile development of innovative business processes.

This chapter discusses characteristics of innovation and how to achieve it through BPM. It explains the importance of process innovation for all forms of creating innovation. You will learn how vBPM serves as a key enabler for business process innovation—one of the key values of a BPM-Discipline.

I stress the aspect of innovation and BPM's role in achieving it since this is an area where I experienced many misperceptions in today's business community. There are still many people who think BPM kills creativity and innovation. This is a huge misunderstanding. The right approach to process management identifies the appropriate degree of freedom for people to deliver the right innovation that moves an organization forward—fast and at minimal risk.

The chapter's focus on innovation as one of the key outcomes of a value-driven BPM-Discipline is visualized in Fig. 2.1. The yellow dot shows that the innovation topic the chapter addresses is closely related to the business strategy of an organization; hence, we discuss important aspects of the link of vBPM to strategy.

2.1 What Has Innovation to Do with Business Processes?

According to Wikipedia [3], the classic definitions of innovation include the following:

- The introduction of something new (Merriam-Webster Online)
- A new idea, method or device (Merriam-Webster Online)

2.1 What Has Innovation to Do with Business Processes?

- The successful exploitation of new ideas (Department of Trade and Industry, UK)
- Change that creates a new dimension of performance (Peter Drucker, Hesselbein)

Innovation as something "new" must be substantially different, not an unimportant change. The change must increase value, customer value, producer value, or a combination of both. These are very straightforward characteristics of innovation, but what has it to do with business process? Why can process management help to drive innovation?

In the last 10 years, more and more companies have been built on the principles of business process innovation, the invention, and successful application of new processes to create significant value. When Dell was founded, for example, the company did not invent the PC. But it did invent new business processes to bring PCs to market, eliminating unnecessary steps in the supply chain, while offering more flexibility and control to the customer. These processes had become Dell's main differentiator in the competitive marketplace. Process innovation was the basis for starting and growing this company. Amazon.com did not invent the book, but it introduced a now popular process of buying books online from the comfort of your living room. This is a process innovation based on digitalization using the Internet with its new capabilities. In a further innovation step, Amazon became a broader online retailer. And now it offers its retail platform to other companies so they can sell new products online. eBay did not invent the auction, but its digital, easy-to-use processes increased the popularity of the auction and the opportunity to make money with it. This is again a process innovation as the basis for a new business. LinkedIn and Facebook invented new processes to manage relationships and personal networks, using this to make money through advertisements or subscriptions.

Traditional companies are also focusing more and more on process innovation. For example, enterprises in the machinery industries offer more convenient and reliable service processes based on Internet connections to their clients or directly to the delivered equipment. Airlines have simplified the ticketing process to reduce cost and increase, or at least stabilize, service levels through online ticketing. This is a process innovation that eventually became the standard, hence an industry best practice. Banks reduce cost and improve their service levels through online banking. An electronic company like Apple becomes more and more of a content provider, reselling music and more in a digital format—through appropriate innovative business processes. Think of all the online travel tools to book hotels, flights, or cars. I am sure you can find many more examples for the power of process innovation.

Examples for the significant impact of business process innovation are shown in Fig. 2.2.

Business process innovation is clearly of highest importance for every company. So we have sown one very strong link between "innovation" and "process management." Let's look at that relation a bit more systematically.

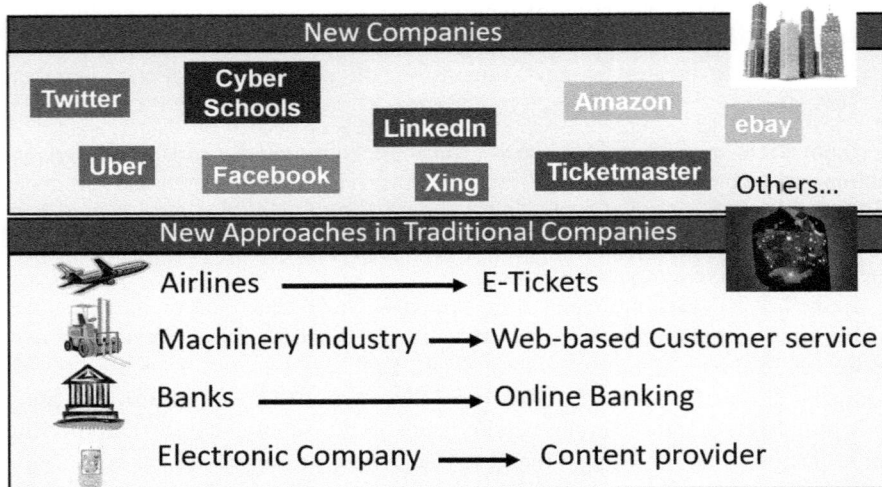

Fig. 2.2 Examples of business process innovation in different organizations and industries

A useful structure to deal with innovation and understand its characteristics is proposed by Davila et al. [4]. According to them, innovation has two major forms:

- Business model innovation
- Technology innovation

Business model innovation includes a new or modified value proposition, new business processes, especially in the supply chain, or new target customers and markets. Let us look at a few examples. Levis Strauss & Co. introduced denim jeans. Because of the company's new process of putting rivets in pants for strength, jeans were introduced as working clothes for farmers and factory workers. Since the first introduction of the denim jeans, the company's value proposition has changed and evolved, as denim jeans have become an expensive fashion product enabling a new business model through a new value proposition. In its PC offerings, Dell's value proposition was the convenient custom configuration and ordering of products—the supply chain processes eliminated dealer networks and enabled individual configuration by the client, while the target customers remained, more or less, the same as those of competitors. Hence, the business model innovation here is achieved mainly through a process innovation. The opening of new markets for existing offerings is another kind of business model innovation. If a company has always sold to the US market but now decides to also provide products to Europe, this is a form of business model innovation, the integration of a new market. Sometimes the pricing approach is considered as an additional component of the business model; however, it can also be seen as part of the general value proposition.

Business model innovation, with processes innovation as a main lever, plays a more and more important role [5]. Many of the previously mentioned examples for the business impact of innovation and the role of processes are mainly business model innovations, realized through the lever of process innovation. But also new value propositions or target customers require in general new or adjusted processes. Hence, the relation between business model innovation and "business processes" is even stronger.

The second form of innovation, technology innovation, has different levers: offerings, including products and services; process technologies; and enabling technologies. New product technologies, e.g., the introduction of digital cameras, are some of the most obvious forms of innovation. Process technologies support efficient and effective business processes. Enterprise resource planning (ERP) systems, for example, were able to make many processes more efficient and effective. Supporting technologies improve either product or process technologies. A good example is the development of efficient relational databases that support the development of integrated application software, such as the aforementioned ERP systems. Technology innovation is what most people still think first about when they hear the term innovation, although business model innovation has become more and more powerful. Technology innovation also requires in most cases the adjustment of processes to realize the full potential of new technologies. Without the right processes, you cannot produce or sell new products, you don't get the full benefits from an ERP system, or you don't end up with the best process technology through enabling technologies. So technology innovation is also closely related to "process" and BPM.

A technology innovation can also enable a business model innovation: the digitization of music in the form of MP3 files and the development of MP3 players opened the way for Apple's development of a new business model for selling music through the Internet [6]. Digital cameras and their digital photos enable new business models focused on the use of "photo data" such as Shutterfly or Snapfish.

Basically, any form of innovation requires new or modified business processes and often business process innovation: processes with new structures; more accurate, granular, or timely data; new organizational responsibilities; new functions; or superior process deliverables. The levers of innovation and their relation to "business process" are shown in Fig. 2.3.

2.2 Some More Thoughts About Innovation and Processes

The close relationship between innovation and business processes is reflected in various innovation theories that are applied in practice, such as Christensen's "value chain evolution" (VCE) theory and his "resources, processes, values" (RPV) theory [7, 8]. Christensen is one of the leading innovation experts. The

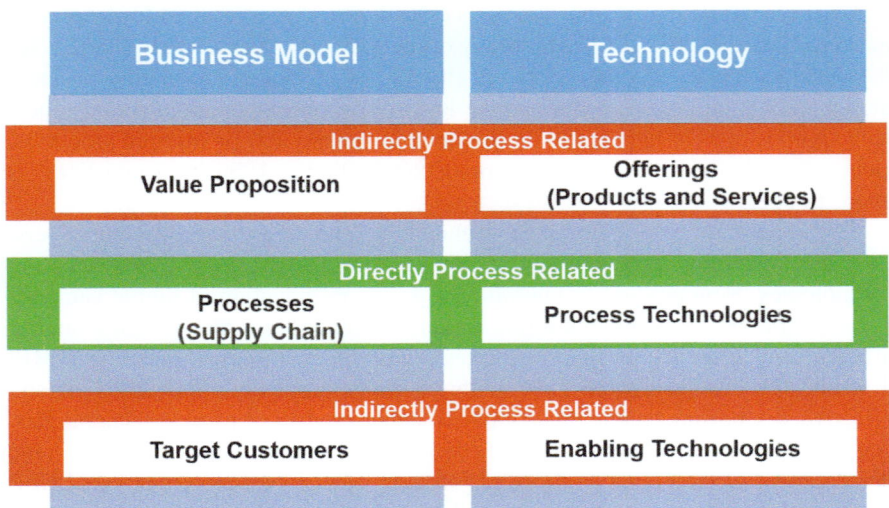

Fig. 2.3 Levers of innovation and the relation to processes

VCE theory is defined around a company's value chain, which is the process beginning with marketing and sales and ending with product distribution and accounts receivables. Customer preferences strongly influence an enterprise's determination of which parts of the value chain process are outsourced and which are executed in-house. The more important the process steps are to the customer, the more likely the enterprise will execute the related process components in-house. Innovation initiatives are focused on the subprocesses executed in-house, making them as competitive as possible. Consequently, business process outsourcing decisions also drive the focus of innovation decisions, especially regarding process innovation. Hence, outsourcing initiatives are another example to show how process management decisions and innovation go hand in hand.

If you outsource an area that is important for your clients, you leave the related innovation basically to your partners. This may in specific situations be justified, but in most cases, an organization should control those key areas and therefore execute them in-house [9]. The VCE theory is visualized in Fig. 2.4.

Christensen distinguishes between sustaining and disruptive innovation. Sustaining innovation strives to improve existing offerings. In that way, "undershot customers," or customers for whom the current offerings are insufficient, can be reached. Disruptive innovation targets "overshot clients" or completely new markets. "Overshot clients" are clients who are not interested in the expensive features of the currently offered products. The present offerings are too sophisticated for them. This distinction is visualized in Fig. 2.5. In the field of process repositories, for example, the ARIS Toolset was one of the first tools on the market. Over time, its functionality had become more and more comprehensive. This allowed new players with simpler tools to enter the market and gain market share. As a reaction,

2.2 Some More Thoughts About Innovation and Processes

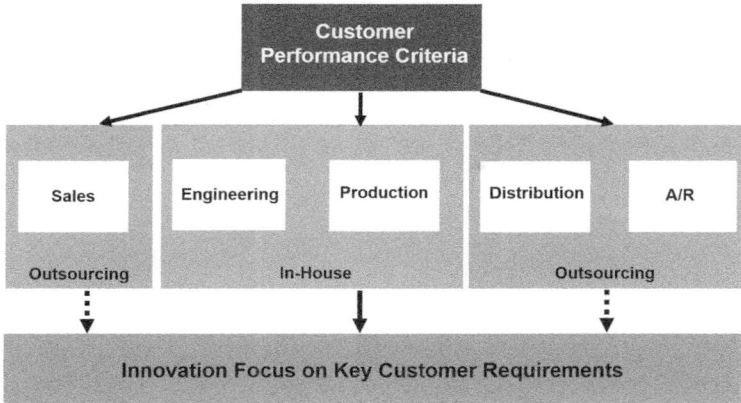

Fig. 2.4 Value chain evolution (VCE) theory

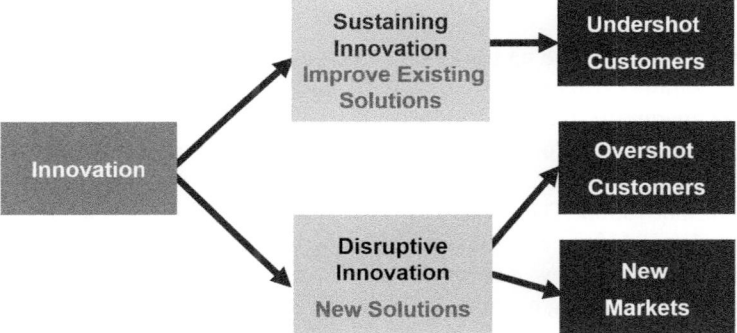

Fig. 2.5 Sustaining and disruptive innovation

IDS Scheer (now Software AG) brought a simplified tool, ARIS Easy Design, to the market to compete in this new segment. However, this answer has, up to date, not been sufficient to prevent the market entrance of start-ups with cheaper simpler solutions like Signavio. Disruptive as well as sustaining innovation is driven through appropriate business process. Disruptive innovation often requires transformational process changes, sustaining innovation can often be achieved through incremental adjustments. BPM is important for both.

The RPV theory demonstrates that innovation is significantly influenced through a company's resources, processes, and values. Resources are transformed through processes from an input to an output. Company values are the basis for setting priorities, thus determining how to use the resources. Successful companies have developed and combined resources, processes, and values to clearly focus on the existing offerings that currently make the organization successful. The result is sustaining innovation that constantly improves existing offerings. But those

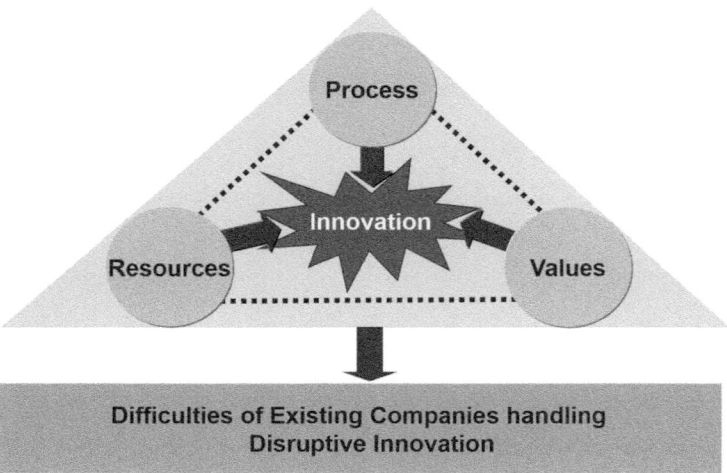

Fig. 2.6 Resources, processes, values (RPV) theory

companies often lose the agility to do something completely new, something that does not simply sustain their existing products. Therefore, if other enterprises introduce disruptive innovations, focusing on new market segments with new solutions, the existing companies are faced with tough challenges. Their focus on sustaining innovation and their lack of flexibility make it difficult to react to disruptive innovation. Their business processes are generally not agile enough to deal with the wide impacts of disruptive innovation or to produce innovations that are really addressing new markets. In this instance, a BPM approach resulting in agile business processes, enabling and simplifying process innovation, can become an important factor for long-term survival. It is important to use the transparency vBPM provides to identify where to innovate to stay competitive and where to conserve existing good and successful practices. The RPV theory is explained in Fig. 2.6. A good example here is Leica: The company had been the leader in high-end optical cameras—but got into trouble because they underestimated the significance of digital cameras. They thought this would only be something for amateurs, not touching their core business in the market for professional photographers—in which they excelled. They have been too focused on their current and past success, used resources accordingly, and aligned processes with that. This almost killed the company. Only a radical shift to delivering optical components for the producers of digital cameras and the entrance into that field saved the prestigious company. The discipline of value-driven BPM is an important enabler of this strategy execution.

"Collaboration innovation" is an extension of business process innovation. In this case, inter-enterprise processes are implemented to support innovative forms of collaborations between organizations [10]. For example, ING is a bank that works together with coffee shops. When customers visit an ING location, they feel like they are in a coffeehouse—with some terminals in the back for banking transactions. Therefore, the BPM infrastructure has to support this collaboration between organizations. Processes of different organizations must be integrated to deliver value to the final client. Thus, process innovation is again the underlying principle of that new form of collaboration. We will discuss inter-enterprise processes and their BPM requirements later.

An important and very specific form of process innovation is the innovation of service processes. A service as rendered by a consulting company, financial services company, etc., is also a process. That means the "product" they deliver to the market is a "business process." Therefore, the innovation of the offering (the service) must be a process innovation—which is consumed directly by the customer. Product innovation in a service company is essentially always process innovation. Therefore, process innovation in such enterprises is even more of a core focus of their activities. BPM enables this innovation.

It is now clear that innovation is tightly linked to business processes—in the form of process innovation and enabler of other forms of innovation: business model and technology innovation. Value-driven BPM provides the management discipline to deal with process innovation successfully. But the discipline of value-driven process management is also important to organize innovation in general and make it part of the daily business of a company. Value-driven BPM enables the "innovation process" of an organization. Let's look into that topic.

2.3 What Is the Business Process of Innovation?

How does an enterprise organize innovation? How does the organization make sure that business model and technology innovation happen systematically, as part of "business as usual"? The answer is process management: the management of innovation within an enterprise is a business process in and of itself. This process must be defined, implemented, executed, and controlled just like any other business process. It goes through the same process life cycle and can be managed using the discipline of value-driven BPM. The "innovation process" is a key process to be managed by vBPM.

A generic example of one such innovation process is shown in Fig. 2.7. The process develops from the preparation of an innovation initiative to the "idea-finding" activities and finally to the execution of the innovation idea. The "innovation manager" identifies relevant megatrends and, on the basis of those, the relevant innovation fields of a company. These innovation fields guide the definition of the company-specific innovation focus. This focus directs the "idea finding," using internal and external resources to come up with ideas for innovations related to the defined focus. The innovation ideas are evaluated, and the most interesting ones become innovation projects. These projects develop prototypes and business cases on the basis of the innovation idea. Then, the innovation team can decide which innovation ideas will be brought to market. These ideas will actually become innovations.

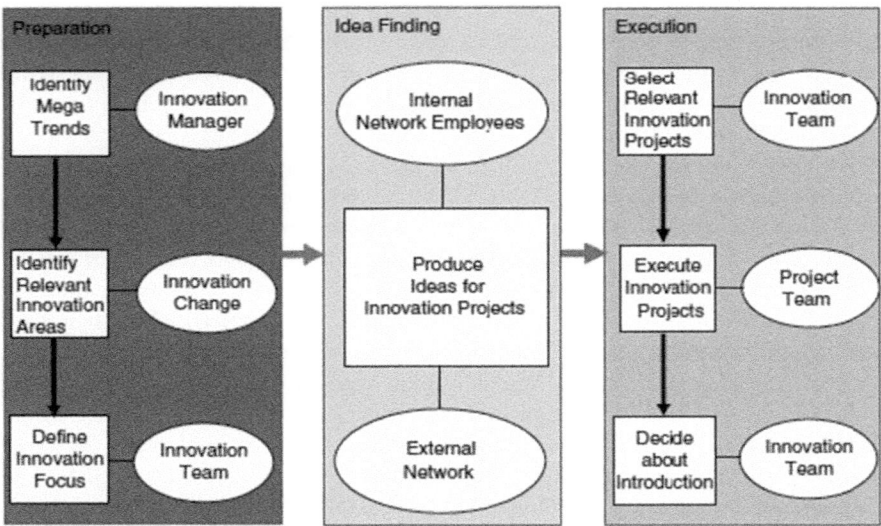

Fig. 2.7 Example of an innovation process

During the idea-finding process, it is key to anticipate the customers' future interests and needs. It is about planning the customer journey. Fingar claims that you should even know customer interests and needs before the customers themselves are aware of them [1] just like Steve Jobs at Apple did [6]. It generally makes sense to include external partners in the innovation process to broaden the input. Examples of such partners include the following:

- Key customers
- Important suppliers
- Additional market partners (e.g., banks)
- Research institutions
- Universities

Generally, the subprocess resulting from idea finding is an emergent process, which cannot initially be defined from start to finish. Later, we will discuss how to manage these processes.

In most cases, however, the step from the idea to the innovation itself is the most challenging. Therefore, the management of innovation initiatives and their evaluation is a key task in the innovation process. An organization can truly achieve competitive advantage by organizing that task carefully, considering the specific company and market context.

Because of the importance of business model innovation and specifically process innovation, the innovation process must support this form of innovation effectively. For many traditional companies, this will require a large shift because they formerly thought of innovation in terms of technology innovation, especially product innovation. This shift can be supported by selecting a specific approach for process

2.3 What Is the Business Process of Innovation?

innovation, for example, based on design thinking [11–13], and appropriate external partners to participate in the innovation process. The structured design of business models and customer value propositions, as suggested by Osterwald, can play a key role here [12, 13].

Davila, Epstein, and Shelton suggest some rules to support and manage the innovation process [4]:

- Implement strong leadership regarding innovation strategy and innovation portfolio.
- Integrate innovation into day-to-day business.
- Align amount and type of innovation with the specific business situation.
- Manage tension between creativity and daily business requirements ("achieve numbers, etc.").
- Control the resistance to innovation and change.
- Form an innovation network consisting of internal and external members.
- Define and manage the appropriate metrics and rewards.

When implementing and improving an innovation process, it is in most cases of highest importance to accelerate the time until the innovation can be introduced into the market. This reduces innovation cost and increases the probability of high revenue effects [14, 15]. At a telecommunication company, for example, it was crucial to reduce the new product launch cycle time by over 50% to stay competitive. BPM has been the key enabler to achieve that.

Hammer, the renowned BPM thought leader, recognized that operational innovation, or business process innovation, is not easy to achieve. For a successful innovation process, he recommends six key factors [16]:

- Business process focus, from the beginning of an innovation initiative
- Definition of process owners, including a senior executive who can make change happen
- Full-time design team
- Managerial engagement, ensuring the implementation of the innovation
- Building buy-in
- Bias for action

Once a process innovation has been implemented, one must recognize that the interrelationship with other processes may require additional change. Therefore, one process innovation initiative may immediately trigger the next process change project.

The innovation process can be centralized in an organization or carried out in decentralized units. The more effective approach has to be defined on the basis of a company's specific context and its strategy.

How can an enterprise provide a "process environment" to support innovation? How can the discipline of process management make a difference and become a key enabler for innovation?

2.4 How Does BPM Enable Innovation Systematically?

Value-driven business process management provides a management discipline delivering the transparency and agility required to enable innovation, especially business process innovation and the closely related business model innovation. BPM also optimizes the performance of the innovation process as part of the daily business. Process management sets the parameters so that an organization is able to react to change fast and effectively. Innovation in general and process innovation specifically are powerful ways of dealing with change—and driving it proactively.

The discipline of vBPM helps to identify the 15–20% of high-impact processes where innovation really matters. It points the innovation activities to the right target to get the best value out of it [9, 17].

The discipline of vBPM identifies the process steps of the innovation process that are purely administrative but necessary. Those areas are managed with the goal of highest efficiency. The subprocesses which really matter for the quality of innovation are optimized differently. Optimizations to achieve best possible results are appropriate. Here, people get the necessary freedom to be creative and develop new ideas.

vBPM enables the right degree of freedom for successful innovation. It also provides the right agility necessary to implement and roll out the new processes. The double impact of the discipline of value-driven process management on innovation is visualized in Fig. 2.8.

As previously mentioned, process innovation is in general customer driven and facilitated through design thinking. Hence, the innovation process is organized around the design thinking principles [11]. A new process idea is developed based on the outside-in customer view, the transfer of experiences from other areas (e.g., other industries or different processes), based on a visionary overall story. The implementation is done through rapid prototyping—which requires the agility vBPM provides. vBPM enables the rapid implementation of process changes to examine the outcomes which drive further improvements. But it is also used to organize an appropriate innovation process, as discussed before. Value-driven BPM treats innovation as a key value it has to deliver.

Value-driven BPM applies the notion of "open BPM," which is the consequent use of business and technology standards around the process life cycle, resulting in an infrastructure that provides optimal process agility at the lowest cost level. This enables an effective implementation and rollout of new "innovative" business processes. Since this is an important success factor for innovation initiatives, the concept of open BPM is discussed now more in detail. The use of standards to support business process management allows business process changes with the lowest effort because the information about the change can be seamlessly transferred through all phases of the process life cycle, from design, implementation, and execution to control of the new processes. The concept of open BPM is shown in Fig. 2.9.

2.4 How Does BPM Enable Innovation Systematically?

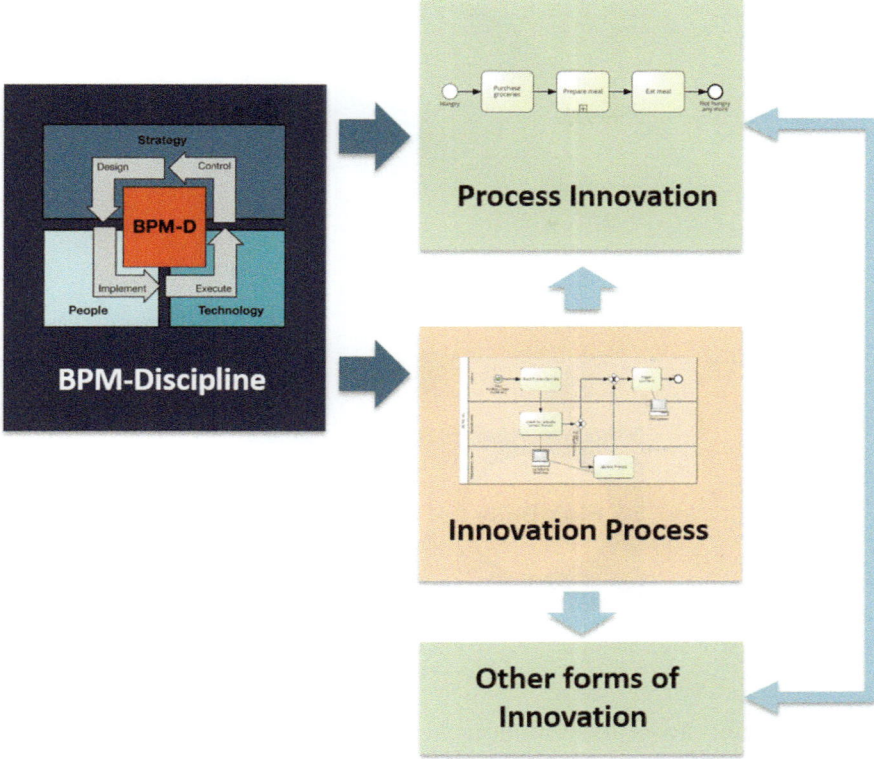

Fig. 2.8 The impact of value-driven BPM-Discipline on innovation

The philosophy of open BPM must be applied to the entire process of vBPM. This includes technology standards for the underlying software tools but also business standards, such as enterprise architecture frameworks, governance processes, or prioritization approaches. Business standards enable the people-based integration of the different process management activities along the process life cycle. Technology standards facilitate seamless integration of the supporting software.

Business standards that can be applied to guide the process design include architecture standards like the SCOR framework developed by the Supply Chain Council, the ARIS Architecture developed by Scheer, or the Zachman Framework [18, 19]. Processes can be described using modeling standards, such as event-driven process chains (EPCs) [20] or the business process-modeling notation (BPMN) [21].

The execution of processes in an open environment is best supported by a "service-oriented software architecture" (SOA) and the technical standards available in this context [22, 23]. This highly flexible next-generation process automation will be later discussed in more detail. The related technology standards directly

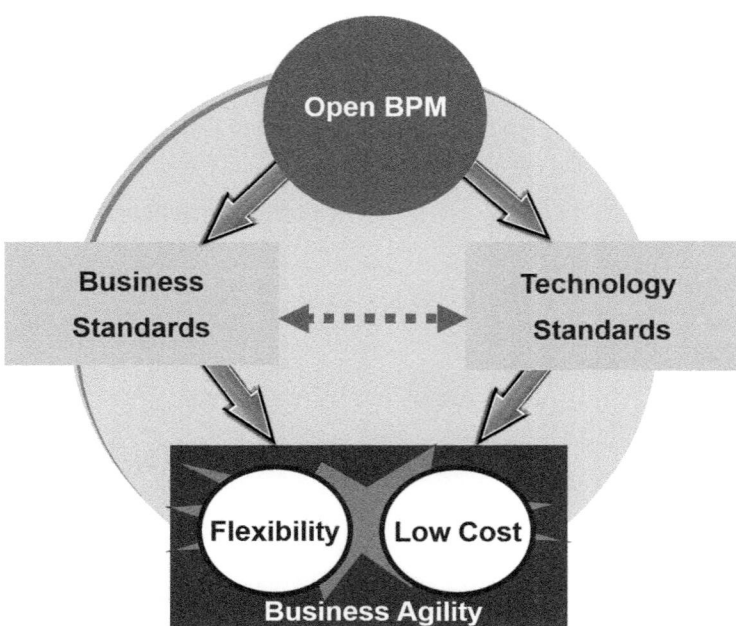

Fig. 2.9 Concept of open business process management

deliver the agility necessary to enable rapid prototyping for an agile development of process innovation.

People enablement plays a central role in the roll out of new processes. The main activities of people change management are information, communication, and training. These activities can be supported by the same process models used for the software solution design, provided that a consistent process-modeling standard is used that is delivering a common language of change. Such formal process-modeling methods can be transferred automatically into process descriptions that are easy-to-understand and easy-to-use, even for employees less familiar with process management methods and tools. Change management encompasses the people side of process execution. Agility in the technical execution of processes requires equal agility from the people working directly or indirectly with those processes and supporting technologies.

Process monitoring and control systems can be linked to the process execution systems through standardized adapters to monitor and measure the business processes [24]. Information, such as cycle times or execution frequency, is monitored. Thus, it becomes easier to provide fast information about potential process issues so that appropriate actions can be taken. This again is very important for rapid prototyping during the innovation process. To measure the appropriate processes or subprocesses, such controlling systems are configured on the basis of the aforementioned process models. They allow the "measurement" of the success of a process innovation and provide the information necessary for "smart" decisions to improve the innovative prototype of a process.

The consequent use of standards within open BPM also supports the management of processes across organizations, resulting in the efficient and targeted collaboration of enterprises [25]. Therefore, collaboration innovation is also enabled through this approach. This can, for example, lead to a new more flexible supply chain process or collaborative research and development. Interactive Web-based applications, as offered by the "Web 2.0" [10] movement, can be used as standards for business processes and support a collaboration environment within and across the organization effectively.

The design of business processes based on modeling standards is a good starting point in process innovation through vBPM. An example is a North American producer of commodity chemicals, such as plastic foils. Differentiation through products is nearly impossible. Process innovation and the competitive advantage it provides are extremely important. Therefore, the company identified process innovation as a key corporate initiative. Every business unit manager delivers suggestions for process innovation in the form of process models in EPC format, so that an evaluation and potential implementation can be carried out easily. Open BPM is key for managing the innovation processes.

2.5 Examples for Innovation Through Appropriate Process Management?

Siemens and Intel, both high-tech enterprises, similarly facilitated the innovation of their mutual supply chain management (SCM). The intercompany collaboration processes were defined on the basis of the SCOR standard delivered by the Supply Chain Council [18]. Innovations included in the supply chain structure enabled an efficient rollout of changes and standards across the organizations. Their approach is visualized in Fig. 2.10. The graphic shows on the top part the supply chains of the companies defined based on the SCOR standard and the collaboration scenarios designed based on this. The lower part of the figure shows the detailed process execution and data exchange based on RosettaNet standards. Open BPM was used as enabler process innovation on the one hand but also to provide the appropriate standards to simplify the innovation process.

Mitsui, a leading Japanese trading company, has followed a similar innovation facilitation initiative. As a service company, process innovation is basically the only effective form of innovation. Mitsui can use its existing BPM environment with the defined standards to transfer innovation ideas from one location to another and to measure the effects of such innovation initiatives. The powerful role of BPM for innovation is directly clear.

Business process innovation has also found its way into the educational and academic practice. Universities, such as Widener University in Philadelphia,

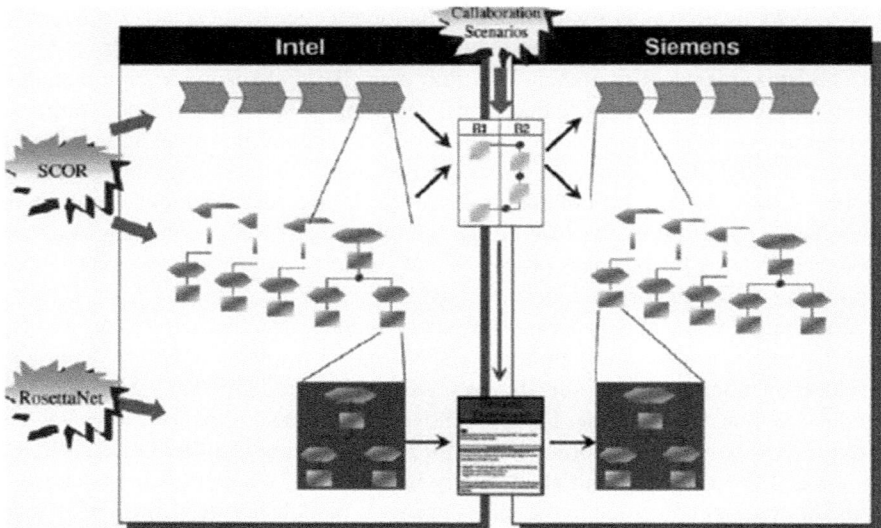

Fig. 2.10 Intel-Siemens: supply chain management (SCM) innovation

Pennsylvania, offer certifications and master's degree programs with a focus on business process innovation [26]. This allows enterprises to recruit employees who are familiar with innovation enabled through business process management.

The role of the BPM-Discipline as enabler of innovation has become an important value proposition for this emerging management discipline. It underlines the importance of process management for strategy execution.

2.6 The Bottom Line

The key messages of this chapter include the following:

- The main types of innovation are business model innovation and technology innovation (Sect. 2.1).
- Business model innovation includes new or modified value propositions, new business processes (especially in the supply chain), or new target customers and markets (Sect. 2.1).
- Technology innovation has the following levers: products and services, process technologies, and enabling technologies (Sect. 2.1).
- Business processes play an essential role in both types of innovation; thus, business process innovation plays a pivotal role in all innovation initiatives (Sect. 2.1).
- Some companies are completely based on the notion of business process innovation (Sect. 2.1).

- Thinking frameworks can help to understand more about the relation of process management and innovation (Sect. 2.2).
- To help ensure long-term business success and high performance, innovation must be part of daily business and an innovation process has to be put in place (Sect. 2.3).
- The innovation process defines the areas of innovation, the development of innovation ideas, and the realization of innovations, based on those ideas (Sect. 2.3).
- Design thinking plays an important role in process innovation (Sect. 2.3).
- The transparency created through the discipline of value-driven process management enables the identification of the right target processes for innovation (Sect. 2.4).
- The innovation process can be managed successfully by applying vBPM (Sect. 2.4).
- Through the use of business and technology standards as part of an "open BPM" approach, vBPM enables optimal agility at minimum cost, thus establishing the basis for successful implementation and rollout of business process innovation (Sect. 2.4).
- BPM has become a key enabler for innovation. This underlines again its strategy execution (Sect. 2.4).

References

1. Fingar, P.: Extreme Competition—Innovation and the Great 21st Century Business Reformation. Meghan-Kiffer, Tampa (2006)
2. Kirchmer, M.: Process innovation through open BPM. In: Pantaleo, D., Pal, N. (eds.) From Strategy to Execution—Turning Accelerated Global Change into Opportunity, pp. 87–105. Springer, Berlin (2008)
3. Wikipedia (ed.): Innovation. In: Wikipedia.org (2015)
4. Davila, T., Epstein, M.J., Shelton, R.: Making Innovation Work. Wharton School Publishing, Upper Saddle River (2006)
5. de Jong, M., van Dijk, M.: Disruption beliefs: a new approach to business model innovation. McKinsey Quarterly, July 2015
6. Isaacson, W.: Steve Jobs. New York, e.a. (2011)
7. Christensen, C., Johnson, M.: Business model innovation. Report to the US Council of Innovation, The Conference Board (2007)
8. Christensen, CM, Raymour, M: The Innovator's Solution: Using Good Theory to Solve the Dilemmas of Growth. Harvard Business School Press, Boston (2003)
9. Franz, P., Kirchmer, M.: Value-driven Business Process Management—The Value Switch for Lasting Competitive Advantage. McGraw-Hill, New York (2012)
10. Wikipedia (ed.): Web 2.0. In: wikipedia.org (2007)
11. Natalie, N.: Viewing Ascension Health from A Design Thinking Perspective. Journal of Organization Design. **2**(3), 23–28 (2013)
12. Osterwalder, A., Pigneur, Y., Bernarda, G., Smith, A.: Value Proposition Design. Wiley, Hoboken, NJ (2014)
13. Osterwalder, A., Pigneur, Y.: Business Model Generation: A Handbook for Visionaries, Game Changer, and Challengers. Wiley, Hoboken, NJ (2010)

14. George, M., Works, J., Watson-Hemphill, K.: Fast Innovation—Achieving Superior Differentiation, Speed to Market, and Increased Profitability. McGraw-Hill, New York (2005)
15. Johnson, M., Suskewicz, J.: Accelerating innovation. In: Pantaleo, D., Pal, N. (eds.) From Strategy to Execution—Turning Accelerated Global Change into Opportunity, pp. 49–64. Springer, Berlin (2008)
16. Hammer, M.: Six steps to operational innovation. In: Harvard Business School Working Knowledge for Business. hbswk.hbs.edu (2005). Accessed 30 Aug 2005
17. Kirchmer, M., Franz, P.: The Process of Process Management—Strategy Execution in a Digital World. BPM-D Whitepaper, Philadelphia, London (2015)
18. Kirchmer, M., Brown, G., Heinzel, H.: Using SCOR and other reference models for e-business process networks. In: Scheer, A.-W., Abolhassan, E., Jost, W., Kirchmer, M. (eds.) Business Process Excellence—ARIS in Practice, pp. 45–64. Springer, Berlin (2002)
19. IDS Scheer A.G. (ed.): ARIS design platform—ARIS enterprise architecture solution. White Paper. Saarbruecken (2006)
20. Scheer, A.-W.: ARIS—Business Process Modeling, 2nd edn. Springer, Berlin (1998)
21. Fisher, L. (ed.): BPMN 2.0 Handbook—Methods, Concepts, Case Studies and Standards in Business Process Modelling Notation (BPMN), 2nd edn. Lighthouse Point, FL (2012)
22. Woods, D.: Enterprise Service Architectures. O'Reilly, Beijing (2003)
23. Scheer, A.W., Abolhassan, F., Jost, W., Kirchmer, M. (eds.): Business Process Automation—ARIS in Practice. Springer, Berlin (2004)
24. Hess, H., Blickle, T.: From process efficiency to organizational performance. ARIS Platform Expert Paper, Saarbruecken (2007)
25. Kirchmer, M.: E-business process networks—successful value chains through standards. J. Enterprise. Manage. **17**(1), (2004)
26. Widener University, School for Business Administration: Business Process Innovation. At: www.widener.edu (2015)

Chapter 3
Digital Technologies for Process Execution

Digitalization is nowadays a key topic in basically every organization. Most business processes are at least partially supported by digital information technology (IT). They are "digital." Applications like enterprise resource planning (ERP), customer relationship management (CRM), supply chain management (SCM), or similar systems are present in most enterprises in one or another way. Many executives are already considering new technology environments on the basis of service-oriented architectures (SOA) or are in the midst of such an implementation. Some companies even take these ideas to the next level, such as procuring their software through "the cloud" or using Web 2.0 applications. But what does it all mean? How do these digitalization components fit into the bigger picture of "strategy execution" and the discipline of value-driven process management?

The entire life cycle of an operational business process is supported by application software systems. Until now, we have primarily discussed the support of the design phase and the transition to the implementation activities through repository-based information modeling and related software tools. However, in practice, most of the interest is in systems that support the process execution and control.

For over 20 years, I have focused on value-driven approaches for ERP implementations and have written many publications about the experiences during those projects of "process-oriented implementations" [1]. In the last years, however, I have been more interested in new software architectures and next-generation process automation [2, 3] with all the opportunities these bring. In this area, I have solid practical experience and conducted a fair amount of research. In this chapter, I share my thoughts regarding digital technologies to support the execution of business processes.

This chapter will explore main process execution approaches and their relation to vBPM. Major topics include ERP, new flexibility of process automation through SOA, the next generation of digital processes with Web 2.0-based "Enterprise 2.0," the impact of the cloud, and other recent developments. The successful value-driven deployment of those solutions for process execution is an important impact

Fig. 3.1 Focus on information technology aspect of value-driven BPM

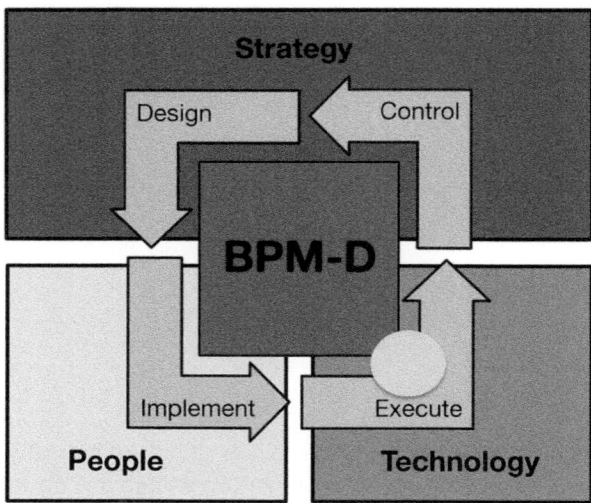

of the discipline of vBPM. The focus on technology-based process execution of this chapter is illustrated in Fig. 3.1.

However, it is important to remember that vBPM is not just about technology, as previously explained. On the one hand, digital technology is a key enabler, but without other components, especially the people involved, the process management and with that the strategy execution will not be successful. On the other hand, without enabling technology, many process improvements, transformations, and innovations would not be possible. I promote the concept of replacing chief information officers (CIOs) through "chief process officers (CPOs)" [4–7]; however, it will be essential for the CPO to have a strong understanding of the business impact of digital technologies and its enabling power for achieving business processes that enable high performance for the organization as a whole.

3.1 The "Traditional" Path to Process Execution: Enterprise Resource Planning (ERP) and More

During the last 15–20 years, an increasing number of business processes have been supported by standard software packages, such as enterprise resource planning (ERP), supply chain management (SCM), or customer relationship management (CRM) systems [1, 8]. The most popular are ERP systems, covering the majority of a company's operational activities, such as sales, material management, production planning and control, maintenance, asset management, finance, financial controlling, and human resources. In this chapter, ERP will be used as the primary example for traditional standard software applications. Major vendors include SAP [9], Oracle [10], Microsoft [11], and Salesforce.com [12]. The use of standard software

3.1 The "Traditional" Path to Process Execution: Enterprise... 49

has numerous advantages when compared with individually developed software systems, including:

- Lower cost of procurement
- Faster procurement and time savings
- Smoother migration of the organization during the software implementation because of best practices in implementation approaches
- Availability of training and other people change management tools
- Lower maintenance cost
- Reduction or elimination of application development backlogs and focus of development on company specifics
- Protection of the investment through continuous support by vendor and large user community
- Delivers necessary functionality and data integration, which enables the support of processes, including process execution and control
- Business skills of the software vendor and the other users: "common practices"
- Often a higher ergonomic and technology standard

Although there are also some disadvantages, like dependence on a software vendor or lengthy implementations, the advantages described above are generally considered to outweigh the disadvantages by far. Most organizations use standard application software wherever possible and develop custom software only for the areas not covered by those systems. Process execution through standard software is especially attractive for the commodity processes of an organization since you want to achieve an industry average performance in those areas. Since over 80% of a company's processes are commodity processes, it is very important to achieve this process performance level as efficiently as possible. Standard application software enables this endeavor [13].

Standard software systems for operational business applications, especially ERP systems, offer the following key business benefits [8]:

- Reduction in cycle times
- Faster information transactions
- More accurate financial management
- Creation of the basis for e-business and inter-enterprise processes
- Visibility of hidden process knowledge

A key advantage of these "traditional" software solutions is that they not only deliver technology to execute a specific process but also provide best or at least common business practices. The software reflects its vendor's business knowledge regarding a certain topic or industry, as well as the experience of the vendor with other customers in the same area.

The successful use of standard software, such as ERP systems, implies the design and execution of business processes, according to the delivered best practices of the software solution. If you buy an ERP system, you do not just purchase a piece of technology; you also buy a set of predefined business processes. In turn, you have to adapt at least part of your organization to the requirements of the

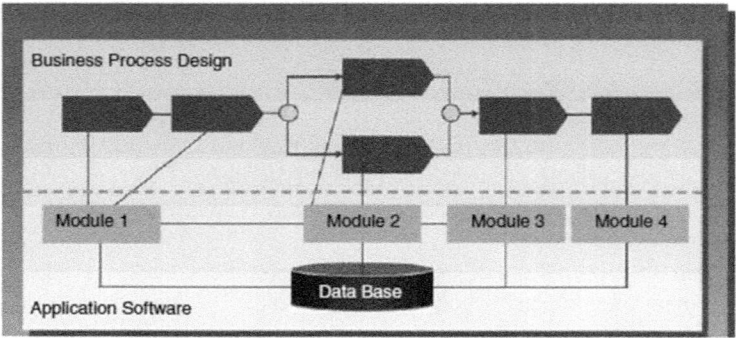

Fig. 3.2 Standard software (e.g., ERP): static integration of process design and technology

software-based business processes. For example, you may be forced to create some material master data before you send out a procurement order. ERP systems include a process definition that is more or less coded in the software. The software only allows limited changes or adjustments of its process definition. These adjustments can be done during the software configuration through the setting of specific parameters. This is an important task of ERP implementation activities.

Modifications to the delivered process logic often result in modification to software that lead, in most cases, to tremendous cost. I have seen companies with departments of more than 30 people solely focused on transferring ERP system modifications from one new software release to the other. Many of the advantages of standard software are lost if you decide to modify that software. However, most of the standard systems allow the integration of "add-on software" through predefined interfaces. But this is, in many cases, insufficient, especially for the support of a high-impact process that is critical to execute on a business strategy and achieve competitive advantage. As a result, key business processes are often not adequately supported by traditional software solutions, which negatively impacts overall business performance.

The process definitions delivered through standard software are more and more often described in so-called software reference models, which document the best and common practices supported by the application system (we will discuss reference models in more detail later). "Next business practices," or process designs that are only starting to emerge in an industry, are generally not supported [2, 3]. These innovative processes were not considered during the standard software development. Only when a next practice eventually becomes a best or common practice, it will be included in the traditional standard software solution and with that into the related reference models.

The tight integration of the business process definition and software technology in traditional standard software systems is visualized in Fig. 3.2.

Although standard software systems, such as ERP systems, can be used to support business processes, the software is still developed in a function-oriented way. It consists of modules that reflect certain business functions, such as a sales module, a shipping module, or a production planning module. There are generally no process modules, such as an "order-to-delivery" module for the "consumer packaged goods industry." Such a process would require the implementation of several modules to be supported properly.

Consequently, the business process support through ERP systems must be accomplished during the implementation. Therefore, vBPM enables a business process-oriented implementation approach for function-oriented developed ERP, SCM, CRM, or similar standard software systems. This means that during the implementation of the software and its roll out into the enterprise, all modules necessary to support an entire business process have to be implemented appropriately.

For example, a company producing industry compressors has identified three core business processes. The "engineer-to-order" processes cover all activities from the customer-order processing, engineering, and production to distribution. The processes are generally optimized on the basis of quality aspects. A customer would be willing to wait days, or even weeks, longer for an engineered-to-order compressor, but it must have the highest quality once it is in the factory. A second process is focused on "make-to-order" compressors, smaller machines that are produced based on customer orders but according to standard specifications. The process does not require engineering activities. It is optimized under cost considerations because competitors build similar products—but for a higher price. The third process is focused on "customer service." It basically supports the distribution of spare parts from stock. Customers in need of spare parts are usually under great time pressure. Therefore, the process has to be optimized under cycle time aspects.

If an ERP system were implemented according to the software structure, all similar activities of the three processes would be treated the same. No specific configuration, just focused on the goals of one of the three processes, would take place. The initially process-oriented designed organizations would be replaced by the functional structure of the software. This can be avoided by a process-oriented implementation approach, as supported by vBPM [1, 8]. It ensures the support of each process through properly configured standard software modules. This approach to the implementation phase is shown in Fig. 3.3. This means that a realistic business process design is used to drive the configuration of the standard software package. The process models delivered through the process design can be used to test and verify the software configuration. This is visualized in Fig. 3.4.

This approach works well, as long as the organization is satisfied with the best and common business practices offered by the standard software, using the predefined adjustment possibilities during the configuration. Experience has shown that this works for 80% and more of all business processes—mainly the commodity processes. Why should one consider company-specific approaches to financial processes that are highly regulated through legal requirements? Also, commodity processes such as human resources administration, procurement of standard materials, are typically not critical in achieving a competitive advantage. Therefore, a common practice-based standard software solution to support the execution is the most appropriate.

52   3 Digital Technologies for Process Execution

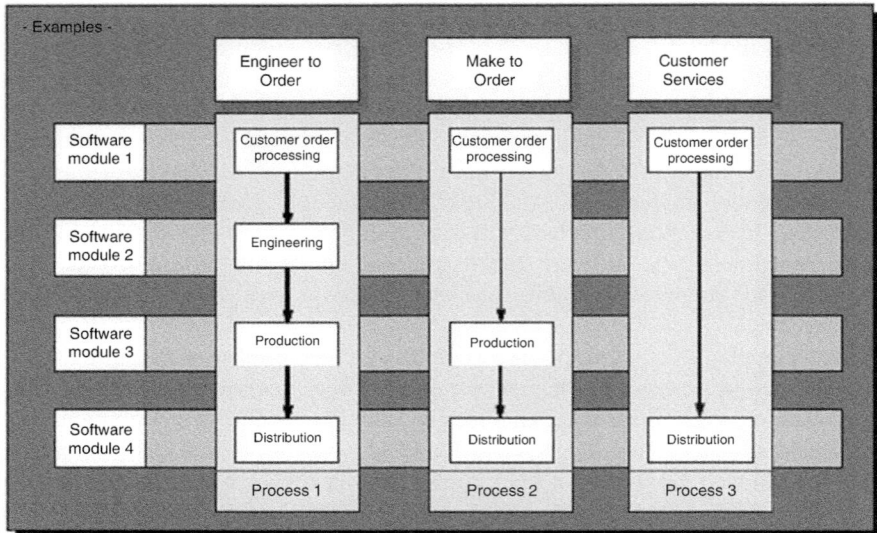

Fig. 3.3 Process-oriented implementation of function-oriented software (e.g., ERP)

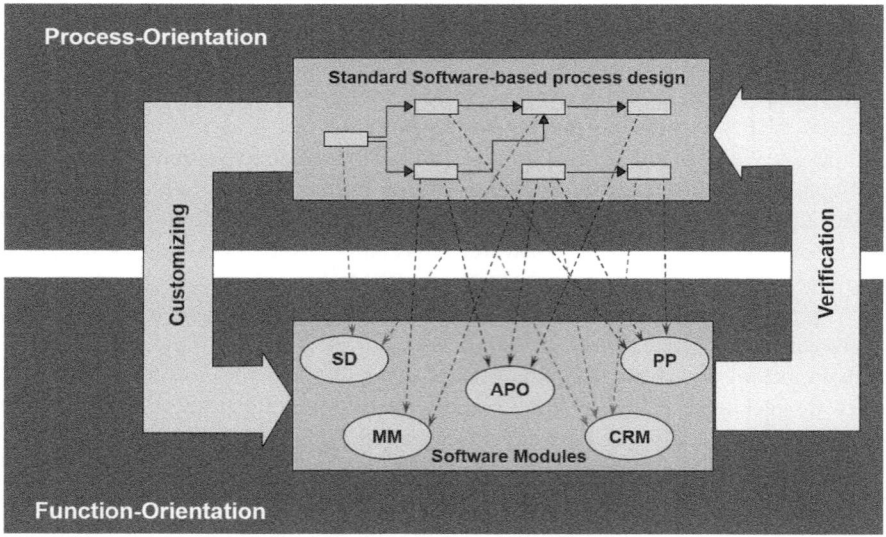

Fig. 3.4 Business process-driven standard software configuration

The standard application software can also be hosted by a third-party company, an application service provider (ASP). This allows an enterprise to focus on the business aspects of the software and outsource the technical tasks. More and more organizations even go a step further: They procure their standard software solution through "the cloud," sharing the software functionality with other organizations while keeping their data company specific. All the mentioned software vendors offer cloud-based solutions and bet their future on those. In this case, organizations have to use "real" standard solutions without company-specific modifications of the software. vBPM as an enabler of a company-specific implementation becomes even more important. We discuss the impact of the cloud more in detail later in this chapter.

But how should one handle the 15–20% of the high-impact business processes that we want to implement and execute on the basis of a unique company-specific design, the processes that are truly important to provide competitive advantage? These processes deliver real competitive advantage but also require more flexible technology support to achieve this. And companies do not really want to share all those competitive business process details with standard software vendors. Until now, the only solution was an individual software development from scratch, followed by the often difficult integration into standard software application and huge maintenance challenges. The next-generation process automation, based on service-oriented architectures (SOA), delivers a solution to that challenge. Let us discuss how that works.

3.2 New Flexibility in Process Execution: Service-Oriented Architecture (SOA)

Key processes tend to be strongly influenced by a company's specific offerings and the related market demands. Consequently, standard software applications like ERP cannot deliver the best possible digital technology support because they reflect the needs of wider user communities and with that common business practices. Service-oriented architectures (SOA) and their technology components offer a solution for those needs. They enable the separation of the business process design and the technology support through appropriate software applications or application components delivered as so-called services. We use "service" as synonym for an application software component, delivering specific results needed to support one or several functions of a business process. This means that application software can be used exactly as required by business processes. SOA provides the environment to integrate the required application components and exchange data between them as necessary to support the overlying business processes design [2, 14–16]. This enables the execution of innovative and company-specific business processes. In other words, it is a digital technology for business process innovation, as Woods and Mattern, some of the first authors of a book about SOA, describe SOA [16]. SOA is an excellent fit to support vBPM's goals of agility and innovation.

The use of SOA can lead to significant reductions in IT maintenance costs because expensive program-to-program interfaces of traditional software environments are avoided. All software components are simply linked into the integration

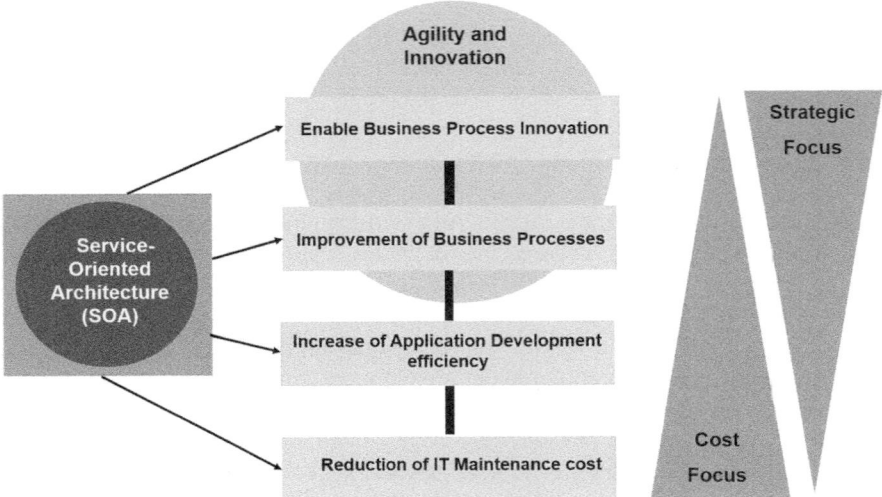

Fig. 3.5 Business impacts of service-oriented architectures (SOA)

environment of the SOA [16]. This resolves many of the issues of extending ERP systems.

These integration capabilities are also the basis for the reuse of software components in the case of custom developments, thus resulting again in cost savings. Once a software component or service is developed, it can be used to support several processes. It can be part of another integrated process-oriented software system.

The true value of SOA, however, is only delivered when the digital environment is used to support business change, to enable agility, process innovation, or even the entire new business models. The design of a business process can be optimized and cost and time efficiently implemented, through the selection and adjustment of the application components needed to support the specific process. New "services" can be added, and others deleted or modified, according to the requirements of the business processes. The same procedure can be used to realize completely new or significantly enhanced processes, thus enabling business process innovation. SOA can become a key component of strategy execution through the discipline of value-driven BPM. Thus, SOA plays a critical role of transferring strategy into operational performance through vBPM. These effects are illustrated in Fig. 3.5.

If SOA is utilized solely to reduce IT cost, the greatest value of this digital solution architecture is missed. SOA only delivers actual strategic impact when it is used to drive process and business model innovation and the related agility in an organization. It must become the compelling force behind business transformation initiatives.

The knowledge about new or modified processes needs to be transferred fast and with little risk of errors into the digital execution components of SOA.

3.2 New Flexibility in Process Execution: Service-Oriented Architecture (SOA)

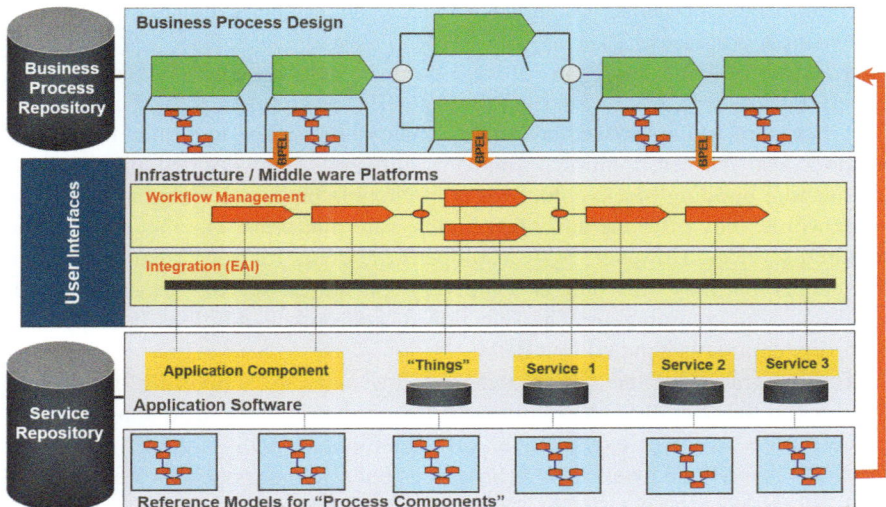

Fig. 3.6 Service-oriented architecture (SOA)

To understand and apply this tight but flexible integration between process design, implementation, and execution, a more detailed analysis of SOA and its components is necessary. The core of SOA is a "middleware" that separates the process design in the form of process models from the executing software services. This middleware consists of a workflow component that allows the definition of the specific process logic and an integration component calling the right software services for each function of the defined workflow. The workflow is identified on the basis of the business process models developed in the process design. This design is supported through "reference model components," describing from a business point of view the subprocesses executed through a specific software service.

SOA also delivers consistent user interfaces for different user groups, independent of the various software services and digital components of the architecture. This supports the integration of people- and technology-based process execution. "Things," for example, machines which produce and understand digital information, can also be integrated into this software architecture. The concept of SOA is shown in Fig. 3.6.

The separation of application software technology and process design through appropriate middleware enables the business-driven use of digital technologies, providing the flexibility necessary for continuous process improvement, transformation, and innovation. vBPM uses this opportunity to align business strategy and technology to establish an ongoing management discipline around business processes.

Services (or applications) can be stored within an enterprise or at a third-party IT environment. In the latter case, they are procured through the Web and thus are called Web services. This makes an enterprise independent from technical changes and new IT developments. A company can focus on the application of IT to support the business processes.

SOA can be built, based on software products, such as SAP NetWeaver [17], Oracle Fusion [18], Microsoft BizTalk [19], IBM WebSphere [20], Pegasystems [21], Software AG's webMethods [22], or many others. The first three mentioned vendors also deliver traditional standard software. They decided to add SOA architecture building blocks to deliver more flexible process-oriented solutions. In other words, they offer the described middleware platforms, but also some of the required services. However, SOA also opens the doors for new, smaller software companies that may only deliver some very specialized services used in a larger vendor's SOA environment. The selection of appropriate solutions for a specific company context is handled by vBPM.

The integration of the design and modeling software supporting the process factory and the overall SOA environment is important for seamless support of the process life cycle. For example, the aforementioned ARIS solution for process modeling is integrated well with webMethods but also other middleware platforms [23]. When selecting a software application for the business process factory, this integration aspect should be an important selection criterium.

Many enterprises utilize not one homogeneous SOA environment, but various SOA-related technology components from multiple vendors or even self-developed SOA software. Some possible reasons for such heterogeneous environments include mergers and acquisitions, different strategies in divisions of an enterprise group, or other historic developments in a company. The use of multiple middleware platforms generally still allows an enterprise to achieve the described benefits of SOA. For example, each platform can support one or several business processes. Or the platforms can be integrated using their own integration technology so that one process can be supported through multiple platforms. However, it is important that the process models, the knowledge about business process, are stored in the overlying process warehouse of the process factory for distribution to the various SOA environments. This is the precondition for an effective enterprise-wide process management as required. The use of multiple SOA environments driven through one process factory is visualized in Fig. 3.7.

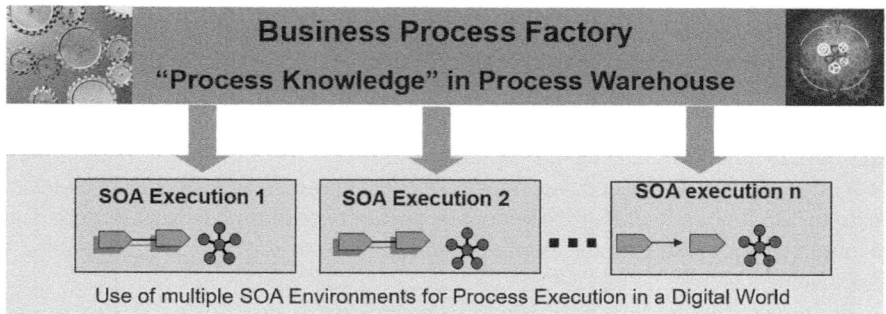

Fig. 3.7 Process factory with multiple SOA environments

SOA delivers a new dimension of flexibility, supporting the goals of vBPM. However, this flexibility does not come without a price. It requires a thorough process design, resulting in semantically and syntactically correct process models. These models are necessary to manage the available flexibility. That is why, a functioning process factory is essential for the use of SOA. Since over 80% of an organization's processes are in general less relevant for achieving competitive advantage, the use of traditional standard software is still appealing for those commodity processes. For many enterprises, the combination of ERP and other traditional software systems with SOA can be the best solution for process execution.

SOA also allows integration with other companies' software applications, for example, by leveraging the Internet. Therefore, it is also an enabler of inter-enterprise processes, like those presented in the Intel-Siemens case in Chap. 2. Such processes across several organizations are key enablers of high-performance enterprises [5].

This is a good point to look into the future—which has already begun. How does SOA evolve? What does the next generation of process execution bring?

3.3 The Next Generation of Process Execution: The Power of Digitalization

Digitalization has become a powerful force in almost every organization. The integration of products and physical objects, people, and processes based on the "Internet of everything" paves the way to disruptive process innovation and new business models. The "Industry 4.0" concept, especially discussed in Europe, applies digitalization to the manufacturing industry by integrating products, equipment, processes, and people [24]. Digitalization enables new business models realizing, for example, affordable mass individualization. A company can produce, e.g., sports shoes, based on the individual requirements of the client stored in transponders fixed to the shoe. The shoe "communicates" to the different machines to trigger the appropriate production activities. The Internet is used to link "everything to everything." Intelligent process management systems react to events, like changes of environmental data [25, 26]. Mobile devices, social media approaches, the handling of huge amounts of data in a short time through "Big Data" approaches, related new analytics capabilities, or the use of cloud-based applications enable and accelerate those developments [25]. The continuously growing computing power enables formerly unimaginable process performance [27].

New IT architectures are clearly driven by the World Wide Web (WWW). The common opinion that the Internet hype would end after the burst of the dot-com bubble in 2001 has proven to be wrong. On the contrary, Web capabilities have continuously improved and the ability to bring people and organizations together in communities has become more important than ever [5]. The new generation of WWW capabilities is often called "Web 2.0."

Web 2.0 can be perceived as the second generation of Web-based communities and hosted services, which aim to facilitate creativity, collaboration, and the sharing of ideas and data between users. The term was created and promoted in a conference organized by O'Reilly Media in 2004 [28]. O'Reilly characterized Web 2.0 by describing the core competencies of Web 2.0 companies [29] as follows:

- Instead of packaged software, services (procured through the web) with cost-effective scalability are used.
- Control over unique, hard-to-recreate data sources, which get richer as more and more people use these sources.
- Trusting users as co-developers.
- Harnessing collective intelligence.
- Customer self-service.
- Software above the level of single devices.
- Lightweight user interfaces, development models, and business models.

A key differentiator of any Web 2.0 service or application continuously improves the results and usefulness as more people utilize it. Therefore, such an application either solicits data directly from the user or finds intelligent data-mining capabilities to continuously produce better data. Those Web pages are called "wikis." Examples of such Web 2.0 applications include the online encyclopedia Wikipedia, created and maintained by its users; social networks, like "LinkedIn"; and Google Search, which improves search results, based on characteristics of past searches [29, 30]. Web 2.0 applications often utilize so-called mash-ups, composite applications using data or functionality from existing Web applications and combining them with new content, delivering additional value to the user without changing the original sources [31]. An example is HousingMaps.com, which combines mapping functionality from "Google Maps" with apartment rental information [31].

Some people are already talking about Web 3.0, which combines the capabilities of Web 2.0 with the so-called Semantic Web [32]. This brings structure to the data masses and enables users to find desired information more efficiently. On the basis of this structure, it will be easier to find the information needed and to make ready use of all the data available through the Web.

Although the aforementioned Web 2.0 applications are more focused on private users, there are already many current initiatives to transfer those capabilities into the business world, targeting enterprise clients. The result is the "Enterprise 2.0." Enterprise 2.0 is a company using the capabilities of Web 2.0 as part of its digitalization approach for its business purposes, including an integrated "business-to-business" (B2B) environment [30, 33]. In this context, the term "Management 2.0" is used to express the idea that these new Web capabilities require an appropriate management approach [34]. In this book, we discuss the Enterprise 2.0"+" to reflect that future Web developments are included in the overall digital technology architecture of an organization.

3.3 The Next Generation of Process Execution: The Power of Digitalization

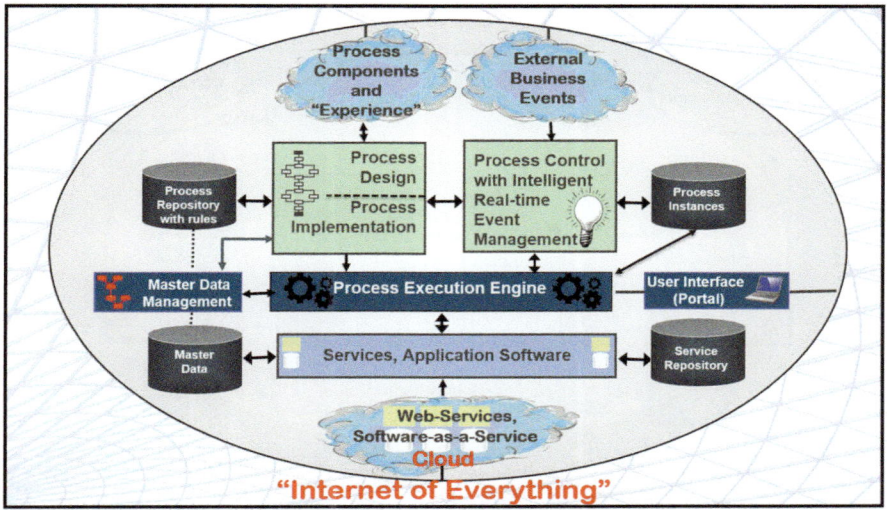

Fig. 3.8 Next-generation IT architecture for process execution—core

Enterprise 2.0+ technologies encompass the following six components [35]:

- Search capabilities: They enable users to easily find the information for which they are looking.
- Links: The information about links between Web pages is utilized.
- Authoring: Users author content of Web pages (e.g., in the form of blogs).
- Tags: Users categorize information through tags to make it more accessible.
- Extensions: Applications automate a part of the categorization work by suggesting content to users, based on past clicks.
- Signals: Users are informed when new content of interest is published.

The vision for a next-generation IT architecture for process execution is shown in Fig. 3.8. The architecture is based on a SOA concept. Core is an integrated process design and implementation component coupled with a component for the management and real-time control of the executed business process instances [36]. The integrated intelligent event management enables the adjustment of the executed process instances to changes in the business environment, such as new customer requirements or supplier issues. Quality issues in delivered materials, for example, may immediately trigger quality assurance or rework processes, or the arrival of a specific customer-order type may lead to certain preparation activities. "Exception events," such as extreme cycle times for an order, may lead to correcting activities related to the specific process instance.

A process execution engine organizes the workflow and links to the various application services, procured through the cloud. This can be small focused application components or larger applications which may be rented for a monthly fee, so-called software as a service. Even the design, implementation, control, and

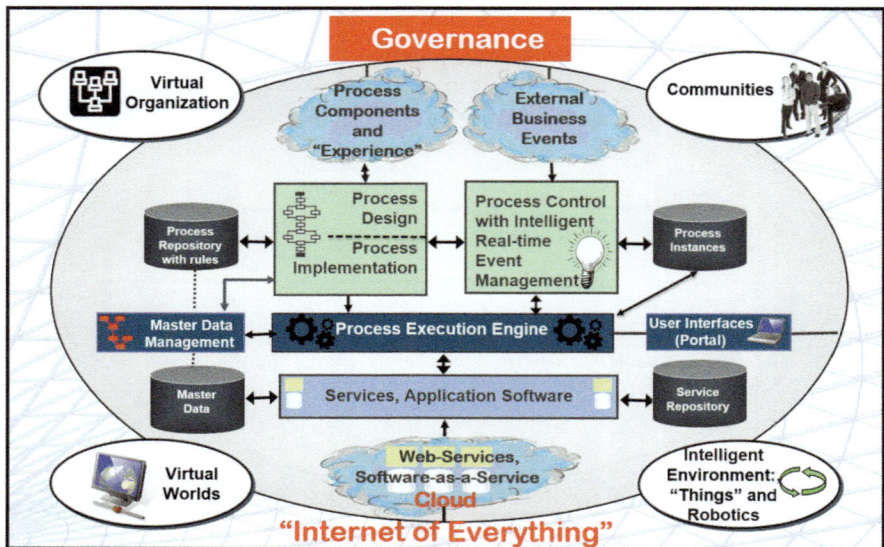

Fig. 3.9 Next-generation IT architecture for process execution—integrated with business environment

execution software could be procured through the cloud to minimize the in-house technology infrastructure and related maintenance efforts. A portal serves as standard user interface that can be accessed through the Web using a variety of devices, like PCs, tablets, or smartphones. This can be complemented through mobile "apps" enabling a more effective access to the process management technology environment.

The master data management (MDM) is handled across all processes to avoid redundancies and inconsistencies. MDM becomes an integrated component of vBPM. This is required to avoid unnecessary process variants and inefficiencies, such as research for missing customer data or delivery issues due to wrong address information [37].

The BPM design component can receive external inputs through the Web. This may include general experiences regarding certain business best and common practices or formal reference models showing relevant business practices. In return, an enterprise also provides this information to others. The BPM event management reacts to more general external events, such as price changes for raw materials, or general macroeconomic events, like changes and trends of currency exchange rates.

The next-generation IT architecture is highly integrated with the business environment to realize the full potential of our digital world. This is shown in Fig. 3.9. A company may be a member of the whole set of online communities. Imagine using an environment like YouTube to exchange business process models. Instead of posting videos, companies could post process models representing their organization's best business practices or other interesting process ideas. The participation at market places, e.g., for the procurement of application software, can help benefit from new developments across the world. The membership in legal communities helps evaluate compliance challenges; HR communities provide newest thinking regarding people management. There is endless opportunity for the exchange of information within and across specific industries. This helps master the volatility of our business environment to stay on a high-performance level.

The Web 2.0 environment could be utilized to make the next-generation enterprise part of a powerful virtual organization. For example, one could create an "innovation network" around the company, including customers, partners, research institutes, universities, etc. The exchange of ideas could be organized through blogs (derived from "Web log"). A blog is a Website where entries are written in chronological order and generally displayed in reverse chronological order [38]. Members of the network make their entries, and the blog facilitator includes them in the overall innovation process.

Until now, most information systems received necessary data through human interaction. For example, a person enters the shipping data of orders. This is often very costly and leads to delays. New technologies, like radio frequency identification (RFID), enable the automated creation of that data. For example, once containers are loaded into a ship, this information is automatically transferred through RFID into a software system and from there becomes available through the Web. But also "machines" become intelligent. They execute specific actions based on the information they receive. Robots "learn" how to manage a warehouse or other more and more unstructured tasks [27]. The result is an "intelligent environment" which is accessible all over the world through the "Internet of things" [39, 40]. Ultimately this leads to business processes of an unimaginable performance level. Similar technologies can also be used to improve products and services, leading to "intelligent products" that behave in a context-sensitive way [39]. An example is cars automatically moving toward a destination and applying the brakes whenever necessary.

This intelligent environment closes the gap between the real and the virtual world step by step. Once you have more and more information about the real world digitized, you can start using this information as building blocks for a virtual world, allowing the realistic test and simulation of new innovative business process as described earlier. You can "live" a new business model before transferring it into reality. The boundaries between the real and virtual worlds begin to blur.

This move to a virtual environment is also reflected in the trend to procure the necessary application software through the cloud—fast, at low risk, and at low price. The cloud has become a major enabler of digitalization and the next-generation enterprise [41]. As a result, more and more of the core information technology moves out of the organization. Companies use the software and concentrate on getting best value out of it. Hence, the key assets which stay in the organization are the business processes. This new reality is visualized in Fig. 3.10. IT experts need to transform into process experts that understand the business impacts and opportunities of the digital technology, less the technology itself. That's also the reason for the emerging new top management role of a chief process

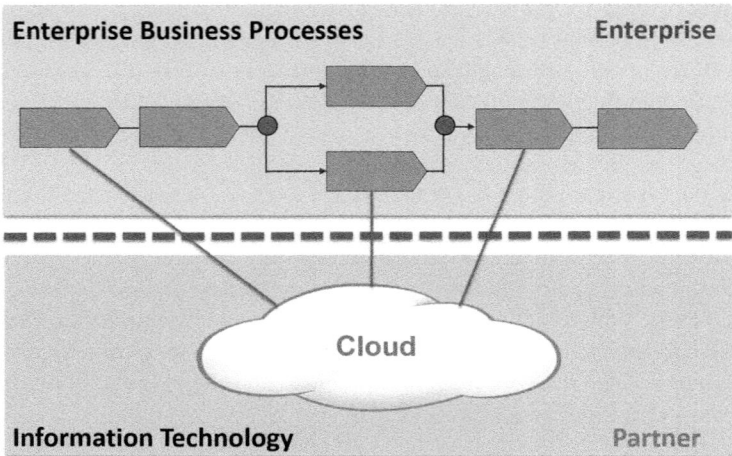

Fig. 3.10 The "cloud": Business processes stay, technology leaves

officer (CPO) [6, 7]. "Enlightened" chief information officers (CIOs) will migrate into that role—others will sooner or later disappear or report to the CPO or a similar role.

A key challenge of next-generation enterprise technology architectures is finding the appropriate governance model. Web 2.0 empowers people and encourages creativity. But how do you ensure they still work toward the company's goals? A traditional governance model, consisting of many inflexible rules and policies, does not work in such an environment. The next-generation enterprise could utilize a governance model similar to that of the online encyclopedia Wikipedia. Users are guided through common goals and control it by themselves. However, it is clear that an enterprise is more complex, so the governance has to be more refined. But the direction of the new governance models is demonstrated by Web 2.0 communities like Wikipedia. We will discuss the topic business process governance in more detail later.

The next-generation enterprise with its open and agile digital architecture is clearly a perfect environment to unleash the full potential of vBPM. It permanently delivers the information necessary for timely decisions and supports the almost real-time execution of the resulting actions. Strategy and operational performance are closely integrated. Agility and innovation are strongly encouraged while still addressing efficiency, quality, compliance, alignment, and conservation of good existing practices.

But the next-generation enterprise also demonstrates that ultimately, high performance depends on people and the way they act within their business processes. They have to feel comfortable with and accept the upcoming change through digitalization and the next generation of technology architectures. Only then will they realize all of its potential. In the next chapter, we will discuss how this change can be managed so that people really feel comfortable with it. They are enabled to see the change as an opportunity, not as a threat.

3.4 Bottom Line

- Traditional standard software solutions, like ERP systems, not only deliver a technology to execute a specific process but also common business practices reflected in the software and its processing logic (Sect. 3.1).
- The use of ERP and similar standard software systems mean you must somewhat adapt your organization to the requirements of the software-based business processes. This works well for most of the commodity processes but creates challenges for the high-impact processes necessary to create competitive advantage because they are mostly company specific (Sect. 3.1).
- A business process-oriented implementation approach is required for ERP or similar software systems. In other words, during the implementation of the software into the enterprise, all modules necessary to support an entire business process must be implemented. Otherwise, the implementation leads back to a functional organization since those traditional software systems are in general functionally structured (Sect. 3.1).
- SOA enables the separation of the business process design and support through appropriate application software components. Consequently, the application software can be used exactly as required by the company-specific business processes (Sect. 3.2).
- The true value of SOA is only delivered when the environment is used to support business transformation, to enable company-specific processes and process innovation (Sect. 3.2).
- The knowledge about new or modified processes can be transferred efficiently and effectively into the technical components of SOA, based on a tight integration of process design software (modeling software) and the SOA execution environment (Sect. 3.2).
- SOA delivers a new dimension of flexibility; however, this flexibility does not come without a price. It requires a thorough process design, resulting in semantically and syntactically correct processes and other information models (Sect. 3.2).
- Digitalization integrates products, people, and processes through the "Internet of everything." It enables new business models for the next-generation enterprise (Sect. 3.3).
- Web 2.0 can be perceived as the second generation of Web-based communities and hosted services, which facilitate creativity, collaboration, and sharing of ideas and data between users. The use of Web 2.0 and related concepts in a business environment leads to the Enterprise 2.0+, an example for the next-generation enterprise (Sect. 3.3).

- The next-generation enterprise is highly integrated with the business environment, participating in communities, acting as part of virtual organizations, and using technologies to digitize the real environment to make it a component of virtual worlds (Sect. 3.3).
- The "cloud" provides necessary application software through the Internet; more and more onsite software and related technology disappears from organizations. Business processes become key assets of an organization (Sect. 3.3).
- The next-generation enterprise with its agile technology infrastructure is a perfect enabler of the full potential of vBPM (Sect. 3.3).
- A key challenge of the next-generation enterprise with its technology architecture is to find the appropriate governance model (Sect. 3.3).

References

1. Kirchmer, M.: Business Process Oriented Implementation of Standard Software—How to Achieve Competitive Advantage Efficiently and Effectively, 2nd edn. Springer, Berlin (1999)
2. Kirchmer, M., Scheer, A.W.: Business process automation—combining best and next practices. In: Scheer, A.W., Abolhassan, E., Jost, W., Kirchmer, M. (eds.) Business Process Automation—ARIS in Practice, pp. 1–15. Springer, Berlin (2004)
3. Kirchmer, M.: Knowledge communication empowers SOA for business agility. In: Proceedings of the 11th World Multi-conference on Systemics, Cybernetics and Informatics, 8–11 July 2007, vol. 3, pp. 301–307. Orlando (2007)
4. Jost, W.: Vom CIO zum CPO. In: Harvard Business Manager (2004)
5. Fingar, P.: Extreme Competition—Innovation and the Great 21st Century Business Reformation. Meghan-Kiffer, Tampa (2006)
6. Kirchmer, M., Franz, P.: Chief Process Officer—The Value Scout. BPM-D Whitepaper, Philadelphia (2014)
7. Kirchmer, M., Franz, P., von Rosing, M.: The chief process officer: An emerging tope management role. In: von Rosing, M., Scheer, A.-W., von Scheel, H. (eds.) The Complete Business Process Handbook—Body of Knowledge from Process Modeling to BPM, vol. 1, pp. 343–348. Amsterdam, Boston, e.a (2015)
8. Davenport, T.: Mission Critical—Realizing the Promise of Enterprise Systems. Harvard Business School, Boston (2000)
9. SAP AG (ed.): http://wwwll.sap.com/usa/solutions/business-suite/erp/index.epx (2007)
10. Oracle, Inc. (ed.): http://www.oracle.com/apphcations/e-business-suite.html (2007)
11. Microsoft, Inc. (ed.): http://www.microsoft.com/dynamics/default.mspx (2007)
12. Salesforce.com Inc (ed): http://www.salesforce.com/products/ (2015)
13. Franz, P., Kirchmer, M.: Value-driven Business Process Management—The Value-Switch for Lasting Competitive Advantage. McGraw-Hill, New York, e.a (2012)
14. Woods, D.: Enterprise Service Architectures. O'Reilly, Beijing (2003)
15. Kalakota, R., Robinson, M.: Service Blueprint: A Roadmap for Execution. Addison-Wesley, Boston (2003)
16. Woods, D., Mattern, T.: Enterprise SOA—Designing IT for Business Innovation. O'Reilly, Beijing (2006)
17. SAP AG (ed.): SAP NetWeaver helps put you ahead of the curve. sap.com (2007)
18. Oracle, Inc. (ed.): Oracle fusion—next generation applications. oracle.com (2007)
19. Microsoft, Inc. (ed.): Your business—connected. BizTalk. Microsoft.com (2007)

References

20. Newman, D.: BPM & SOA: Real world stories of business success. In: IQPC (ed.) Proceedings of the Business Process Management Summit, Las Vegas (2007)
21. www.pega.com (2007)
22. Software AG (ed.): http://www.softwareag.com/corporate/products/default.asp (2015)
23. Software AG (ed.): http://www.softwareag.com/corporate/products/aris_alfabet/default.asp (2015)
24. Scheer, A.-W.: Industry 4.0—From Vision to Realization. Scheer Whitepaper 5, Saarbruecken, May 2015
25. Sinur, J., Odell, J., Fingar, P.: Business Process Management—The Next Wave. Meghan-Kiffer Press, Tampa (2013)
26. Fisher, L. (ed.): Intelligent BPM Systems—Impact and Opportunity. Future Strategies, Lighthouse Point (2013)
27. Brynjolfsson, E., McAffee, A.: The Second Machine Age—Work, Progress and Prosperity in a Time of Brilliant Technologies. W.W. Norton, New York (2014)
28. Wikipedia. (ed): Web 2.0. www.wikipedia.com (2007)
29. O'Reilly, T.: What is web 2.0—design patterns and business models for the next generation of software. www.oreilly.com (2005)
30. Heuser, L., Alsdorf, G., Woods, D.: International Research Forum 2006—Web 2.0—IT Security-Real World Awareness—IT as a Tool for Growth and Development. New York (2006)
31. Bradly, A., Gootzit, D.: Who's who in enterprise 'Mashup' technologies. In: Gartner Research, ID Number: G00151351 (2007)
32. Wahlster, W, Dengel, A.: Web 3.0 convergence of web 2.0 and the semantic web. In: Technology Radar Feature Paper, Edition 11/2006, Germany (2006)
33. Heuser, L., Alsdorf, C., Woods, D.: Enterprise 2.0, The Service Grid, User-Driven Innovation, Business Model Transformation—International Research Forum 2007. New York (2008)
34. Lochmaier, L.: Management 2.0 und der intelligente Schwarm. manager-magazin.de (2007)
35. McAffee, A.: Enterprise 2.0: the dawn of emergent collaboration. In: MIT Sloan Management Review, vol. 43, no. 3, Spring (2006)
36. Carter, S: The New Language of Business—SOA & Web 2.0. IBM Press, Upper Saddle River (2007)
37. Packowski, J., Gall, J., Baumeister, H.: Enterprise Process and Information Governance—Integration of business process and master data governance as competitive advantage—Study Results, Camelot Whitepaper (2014)
38. Wikipedia. (ed): Blog. www.wikipedia.com, 12/2007
39. Fleisch, E., Christ, O., Dierkes, M.: Die betriebswirtschafthche vision des internets der dinge. In: Fleisch, E., Mattern, F. (eds.) Das Internet der Dinge—Ubiquitous Computing und RFID in der Praxis, pp. 3–37. Springer, Berlin (2005)
40. Mattern, F: Die technische Basis fuer das Internet der Dinge. In: Fleisch, E., Mattern, F. (ed.) Das Internet der Dinge—Ubiquitous Computing und RFID in der Praxis, pp. 39–66. Berlin (2005)
41. Abolhassan, F. (ed.): Was treibt die Digitalisierung? Warum an der Cloud kein Weg vorbeifuehrt. Springer Gabler, Wiesbaden (2016)

Chapter 4
People Enablement for Process Execution

Change is the only constant in today's business environment. Mastering this change successfully is a main driver for establishing business process-oriented management approaches in enterprises striving for high performance. New, flexible digital information technology (IT) architectures provide the necessary agility and innovation from a technology point of view, as we have discussed in the previous chapter. But how can you prepare people and help them cope with impending adjustments? How can people benefit from the opportunities of change and avoid the threats? People enablement through appropriate change management provides the answer to those questions. People change management has become one of the greatest challenges for organizations on their journey to high performance in our digital world. Companies have to manage their talent with caution and enable continuous learning, as well as help adjust to different business and work environments.

People need to master change triggered through different business situations with different impacts on the members of an organization. Typical examples for such triggers of change are the following [1]:

- New or changing customers, suppliers, or other market partners
- New or altered market offerings (goods, services, information, etc.)
- Changing legal regulations
- Availability of new or modified technologies, like application software or other digital technologies
- Outsourcing of processes or subprocesses
- Mergers and acquisitions
- New business models, e.g., enabled through a major digitalization
- Cultural differences in new enterprise locations
- Internationalization with various country requirements

All of the resulting changes affect one or several business processes. The execution of most of the processes requires a combination of people and technologies. Therefore, an effective people change management is required, enabling

Fig. 4.1 Focus on people aspects of vBPM

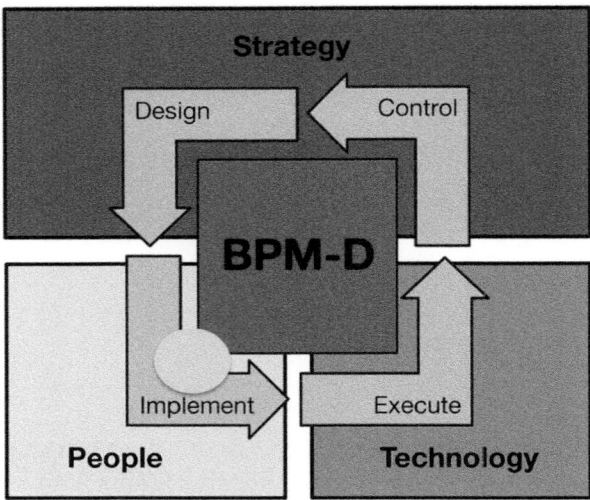

everybody to drive high performance. Even if a digital initiative leads to the automation of an entire process, this may result in process changes for employees in the technology department or in other business processes. Again, effective people change management is necessary.

In this chapter, we will discuss how to handle the people side of such process changes. We will show how people are enabled to drive the success in our volatile business environment. People are a key asset when establishing the discipline of vBPM [2]. The focus of this chapter is shown in Fig. 4.1.

4.1 What Is Business Process Change Management?

Let us look at a few examples of business process changes. The business-driven implementation of new digital technologies, like "mobile business" (m-business), can result in many business process changes [3]. An example is shown in Fig. 4.2. In a traditional process, a truck with office supplies arrives at an office supply store. Then, the truck driver checks with the store clerk, who consults his IT system to find out which supplies are needed. The truck driver documents the necessary inventory changes and fills the store shelves. Then, the store clerk books the inventory adjustments for his shop. The m-business process improves this procedure. With his mobile device, the truck driver accesses the store application systems so he can do all bookings by himself.

Cultural differences with different market expectations can drive the adjustment and change of business processes as well. An example for this is visualized in Fig. 4.3. In a process typical of Japanese environments, there is a high focus on quality. The quality assurance activities are carried out twice: on the customer side

4.1 What Is Business Process Change Management? 69

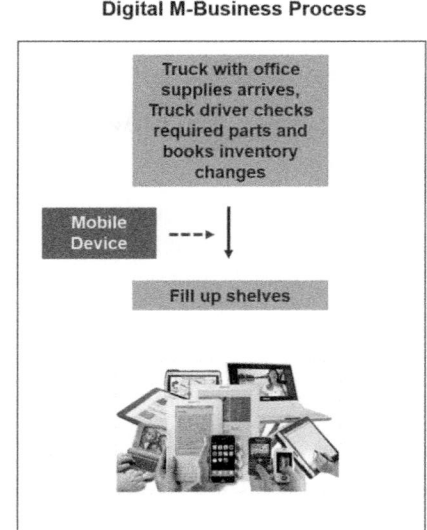

Fig. 4.2 Digital m-business—technology drives business process changes

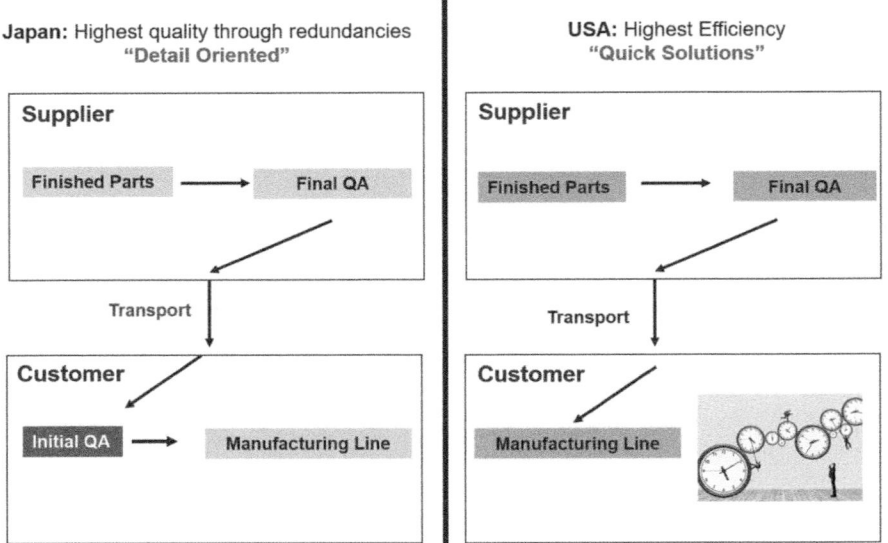

Fig. 4.3 Business processes can reflect cultural differences

and on the supplier side. The redundancy ensures the highest-quality standards and demonstrates the characteristic Japanese attention to details, although the process is not 100% efficient. If efficiency is the main goal, these redundancies are eliminated. Depending on business goals and the cultural environment, one of the processes may be changed to the other. This is a question global companies would have to answer (we will discuss the effects of globalization in detail later on).

All the described changes require the related modifications of existing business processes or the creation of new ones; thus, business process change management is necessary. To ensure that such a change is really effective for an organization, the following conditions should be fulfilled [4]:

- There must be a perceived advantage of the change that can be identified by the people who will have to make the change.
- The change must be compatible with the involved people's thought process.
- The change must be as easy-to-understand as possible.
- The change must be divisible and executable in phases or by different people.
- It must be possible to communicate the change clearly without using a new vocabulary with which people are not familiar.
- The change must be reversible and can be undone if things do not work out as expected.
- The change should be as cost efficient as possible and require as little time as possible from the people involved.
- The change has to treat people with respect; it must not result in embarrassment for the involved people.
- The initiator of the change must have credibility or a reputation of success.
- The change must be realistic and really do what it is supposed to do.
- The consequences of failure must be minimized.

In most business situations, it is not possible to fulfill all those requirements. However, experience has shown that at least seven to eight [4] of the requirements should be met in order to make a change truly successful. Change management then ensures the following conditions to achieve a successful process change [5]:

- Necessary actions are initiated with an acceptable delay after the external change has occurred.
- Necessary actions are executed in a fast and effective way.
- All reactions and actions are initiated and executed in a controlled manner.

As explained, the effective management of the permanent change is a key success factor for an enterprise and a precondition to move from "good to great" [6]. It is of fundamental importance that the people involved in changing processes are able to understand and accept those changes and, ultimately, make them happen. Therefore, the most appropriate definition of change management includes the combination of the following activities [1, 7]:

- Information
- Communication
- Training

People must be informed of the changes and invited to provide feedback. An intense communication period typically occurs at this point. And finally, people

4.1 What Is Business Process Change Management?

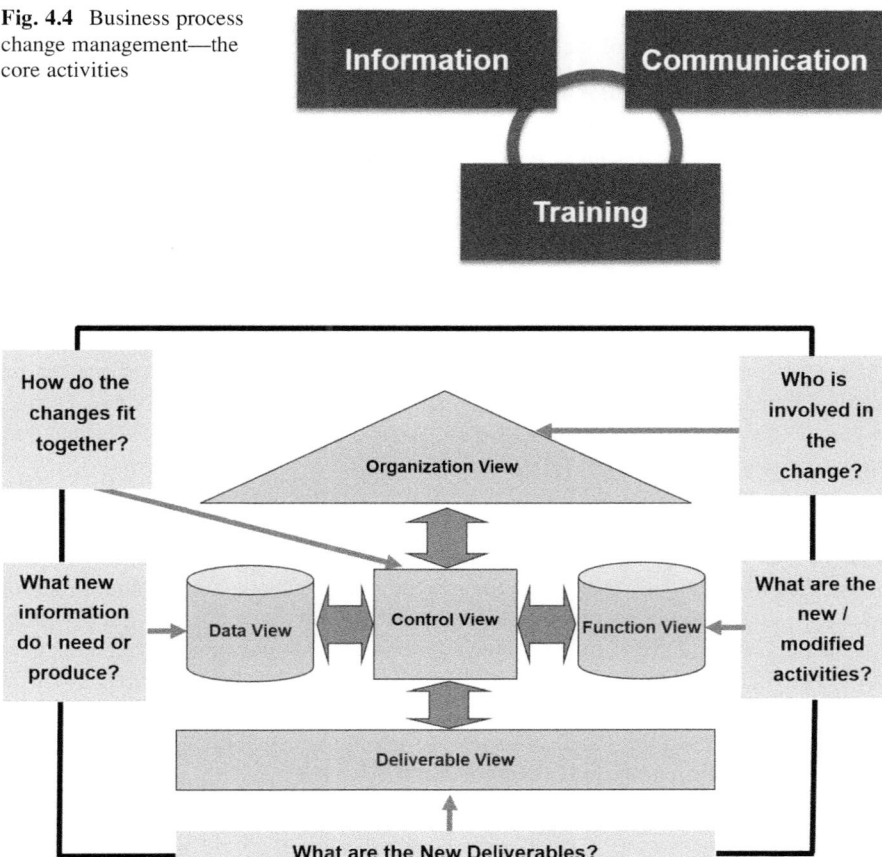

Fig. 4.4 Business process change management—the core activities

Fig. 4.5 Business process change management based on the ARIS Architecture

have to be trained to be successful in the new business process environment. Figure 4.4 visualizes this basic definition for business process change management.

The content of the relevant information, communication, and training concerning specific business processes can be structured using the ARIS Architecture, previously discussed [7, 8]. This ensures that all relevant process aspects are addressed. The major questions to be handled in change management activities can be directly deducted from the ARIS information system views, as shown in Fig. 4.5:

- Who (people, departments, different enterprises, etc.) is involved in the change (organization view)?
- What are the new or modified functions and why are they better (function view)?
- What new or modified information is needed or produced and why is it better (data view)?
- Which new or modified deliverables are expected and why (deliverable view)?

- How do the changes fit together and how do they influence and improve the overall process (control view)?

This structure for change management based on ARIS also ensures the overall integration into vBPM because vBPM also applies the ARIS framework and its principles to describe business processes. This leads to an overall consistent and integrated approach, which supports the required effectiveness of the approach as part of the overall process of process management [9]. People-related activities are based on the same business process knowledge assets as technology-related activities.

Business process change management is again a process in and of itself. Information, communication, and training are subprocesses. Therefore, process-oriented methodologies and approaches (e.g., for the design or the implementation) can be applied to manage business process change. The principles of vBPM can be used to organize the process change management. BPM-related software can be utilized to support change management [10].

Once people have to start working in a new transformed process, a learning curve with a performance decrease is almost unavoidable. vBPM manages the change management process in a way to minimize the time required for this learning period and to minimize the performance effects during that time. In addition, vBPM manages change management to reduce the risk of not reaching the desired outcomes. It enables people to create the planned value through the new process. This aspect of managing the process of people change management is shown in Fig. 4.6.

We will now examine the elements of change management in more detail, starting with information and communication.

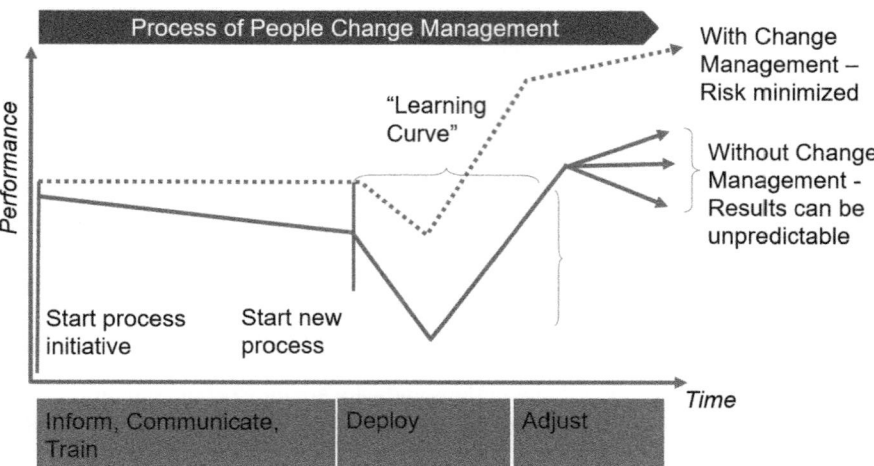

Fig. 4.6 Business process change management based on the ARIS Architecture

4.2 How Do You Provide Information and Communication?

The starting points of most change management activities are information and communication. Both must be adapted to the cultural environment of the enterprise and its specific situation. For example, you may need to act cautiously in a company that is in a bad economic situation because people may fear for their jobs. In a software enterprise founded only a few years ago, people may be more accustomed to change and accept it easily. In a 100-year-old traditional manufacturing company, people may be much less accustomed to and less open to change. The situation in the public sector is also different because of numerous legal requirements and policies.

The following general guidelines are related to the preparation of information and communication activities in an organization [7] starting a business process change management initiative:

- Segment the audience—Different groups of people must be addressed differently in their "language" and consider their specific situation.
- Use multiple channels—People have personal preferences regarding where they like to get their news; some may prefer e-mail or other kinds of computer-based communication, while others are more open to phone or face-to-face communication.
- Use multiple voices—Switch between various "messengers" who may each address people in a different style that facilitate a high level of acceptance.
- Be clear—Set understandable expectations to avoid later misunderstandings and disappointment.
- Honesty is the only policy—Sooner or later people will find out the truth anyway, so do not hold it back.
- Use emotions, not just logic—You are dealing with human beings who have feelings about situations, which is something you can use to your advantage.
- Encourage—Change is always difficult; nevertheless, people have to feel good about the situation to be successful.
- Make the message tangible—Tell people specifically what will change for them and their work environment and what the specific expectations are.
- Listen, listen, listen—Your people likely know more about their processes and the consequences of change than you.

The basis to apply all these guidelines is the audience segmentation. Once you know exactly who you are addressing, you can optimize your information and communication activities accordingly, applying the presented guidelines. The following questions facilitate audience segmentation [7]:

- Who is in the segment?
- How will people be affected?
- What reaction will they have?

- What behavior will we need from them?
- How can we stimulate this behavior?
- When shall we inform/communicate?
- What medium should we use for each message?
- Who should communicate the message?

Challenges for successful change management activities result from the following aspects:

- Disbelief
- False familiarity
- Fear
- The "rumor mill"
- Incomprehensibility
- Abstraction
- Complexity
- Use of cliches

The business process factory of vBPM delivers the necessary content for the information and communication activities in the form of business process models. The models can then be used as a common "language of change." The language of change facilitates the communication between various groups involved in a process change management initiative, such as business experts and managers, executives, technology experts, software vendors, and consultants. The use of formal methods, such as event-driven process chains (EPCs) or the business process-modeling notation (BPMN), helps to support clear, straightforward communication and minimizes misunderstandings. These modeling methods promote communication across company boundaries or between locations in various countries since they are well-established standards.

For example, a well-known pharmaceutical company uses process models widely as a communication basis. The company develops all job descriptions, based on process models. On the one hand, this ensures that the change documented in the models is actually implemented. On the other hand, it ensures that only realistic, achievable change suggestions are defined. Because the same business process models drive the people change management and the IT change, e.g., through a SOA environment, you end up in a holistic business process transformation.

To use those process models effectively for change management, the graphical representation of the models may have to be adjusted to the specific target segment of the information and communication activity. People who work in a warehouse or manufacturing environment may not be accustomed to process models consisting of rectangles, diamonds, ovals, and other abstract objects. They may even get anxious about them. Therefore, those abstract symbols could be replaced by more concrete objects, like a desk for a function or a picture of a person for an organizational unit. BPM tools used to support vBPM deliver a transformation from one model representation to another automatically [11] without changing any semantic content. An

4.2 How Do You Provide Information and Communication?

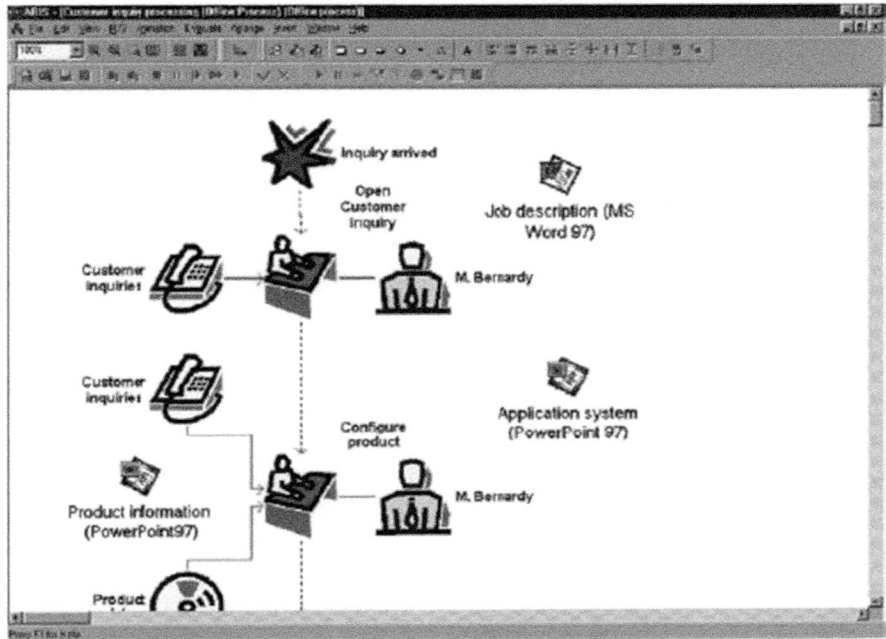

Fig. 4.7 Business process model in a less abstract format (in ARIS Toolset)

example of such process models in a less abstract format using the design functionality of the ARIS Platform is shown in Fig. 4.7.

Because the business process models are in a digital format, they can be distributed via the Internet, again using the process factory modeling environment [11]. This enables fast distribution of information, as required by vBPM, and the easy update of information because it is centralized in the process warehouse. This results in increased efficiency in the change management process.

In international company environments, cultural differences between locations in different countries must be taken into account. Therefore, different process model representation may be used in different countries. However, the semantic content of all the models remains the same; just their modeling format changes.

The unique effects of the global business environment and their impacts on vBPM will be discussed later.

Now, we will have a look at the training activities in a business process change management initiative. Information and communication pave the way for successful training regarding the new business processes.

4.3 How Do You Provide Process Training?

Training ensures that people can do their jobs as required by the altered or newly established business process. Training activities must also be organized with a business process-oriented approach and address the relevant changes of the existing as-is processes or the integration of a new process into the overall process landscape. Business process-oriented training can be divided into four major activities [12]:

- Basic training—business background
- Basic training—enabler (e.g., newly implemented application software or digital devices)
- Business process training
- Kick-off training

In basic business training, the changing business background is explained. This allows people to understand the motivation for the change and ensures they have the necessary general business knowledge to be successful in the new environment. For example, a manufacturing company that previously executed material requirements planning (MRP) manually implements an ERP solution, including the use of MRP functionality. This means employees who formerly did simple straightforward calculations of the quantities of required parts now have to decide how those parts should be ordered (e.g., based on a specific minimum stock or based on demand). They must set the appropriate parameters in the software application. The work requires more developed business skills, which are provided in the basic business training.

The basic "enabler" training is an introduction to new technologies or other enablers to be used in the changed processes. This training phase includes topics such as the handling of application software products or the use of new digital process performance tools like transponders. This training is less focused on "what to do" and more on "how to do things" in the future, in the changed business environment. In the past, this training phase was often considered very relevant. However, with easier to use IT systems, the importance of this training activity is less crucial. The focus then moves to the business and the process training.

The most important training component is clearly the business process training. This training empowers people to do their new or modified jobs in the changed process environment. These training activities explain how to apply the business knowledge using the new enablers in a business process to achieve the defined change and its business benefits. Hence, it makes the overall training value driven. It involves all aspects concerning the execution of the new business processes, as well as monitoring and controlling this process. This training phase ensures that people have the appropriate understanding of the end-to-end business process helping them to realize the impact of their work and the tasks of others involved in the process and on the final result of value for an internal or external customer.

4.3 How Do You Provide Process Training?

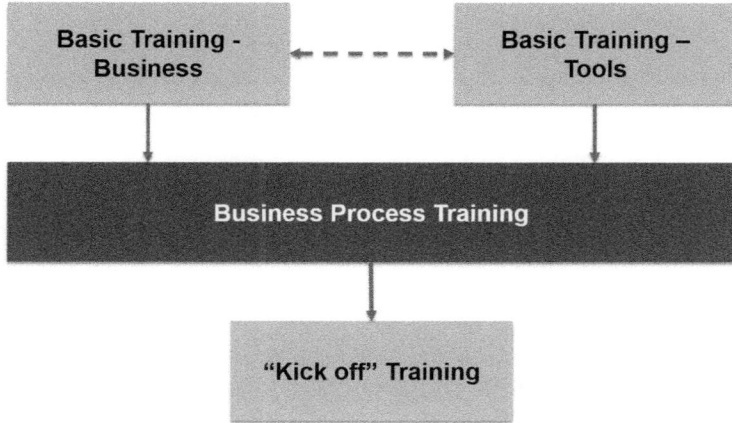

Fig. 4.8 Business process-oriented training

This training phase makes the overall training approach a key element of vBPM business process change management.

Kick-off training ensures that people recall the key aspects of the change before the "go live." This training chiefly prepares people for the first time phase when the changed business environment may not be 100% stabilized, e.g., due to initial technical issues. This includes information such as who to contact with questions or other work-arounds that may be necessary to keep the operational process functioning in spite of the issues.

The structure of the business process-oriented training is shown in Fig. 4.8.

In many instances, the delivery of the necessary training is the most expensive change management challenge for an enterprise. Frequently, thousands of people need training in new business processes and new enablers, such as ERP systems or new digital processes. Therefore, the introduction of computer-based training (CBT) has become more and more important and often replaces face-to-face classroom training [13]. Although it is important to increase the efficiency of vBPM, there may also be situations when face-to-face training is more appropriate. For example, it may be important to have spoken with some of the key experts personally to more easily ask questions at a later time. Also, face-to-face discussions are sometimes more effective. Therefore, a hybrid training approach, combining CBT and face-to-face training, is an excellent solution.

In combination with CBT, concepts of distance learning using the Internet as an enabler have also become increasingly more important [13–15]. This approach reduces logistical challenges significantly and ensures constant and consistent training quality. Therefore, this approach is again very relevant to ensuring the efficiency of vBPM. It has to be used in the right overall delivery mix for the various training sessions.

Distance learning via the Internet basically enables people to obtain the best education possible from wherever it is available. Universities in some countries may offer classes about relevant business topics that are not available in other countries. This is no longer an issue. Enterprises have the choice [16]. They can use education offerings from institutions around the world via distance learning.

Much of the process training can also be integrated in the enabling technology itself, e.g., the SOA environment. People can view the process models and the process steps on which they are working, as well as the next activities to be executed. They can acquire necessary background information, submit questions, and learn about the process. This results in individualized, on-the-job training focused on relevant business processes.

Such an approach of integrated training also supports the concept of lifetime learning. Continuous change in the business environment, leading to process change, requires continuous training. Training becomes part of the day-to-day work. This is an important aspect for vBPM because it ensures the continuous integration of strategy and execution, resulting in high performance in our digital world.

For business process training, the use of virtual worlds could become an increasingly important method for delivery. The process models of the process factory could be used to configure a virtual environment where people can learn how to execute future processes. They "live" their future processes, just as pilots are trained using flight simulators [17].

4.4 Digitizing the Process of Change Management

The people enablement through the process of change management is a key subprocess of the BPM-Discipline that has a major impact on the outcomes of an improvement initiative. Hence, it is worth to invest in this process to innovate and optimize in this area. Therefore, organizations start to digitize the change management process itself, as already indicated at different occasions in this book.

The joint development and use of the information models in the process repository to identify the content for information, communication, and training, the collaborative publication of process models through the Internet, and the rollout of Web-based training and other learning tools are key examples for the direct digital support of change management. Especially the early involvement of many people in process design by using Web-based process-modeling and repository tools can be very helpful since it makes people part of the change and gives them a maximum of time to deal with it.

There are many more opportunities to improve this vBPM process, for example, through the management of process communities leveraging digital collaboration platforms, the use of process monitoring to show business progress of an initiative, or the application of process mining to identify issues with new business processes and suggest proactively solutions to the related people.

Innovative and digitized change processes bring important advantages [18]:

- Just-in-time feedback to people affected by the changes
- A personalized experience throughout the entire change period
- The management of change independent of existing hierarchies
- Communities of empathy that overcome change issues easier
- Continuous demonstration of progress

People enablement in general and the process change management in specific will continue to play a high-impact role in traditional and digital transformations. The change management process has started to benefit itself from our digital world.

4.5 The Bottom Line

- Business process change management is the combination of information, communication, and training regarding changes in existing business processes or the creation of new processes (Sect. 4.1).
- Change management ensures that the necessary actions are initiated with an acceptable delay, required actions are executed in a fast and effective way, and all reactions and actions are initiated and executed in a controlled manner to enable high performance (Sect. 4.1).
- The content of information, communication, and training concerning specific business processes can be structured using the ARIS Architecture (Sect. 4.1).
- Business process change management is a process in and of itself. Therefore, process-oriented methodologies and approaches can be applied. Business process management software can be used to support change management (Sect. 4.1).
- The change management processes need to be managed to minimize the period during which the change has a negative performance impact, and it must minimize this effect, as well as related risk (Sect. 4.1).
- Information and communication in a business process change management approach should be well prepared, including an audience segmentation (Sect. 4.2).
- The business process models delivered through the process factory can be used as a common "language of change" (Sect. 4.2).
- To use those process models effectively for change management, it may be necessary to adjust the graphical representation of the models to the specific target segment (Sect. 4.2).
- Business process-oriented training can be divided into four major activities: basic training concerning the business background, basic training concerning used enablers, business process training, and kick-off training (Sect. 4.3).
- The most important training phase is the business process training. It explains how to apply the business knowledge using the new enablers in a business process to achieve the defined change (Sect. 4.3).

- A hybrid training approach, combining CBT and face-to-face training, is generally an excellent delivery mode. Also, concepts of distance learning using the Internet as enabler become increasingly important (Sect. 4.3).
- The change management process itself is subject to innovation and optimization through digitization efforts (Sect. 4.4).

References

1. Kirchmer, M., Scheer, A.W.: Change management—key for business process excellence. In: Scheer, A.W., Abolhassan, E., Jost, W., Kirchmer, M. (eds.) Business Process Change Management—ARIS in Practice, pp. 1–14. Springer, Berlin (2003)
2. Franz, P., Kirchmer, M.: Value-driven Business Process Management—The Value-Switch for Lasting Competitive Advantage. McGraw-Hill, New York, e.a (2012)
3. Kalakota, R., Robinson, M.: M-Business—The Race to Mobility. McGraw Hill, New York (2002)
4. Oleson, J.: Pathways to Agility—Mass Customization in Action. Wiley, New York (1998)
5. Spath, D., Baumeister, M., Barrho, T., Dill, C: Change management im Wandel. In: Industrie Management—Zeitschrift fuer industrielle Geschaeftsprozesse, pp. 9–13 (2001)
6. Collins, J.: Good to Great—Why Some Companies Make the Leap…and Others Don't. Harper Collins, New York (2001)
7. Hammer, M., Stanton, S.: The Reengineering Revolution. Harper Collins, Glasgow (1995)
8. Scheer, A.W.: ARIS—Business Process Modeling, 2nd edn. Springer, Berlin (1998)
9. Kirchmer, M., Franz, P.: The Process of Process Management—Strategy Execution in a Digital World. BPM-D Whitepaper, Philadelphia (2015)
10. Exel, S., Wilms, S.: Change management with ARIS. In: Scheer, A.W., Abolhassan, E., Jost, W., Kirchmer, M. (eds.) Business Process Change Management—ARIS in Practice, pp. 23–18. Springer, Berlin (2003)
11. IDS Scheer, A.G. (ed.): ARIS Platform. Product Brochure. IDS Scheer, Saarbruecken (2007)
12. Kirchmer, M.: Business Process Oriented Implementation of Standard Software—How to Achieve Competitive Advantage Efficiently and Effectively, 2nd edn. Springer, Berlin (1999)
13. Kraemer, W., Mueller, M.: Virtuelle corporate university—executive education architecture and knowledge management. In: Scheer, A.W. (Ed.) Electronic Business und Knowledge Management—Neue Dimensionen fuer den Unternehmenserfolg, pp. 491–525. Physica Verlag, Heidelberg (1999)
14. Kirchmer, M.: e-Business Process Improvement (eBPI): Building and managing collaborative e-business scenarios. In: Callaos, N., Loutfi, M., Justan, M. (eds.) Proceedings of the 6th World Multiconference on Systemics, Cybernetics and Informatics, vol. 8, pp. 387–396. Orlando (2002)
15. Kraemer, W., Gallenstein, C., Sprendger, P.: Learning management fuer Fuehrungskraefte. In: Industrie Management—Zeitschrift fuer industrielle Geschaeftsprozesse, pp. 55–59 (2001)
16. Fingar, P.: Extreme Competition—Innovation and the Great 21st Century Business Reformation. Meghan-Kiffer, Tampa (2006)
17. Greenbaum, J.: SimEnterprise: The video gamer's guide to SAP's business-process revolution. SAP NetWeaver Magazine, vol. 2 (2006)
18. Ewenstein, B., Smith, W., Sologar, A.: Changing Change Management. McKinsey Digital, July 2015

Chapter 5
Business Process Governance

Today, many enterprises still use concepts of business process management (BPM) for one-time transformation and improvement projects or short-term initiatives. An increasing number of organizations, however, recognize its power as a fundamental management discipline which is instrumental in achieving strategic goals for competitive advantage and long-term success. BPM becomes the discipline of strategy execution. This demands ongoing attention to deliver high performance in our digital world. The "process of process management" has to be managed as part of the day-to-day business. Organizations must orchestrate and adapt their overall management approach to realize the full potential of the BPM-Discipline. These organizational aspects about granting power, making decisions, acting on them, and controlling the results are referred to as business process governance (BPG). BPG enables the effective management of the process life cycle and with that the achievement of high performance.

Andrew Spanyi, a well-known expert in BPM and the author of several related books [1, 2], and I have worked closely together on the topic of BPG. I had approached the field of BPG from a general organizational and infrastructure point of view, while he had focused on necessary leadership behavior. We discussed the topic and decided to combine the various aspects: leadership, required tools and technologies, and governance approaches with the resulting governance processes [3, 4]. The findings of our research are the basis for the discussions in this chapter, combined with recent developments and experience [5, 6].

BPG represents the overarching approach for the management of BPM. It defines the allocation of power and authority in the enterprise to establish a process-oriented "value network" across the mainly functional and traditional organization. BPG does not replace the existing organization. It adds an additional market- and customer-focused view that enables value through process management. Business trends, corporate strategies, legal requirements, and other aspects, like the use of specific standard software packages, influence the design of process governance. BPG sets the stage for the successful and business-driven use of next-generation process automation environments, such as service-oriented architectures

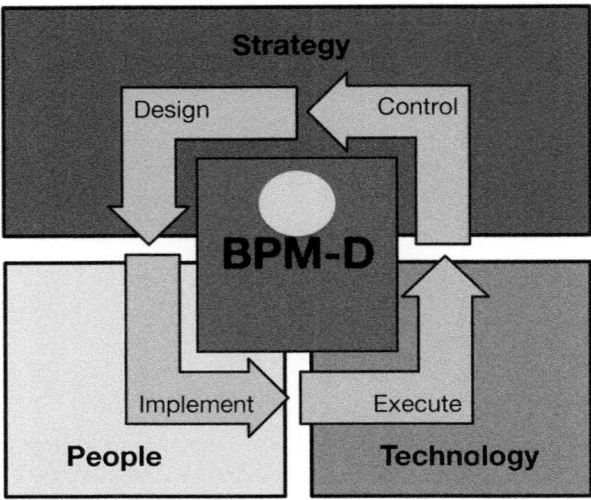

Fig. 5.1 Focus on organizing the BPM-Discipline

(SOA) or cloud-based applications. It is key to enable the value of digitalization [7]. BPG is also essential for effective change management since it helps to establish people enablement as ongoing capability of an organization. This is crucial in a permanently changing digital world [8].

BPG drives the entire BPM-Discipline. It is at the core of this management approach. This positioning is shown in Fig. 5.1.

You may wonder why this important strategic concept was not introduced earlier in this book. The reason is because it is easier to comprehend the concept and impact of BPG with an understanding of the approach of the discipline of value-driven BPM. There are many company-specific aspects to consider when you manage a successful BPM-Discipline in an organization. Therefore, successful BPG is always established in a way considering the specific company context.

But what exactly is BPG and why do you really need it? How do you establish and maintain it? We will now discuss the answers to these questions.

5.1 Business Process Governance: What Is It and Why Do You Need It?

Governance in general relates to procedures and decisions that seek to define actions, grant power, and verify performance [9]. If we transfer this definition to the field of business process management, "process governance" can be defined as the procedures and decisions that seek to define actions, grant power, and verify performance related to the "process of process management," hence the BPM-Discipline. BPG is a set of guidelines and definitions focused on organizing all BPM-related activities of an organization to manage its business processes toward achieving the strategic goals. The resulting governance framework provides the frame of reference to guide organizational units of an enterprise and enable ownership and accountability related to the discipline of process management. In its simplest terms, BPG can be considered the "definition" layer of the BPM-Discipline. It contributes to the allocation of power and authority in the entire enterprise by specifying the governance. It especially balances the power between functional responsibilities which are in general more focused on resource efficiency and process responsibilities which are market and client driven. BPG involves the following enabling components:

- A high-level identification of the company's main, cross functional business processes
- Clarity on the high-level goals to frame the definition of key performance indicators (KPIs) of these business processes
- Accountability and ownership for the management of business processes, combined with the appropriate empowerment, control, and guidelines
- Management of the knowledge about processes (process models, KPIs, etc.) to achieve the necessary transparency and visibility of the processes
- Aligned recognition and reward systems
- A set of priorities in improving key business processes and their subprocesses

The primary objective of BPG is to set the stage for the effective deployment of the BPM-Discipline to execute the company strategy and with that create value for customers, shareholders, employees, and other stakeholders. BPG ensures that BPM delivers consistent business results to satisfy and exceed the expectations of an organization. Thus, BPG "governs" BPM. It is responsible for the management of the BPM processes, the "process of process management." BPM again drives the success of all other business processes, including specific high-impact processes relevant for a company's competitive positioning. The interactions between BPG, BPM, and an organization's other operational business processes are visualized in Fig. 5.2.

BPG is established through governance processes. Let us look at a simple example regarding a restaurant that we want to manage in a process-oriented way. Two governance processes are depicted. The first process requests the automation of a business process but also requires the definition of a manual backup process to reduce or even eliminate the risk inherent to process automation. The second governance process presents the scenario for the manual process to be used. Should the automation technology malfunction then the backup process needs to be executed to ensure the delivery of the process results. These governance processes encourage efficient, automated processes that use the power of our digital world and simultaneously mitigate the risk of process automation. BPG drives the execution of the strategic goals of superior customer satisfaction. The governance processes, in the format of event-driven process chains (EPCs [10]), are shown in Fig. 5.3. The diamonds represent business events, the rectangles are functions, the ovals are organizational units, and the rectangles with the double line information objects are used or produced by a function.

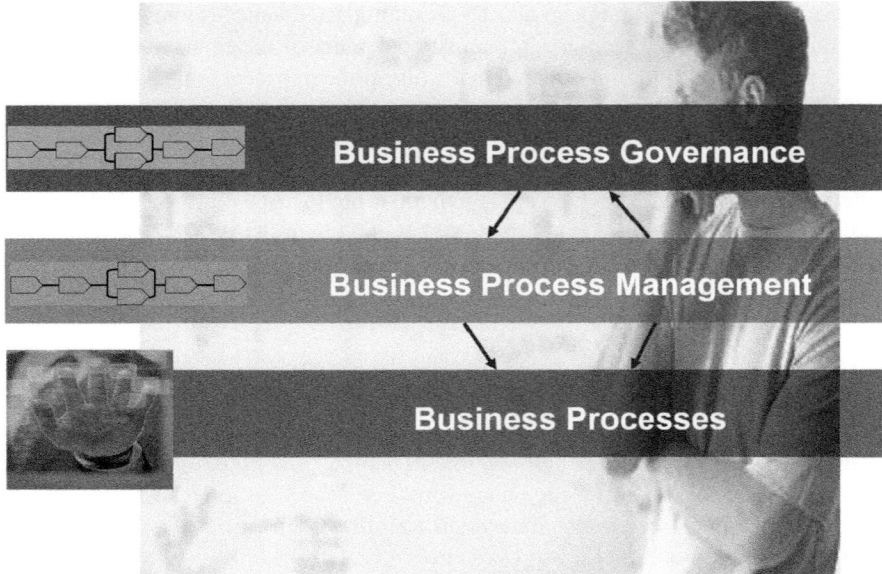

Fig. 5.2 Business process governance: Managing business process management

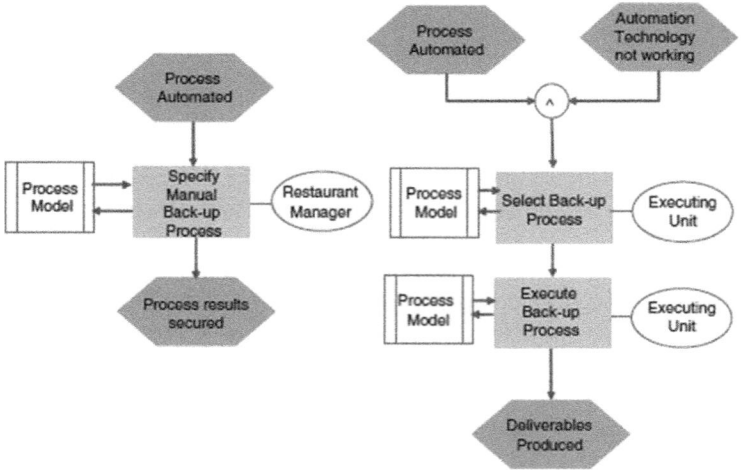

Fig. 5.3 Examples of governance processes for a restaurant

In the process design of a BPM initiative, those BPG processes lead to the design of processes for leveraging digitalization opportunities while mitigating the resulting risks. The waiter uses PDA, such as a tablet computer, to transfer the customer orders wirelessly to wherever the information is needed. This saves time and ultimately leads to high customer satisfaction. The backup processes are

5.1 Business Process Governance: What Is It and Why Do You Need It?

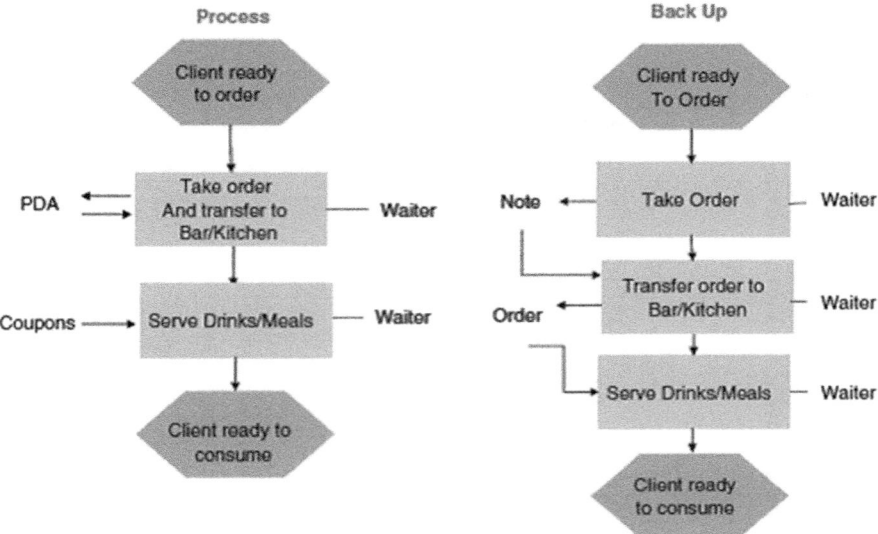

Fig. 5.4 Example of the design of selected restaurant processes

manual, independent of the implemented technologies, but still effective. They keep the restaurant running even in case of technology issues. The process is a traditional order process in the restaurant. Examples are shown in Fig. 5.4.

In both scenarios, the customer receives the ordered products. However, the manual processes are more time-consuming, inefficient, and susceptible to human error and hamper productivity. That's why they are only backups for the digital processes—which reduce potential risk.

In reality, if a patron visits our restaurant, the business processes are executed, based on the process design we just discussed. The information models developed through our BPM-Discipline are carried out in practice. If possible, the waiter ensures the efficient digital process. In the case of a technical problem, he also knows how to proceed to fulfill the customer demands. The result is optimized customer satisfaction.

BPG is relevant for all phases of the process life cycle: design, implementation, execution, as well as monitoring and controlling of processes. Each subprocess of the process of process management is guided by BPG, leading to its overall orchestration and driving the realization of strategic goals. These guidelines may target the content of process design and models (e.g., operationalizing strategic goals, identifying and mitigating risks, defining scope) or purely formal aspects of process management (e.g., each function of a process model must be assigned to the responsible and accountable organizational unit, designing escalation procedures in case of conflicts between functional and process leaders). This is visualized in Fig. 5.5.

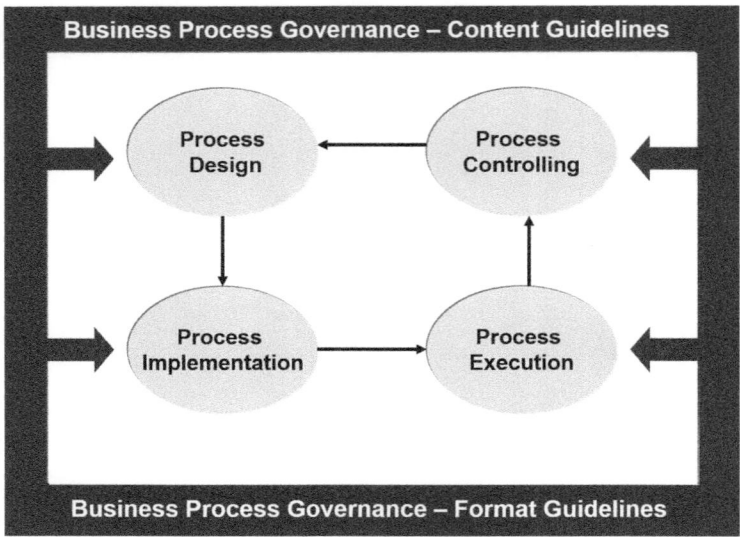

Fig. 5.5 Process governance: guidelines for each phase of business process management

An example of a BPG guideline for process design is "identify operational risk in process models." A process implementation example is "deploying the Enterprise Resource Planning (ERP) system xyz to support commodity processes, add additional digital technologies for high impact processes as long as these technologies impact one or several strategic value-drivers." The result is a "process-oriented implementation of digital technologies" [11]. "Any change of the process flow must be approved by the process owner; involved functional managers need to be consulted" is an example of a guideline for process execution. "Process performance indicators need to relate to the result of value of a business process and must trigger actions if target values are not achieved" guides the continuous process improvement in the controlling phase of the process life cycle.

What is the broader background of process governance? BPG is the required foundation to enable the sustainability of process improvements and the continuous focus on creating value for all stakeholders, such as customers, business partners, employees, and executive leaders. Process governance makes the BPM-Discipline real by establishing it as a value network across the functional organization. The importance of governance has already been recognized in one-time improvements to managing individual business processes, such as order to cash, source to pay, or new product development. Its importance increases significantly when an organization decides to deploy the BPM-Discipline on an enterprise level to achieve sustainable competitive advantage, at pace with certainty.

BPG ensures and guides the enterprise-specific execution of the process of process management. It is an essential component of the overall leadership approach. Therefore, general principles for execution of strategies and management tasks must be considered when defining BPG for an organization [12]:

- Know your people and your business
- Insist on realism
- Set clear goals and priorities
- Follow through
- Reward the doers
- Expand the capabilities of your employees

To develop BPG for an organization, it is crucial that the leadership team knows the people and the business of an enterprise within the context of key business processes. Vital stakeholders need to have a consistent view on those key business processes as a basis for an appropriate governance approach especially when it comes to new and innovative business models. A focus on realism and achieving a shared understanding of the organization's business processes is required when developing BPG guidelines; otherwise, the guidelines are worthless. At a minimum, the leadership team must have a common understanding of the high-level business processes, including clarity on organizational responsibilities, deliverables, inputs, outputs, key functional steps, dependencies, and KPIs. Within BPG, clear and strategy-based goals and priorities must be set so that people's efforts in executing BPM activities are as effective as possible—and provide the best value. These priorities are often defined in a BPM roadmap or agenda, identifying "target processes" for improvement and necessary BPM capabilities to achieve them [13, 14]. BPG ensures that business performance management activities create value by executing on the overall strategy and the "doers" or people who accomplish them are rewarded. This really makes the BPM-Discipline a part of how the organization gets things done. It becomes the discipline of strategy execution. BPG should include guidelines for people enablement, especially training and education, to expand the capabilities of employees and call attention to the importance of cross functional collaboration.

The leaders of organizations that chose to deploy BPM as a management discipline appreciate that value is created and strategic goals are accomplished via the organization's business processes. They recognize the importance of BPM to topics, such as innovation, growth, performance, productivity, compliance, agility, effective collaboration with partners, and the integration of mergers and acquisitions. These topics typically preoccupy the thoughts of leadership teams—the people of an organization responsible for making a value-driven BPM-Discipline happen—as core component of high-performance businesses.

Thoughtful leaders recognize that BPM enables clearer formulation and execution of strategy. As far back as 1985, Michael Porter emphasized the concept of the value chain and noted, "Activities, then, are the basics of competitive advantage. Overall advantage or disadvantage results from all of a company's activities, not only a few" and then went on to say, "The essence of strategy is choosing to perform activities differently than rivals do" [15]. Strategy must be based on a thorough assessment of external and internal business environments. Overall business strategy drives the design of BPG, and BPM enables the execution of strategy. This aspect supports vBPM's key role as the link between strategy and its execution.

When it comes to sustainable organic growth and innovation, leaders also recognize that BPM is equally important. Rapid, sustainable growth requires a systemic view of the business and broad collaboration, which requires immense effort from many businesses. The design of BPG must recognize that focusing on goals, such as flawless delivery responsiveness, is essential in providing existing products or services to existing or new markets. Hence, BPG is key to establishing new business models successfully.

When growth is planned through mergers or acquisitions, the integration phase is essential to success. Perceptive leaders appreciate that an important reason for the success of mergers or acquisitions is the ability of the merged firm to perform for and meet the needs of their customers. It is in the "integration phase" that BPM can play an important enabling role. This is related to the fact that merged firms often have an opportunity to gather specific information on comparative core business processes and their relative health and address customer-facing issues in the premerger due diligence period. It is now that you standardize and harmonize processes for best post-merger results [8].

BPG plays a key role in vBPM and enabling high performance for an organization. Organizations elect to invest energy in establishing BPG because it is the management infrastructure that enables them to address critical topics for their strategy execution through the improvement and management of the corporation's core business processes. BPG sets the stage to achieve competitive advantage through BPM—fast and at low risk.

So, how does an organization establish BPG? What is necessary to get started with an effective process governance approach?

5.2 How Do You Establish Business Process Governance?

BPG is the cornerstone for establishing a BPM-Discipline in an organization. There are three essential activities to begin BPG, a subset of the previously discussed components of BPG:

- High-level enterprise process model that identifies the key process of an organization
- Set of goals to frame the definition of KPIs
- Management plan, including an enterprise or process architecture structure, priorities, as well as the organizational responsibilities, accountabilities, and related structure for people involved in BPM activities

The other components of BPG can be added over time, depending on the specific needs of an organization and the evolving maturity. In general, enterprises require a set of cross functional leadership behaviors that facilitate the development of

5.2 How Do You Establish Business Process Governance?

critical BPG components and contribute directly to the success of BPM and its role as discipline of strategy execution.

The development of a robust, compelling, and visually striking enterprise-level business process model is one of the key components of BPG. In the absence of such a model, leadership teams will rely on the one model that most companies do have—the organization chart—and that will unduly and adversely influence their thinking. In most cases, this will result in a traditional, functional approach with all of its disadvantages. The enterprise-level definition of processes includes core, support, and management processes [16], as well as the necessary governance processes.

Primary processes are typically customer touching (e.g., "order-to-delivery" and "idea-to-new product launch"). Supporting processes typically enable the performance of the primary customer-touching processes. Examples of supporting processes include "hire-to-retire," "record-to-report," or "idea-to-software application." Management processes generally create the framework for BPM such as "business needs-to-budget" or "monitor-to-action." BPG delivers the governance processes relevant to manage BPM activities. We discussed such examples previously.

The development of KPIs for the set of business processes in the enterprise-level process model must involve balance between what is important to customers (and their enterprises) and what is important to the company itself. However, it always focuses on the result of value for a client at the end of a process. This is dramatically different than what occurs in conventional organizations, where traditional financial measures of revenue, expenses, earnings, and cash flow dominate. The metrics that really matter to customers, such as "on-time receipt of product or service," "complete, defect-free delivery," "an accurate and user-friendly invoice," "rapid and courteous responsiveness," or similar KPIs, often are not included in the front page of the executive dashboard or scorecard. In traditional companies, even when the metrics that matter to customers are monitored, the next level of diagnostic measurement is usually missing, and the infrastructure for corrective action is either lacking or flawed.

In contrast, the development of BPG requires a broad range of KPIs, including cost, quality, timeliness, and productivity metrics, in the measurement of the key deliverables for each enterprise-level process, and the means to cascade these performance metrics to the subprocess level. Furthermore, a realistic assessment of current performance is needed for each end-to-end process.

The combination of the clear definition of enterprise-level processes in the process model and the clarity on KPIs are prerequisites for the management plan, which is the third basic component in establishing BPG. The process management plan must answer three fundamental questions:

- Which of our business processes need to be improved, by how much and by when, in order for us to achieve our goals?
- Who will be accountable for the improvement and management of each key business process?

- How will we organize to fully engage our people in the improvement and management of key business processes? What are the new or modified roles?

To determine which business processes need to be improved or transformed, by how much and by when, in order to achieve which business goals, the leadership team needs to express its strategic goals in a process context and assess the size of the gap between current performance and desired performance. This can be done by identifying high-impact processes and their maturity level related to the desired strategic impact, as well as the maturity level of commodity processes in comparison of the industry average [8, 13]. This step involves making difficult choices to prioritize key projects and resource allocation. But budget, time, and other resource constraints make these choices necessary.

Similarly, key decisions need to be made to determine the executive accountability for the improvement and management of business processes and the development of the appropriate process management organization—the value network. Although there are various approaches to assigning accountability or ownership, the two most common might be called the "two hats line" and the "one hat staff approach." In the "two hats line" approach, a senior line executive assumes responsibility for an end-to-end process, as well as retaining accountability for his or her functional area. Clearly, this approach relies on "matrix management" principles. In the "one hat staff" approach, a senior executive is appointed to a full-time staff position of "process owner" or "process steward" for an end-to-end business process. The process owner is one of the most important roles of the BPG organization with some of the most important responsibilities, for example:

- Initiate process improvements or transformations based on external events.
- Review proposed changes to the Process and Governance Structure.
- Review integration issues between the various processes.
- Communicate changes to the Process and Governance Structure.
- Promote the business process management vision to senior management.
- Function as a point of escalation when required.
- Approve and initiate training when required.
- Recruit and coach staff to support the process where needed.
- Attend all key management meetings to assess the impact of organizational decisions on the process environment.
- Schedule and attend meetings according to the Process and Governance Structure; engage and manage the "value network" around the business process.
- Analyze and distribute reports.

An organizational core unit ensuring the implementation and execution of BPG and the underlying process management is generally necessary to fully engage people into a process management. This core unit has to support the employees involved in daily BPM-related management and administration activities to make sure they don't get overwhelmed. Sometimes they may even need to push things a bit to keep making progress with the process management journey. In many cases, a "BPM Center of Excellence," "BPM Center of Expertise," or "Strategy Execution

5.2 How Do You Establish Business Process Governance?

Team" is founded. A pragmatic approach to this is to start with an existing team and migrate its members into such a BPM core organization unit. This saves time and effort. The naming should be chosen in the company context so that it has a positive connotation. We will discuss the systematic setup and rollout of such a vBPM core organization unit later in this chapter. At the beginning this is in many cases a small team, often only one to three people, supporting process initiatives as needed.

The head of the entire BPM organization and the BPG needs to be somebody with a good standing in the organization, best a top executive, who provides process-oriented input into the overall business strategy, drives the idea of value-driven process management into the company, and positions its full power for people- and technology-based strategy execution. We refer to this emerging top management role as the chief process officer (CPO) [6, 17].

To apply the defined process approach on a company-wide level, the high-level process model should be the entrance point into a structured description of processes at all levels of detail—as required by different business process initiatives. This can be supported by enterprise architecture (EA), which is a framework to describe all aspects relevant for a business process at various levels of detail. We use enterprise architecture in a wide sense, including business and technology information—contrary to other approaches that focus EA on technology aspects. Examples for predefined architectures are the ARIS Architecture, the Zachman Framework, or the US Department of Defense Architecture Framework (DoDAF) [10, 18–21].

In most cases, those general frameworks are then adjusted to company-specific needs. The following key activities are used to build an EA in an organization:

- Identify what to use the architecture for to drive the following steps through the desired outcomes.
- Define architecture requirements (e.g., which aspects of a process should be included: business, IT, legal, etc.—hence the content of the architecture).
- Select the right existing EA framework (ARIS, DoDAF, Zachman, etc.—the structure).
- Tailor the selected architecture (which information is needed in which level of detail—detail structure).
- Choose the right methods/notations (methods that deliver the needed information, easy to use, etc.—define how to get information into the structure).
- Define the architecture governance required to keep the information up to date.
- Select the appropriate architecture software tool to implement the framework.

The application of an EA is facilitated through specialized software tools, such as the ARIS Platform [22, 23] or Signavio [24], both introduced before in Chap. 1. EA can be seen as a tool to enable the transfer of BPG into the operational process management since it provides the required transparency to execute a process governance approach. This mechanism is part of the overall value-driven BPM-Discipline. This is visualized in Fig. 5.6.

The definition of BPG is generally influenced by the following factors:

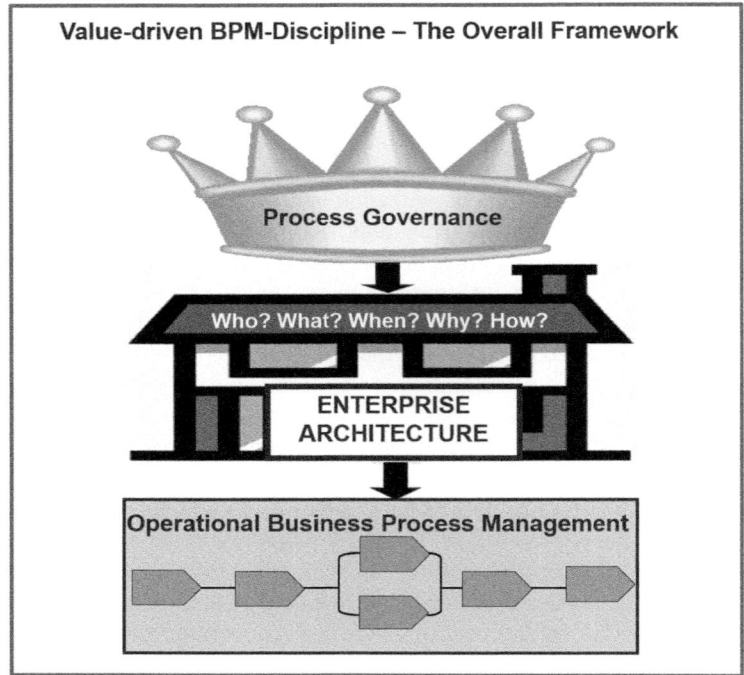

Fig. 5.6 Enterprise architecture: transfer of BPG into operational business process management

- Enterprise strategy, e.g., revenue growth through customer-centric organization and real-time business, higher margins through cost reduction and appropriate quality standards, product strategy, or specific innovation goals
- Legal requirements, e.g., Sarbanes-Oxley (SOX), Basel II, or FDA regulations
- "Megatrends," e.g., digitalization, omni-channel approaches, globalization, or mobility
- Other corporate factors, e.g., ERP systems in use, enterprise culture, or regional locations

These factors are shown in Fig. 5.7. Once the general influence factors for BPG are identified, concrete requirements must be defined. Some requirements are relevant for all enterprises within an industry sector or even across industry boundaries—others are company specific. Therefore, it is very important for each enterprise to develop a BPG, suited to the specific culture and business situation.

The development of BPG to govern an organization's BPM efforts is still not a general management practice, although more and more organizations are moving in this direction. In many cases, companies start establishing BPG without calling it by name. For example, they develop "method handbooks" as part of their BPM projects and keep on applying and controlling the related rules and guidelines. Hence, they start rolling out a process governance approach as a "side effect" of process

5.2 How Do You Establish Business Process Governance?

Fig. 5.7 Key factors influencing process governance

improvement or transformation projects. However, to reach the full potential of a BPM-Discipline and use it for systematic strategy execution, a well-thought-through process governance approach is required.

In spite of the compelling logic that customer and shareholder value is created by means of business processes—not just individual functions, current leaders at many organizations continue to support a traditional, functional view of the business and act accordingly. Why? There are at least four possible reasons [1, 2]: leaders do not care; leaders cannot focus; leaders do not know how; and leaders have been conditioned.

If leaders really cared, were focused, and knew how, would they not behave differently? Would they not measure what is important to customers in a disciplined way, in addition to monitoring the traditional financial metrics, such as revenues, earnings, and cash flow? Would they not assign accountability for the performance of the company's large business processes, instead of opting to assign accountability purely in terms of functional or business unit lines? Of course leaders would do these things if they cared enough to invest the time and energy, were able to devote sufficient attention for sustainability, and knew how to do so. They would do all of this if they recognized that business processes are core assets of an organization.

However, in many companies, leaders have been conditioned by both their academic and business experience to think and act in traditional, functional terms. Most leaders studied a particular academic discipline in college, such as marketing, finance, IT, or engineering. Then, for the most part their first job was in the same functional area that they studied—marketing, finance, IT, or engineering. In most cases, career progression was based on demonstrating excellence in that same area of functional responsibility.

It is this experience that leads to "silo" behavior and "turf protection." So it should come as no surprise that many leaders view the world through a functional bias. Although more and more universities and academic institutions, as well as professional organizations, are offering BPM-related educational programs, this is still not the norm. But things are starting to change, and process orientation is increasingly recognized as key for graduate and postgraduate education. BPM-D, the consulting organization I co-founded to help organizations realize the full potential of the BPM-Discipline, has educated over 300 executives in the last 2 years in the power of process management and its role as discipline of systematic strategy execution.

Leaders who chose to deploy BPG to establish a BPM-Discipline recognize the importance of shifting traditional functional thinking at both executive and middle-management levels. They practice a set of leadership behaviors to shift conventional wisdom and invest significant time and energy in this respect. This is the leadership aspect of process governance, related to various BPG aspects discussed before.

Leading firms appear to practice the following three distinct leadership behaviors in establishing BPG:

- Wide-range communication of a robust, enterprise-level process definition
- Discipline in performance measurement
- Commitment to broad-based education on process management

The first leadership behavior in establishing BPG involves leadership commitment to a wide-range communication of a robust, enterprise-level process definition, and the related enterprise architecture. A prerequisite is the aforementioned enterprise process model and clarity on the ownership of the principal business processes depicted in this model. Such a process model is central to broad-based communication, but it is the leadership team's shared understanding of the underlying details on the definition of the business processes and the size of the performance gap that needs to be bridged that drives deep commitment to deploying BPM as a management discipline that moves strategy into execution.

The second essential leadership behavior in establishing BPG is to exercise discipline in performance measurement and achieve balance between measuring what matters to customers and what matters to the company. Then the leadership team exercises discipline in reviewing results on a regular basis and takes corrective action when actual results are below targeted levels. It is not about having as many metrics as possible but about having a few important performance indicators that really drive action when necessary.

The third key leadership behavior in this context is related to leadership commitment to broad-based education on BPM, the value it provides, and the BPM processes necessary to make it happen on an ongoing basis. In leading firms, executives are directly involved in sponsoring, introducing, and even delivering process-oriented education to senior and middle managers. In a leading financial institution, for example, the responsible executive vice president opened the training session for the team of business analysts, delivered by an external partner he and his management team had selected. The resulting motivation and psychological effect has been as important as the training content itself.

Although the set of these three leadership behaviors requires a significant investment of executive time and energy, the return on effort invested can be considerable—if it results in a functioning BPM-Discipline. What does it mean to sustain BPG and, with that, enable a long-term successful BPM-Discipline in an organization?

5.3 What Does It Mean to Sustain Process Governance?

The central goal of BPG is to ensure that BPM delivers consistent business results in strategy execution to satisfy and exceed the expectations of customers and other stakeholders. BPG is successful when the BPM-Discipline delivers on the strategic goals of the organization. BPG "governs" the process of process management on a day-to-day basis.

Success in establishing and sustaining BPG relies on both leadership attitudes, as discussed above, and organizational skills in the deployment of the required management discipline. In terms of sustaining BPG, digital technology matters tremendously. Not only is it important to use a process-modeling and repository tool to manage the enterprise architecture as previously discussed, it is equally important that the selected tool is able to link directly to a company's execution environment, which can be ERP based or use a more advanced technology architecture, as discussed in Chap. 3. The degree of complexity in most, even small and medium businesses, requires the use of a robust modeling tool to effectively cascade BPG principles across the organization.

BPG enables the discussed concept of open BPM [25] within value-driven BPM by requesting and identifying open standards to be used. These selections must be reviewed on a regular basis to reflect the newest developments regarding technology and business standards. The measurement of defined KPIs should be automated as far as possible to enable the effective implementation of BPG guidelines in a cost- and time-efficient way [22].

The definition of BPG processes and guidelines for each phase of the BPM approach can be used to drive an "execution-oriented" culture into an enterprise [12]. BPG sets the stage for getting things done. An enterprise must define how process governance and the resulting BPM-Discipline affect the organizational structure. BPG-related activities and BPM in general may be centralized for the entire organization or decentralized (e.g., a process governance approach for every business unit). Alternatively, a combination of both extreme approaches can be

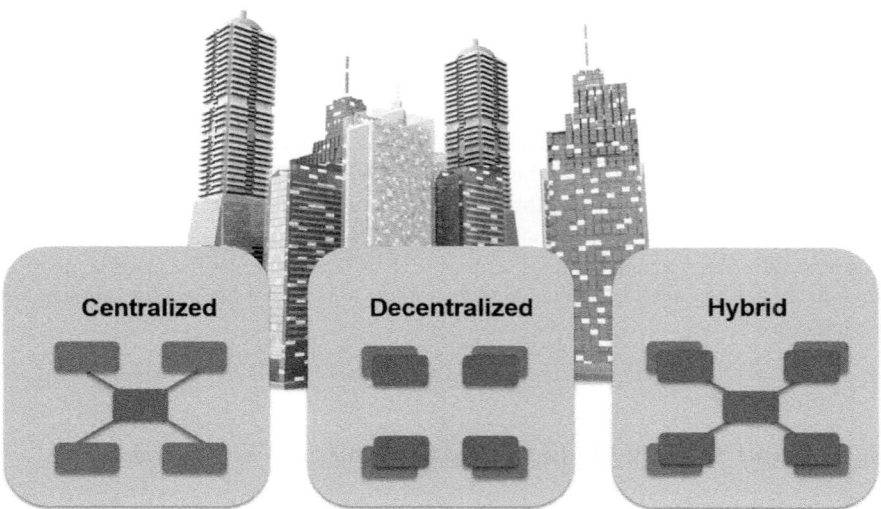

Fig. 5.8 Options to include process governance and the BPM-Discipline into the organization

applied and rolled out as a hybrid organizational model. This is visualized in Fig. 5.8.

The decision about the centralization or decentralization of BPG activities can be made on the basis of the same principles used in process management to make decisions about the degree of centralization [11]:

- Coordination requirements
- Relevant time periods
- Actuality of data (yearly, monthly, etc.)
- Data volume

Over time the organizational integration of BPM may change based on the maturity level of the company. Many businesses start with a focused central approach, e.g., targeting just one business unit, and move over time to a hybrid approach keeping a small centralized governance organization to enable synergies and move most activities into decentralized product or geographical units to be close to the operational business.

The organization of BPG may lead to new departments like the mentioned "BPM Center of Excellence" or to new roles, e.g., the formerly mentioned chief process officer (CPO), process owners, process architects, business process analysts, process repository manager, and more [5]. The steps necessary to formalize and roll out such a Center of Excellence while the BPM-Discipline gets more mature are shown in Fig. 5.9.

While the initial BPM core organization or Center of Excellence (CoE) is more or less defined very pragmatically through the initial governance and BPM support needs, this organizational unit will soon need to be more formally defined to

5.3 What Does It Mean to Sustain Process Governance?

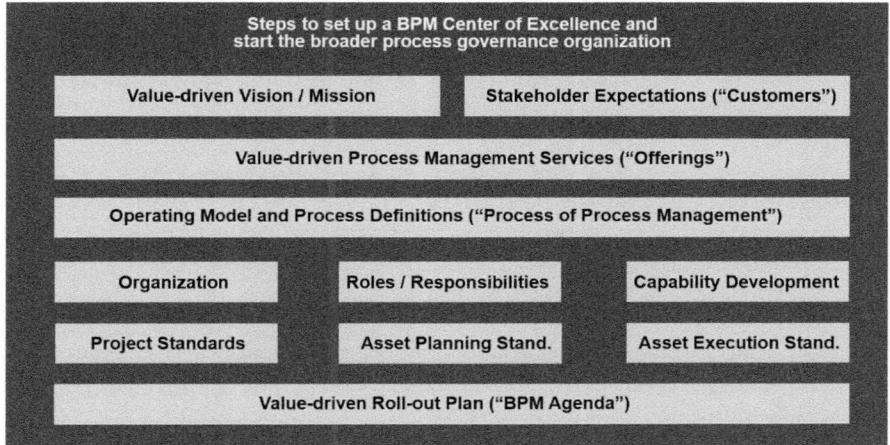

Fig. 5.9 Steps necessary to set up and roll out a BPM Center of Excellence

become a sustainable organizational unit. At this point it is key to demonstrate clearly to the organization that we don't just create another overhead unit but a value-driving strategy execution organization. It is important to define a BPM Center of Excellence in a "market-driven way," considering the company as its "internal market." By defining internal offerings that such a center brings to the organization, you set the appropriate expectations. Typical offerings of such a unit are improvement and transformation initiatives, prioritization initiatives, process innovation, support of an enterprise wide-system rollout, post-merger integration, standardization and harmonization of processes, providing transparency through appropriate process repository management, integration of process and data governance, or enabling process-oriented training. The head of this center is basically the owner of the process of process management. The offerings are determined based on overall vision and mission of the CoE, as well as the related stakeholder expectations. Once the offerings are defined, you can establish the supporting process of process management as the operating model. An example of such a process of process management and its subprocesses is shown in Fig. 5.10 [26]. It divides the subprocess of the BPM process into project-focused, directly value-creating subprocesses and asset-focused enabling subprocesses. Each group is again segmented into planning and execution processes [26]. The BPG processes are part of this process of process management providing the organizational infrastructure. Finally, you need to go through all the other steps necessary to set up a new organizational unit, shown in Fig. 5.9—in general, a relatively straightforward exercise.

The implementation and execution of BPG are also enabled by specific governance applications, for example, Sarbanes-Oxley (SOX) Process Audit Management Systems or other systems supporting the process of process management [26]. These systems support the process governance similar to how BPM is enabled

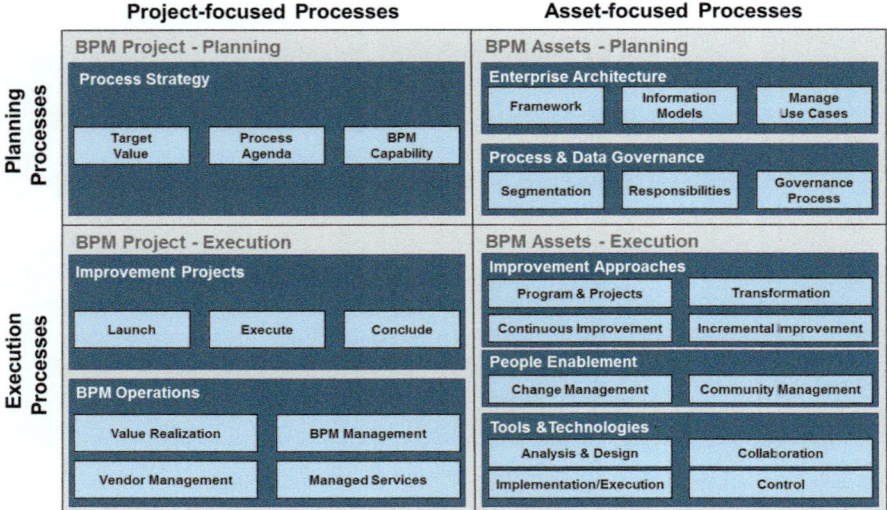

Fig. 5.10 BPM-D process framework—Example for a process of process management definition [26]

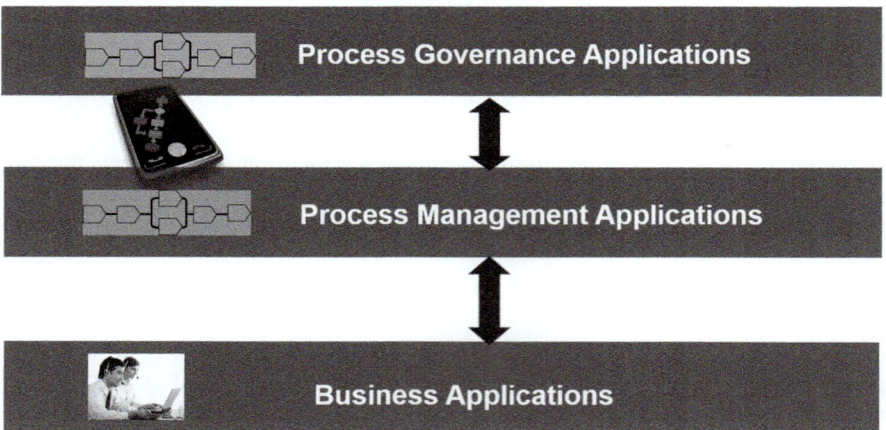

Fig. 5.11 Software application hierarchy, starting with process governance software

by BPM applications like repository tools and the execution of processes by systems like ERP or next-generation process automation. Process governance applications are basically "meta" applications to enable a faster less risky management of operational processes. This application hierarchy is visualized in Fig. 5.11.

BPG applications require appropriate implementation approaches. Although the general concepts of a process-oriented implementation of standard software can be utilized [11], the following specific aspects must be included in the BPG application approach:

5.4 The Bottom Line   99

- Close integration with BPM tools (e.g., a BPG application could prioritize BPM initiatives or carrying out a consistency check of process models)
- Documentation requirements to prove compliance with BPG processes and guidelines (e.g., executing SOX-relevant checks is insufficient—these requirements must also be documented)
- Change management to make BPG part of the overall enterprise culture (e.g., BPG guidelines may also need to be applied "manually" by employees working on BPM initiatives; thus, BPG tools simply deliver the necessary information)
- Integration of guidelines not supported and enforced by applications (e.g., the requirement to use a specific modeling method)

BPG is a key element of a successful enterprise management focused on systematic strategy execution. It ensures the appropriate and targeted use of BPM throughout the entire business process life cycle. Therefore, it has to be maintained on a day-to-day basis as part of an organization's daily working activities. Hence, BPG makes BPM a real management discipline—the discipline of strategy execution.

5.4 The Bottom Line

- Business process governance (BPG) relates to guidelines and decisions that seek to define actions, grant power, and verify performance related to the process of process management. It is a set of guidelines focused on organizing all BPM activities and initiatives of an organization to manage its business processes (Sect. 5.1).
- BPG ensures that BPM delivers consistent business results for strategy execution to satisfy and exceed the expectations of an organization (Sect. 5.1).
- Some of the guidelines of BPG can again be processes, so-called BPG processes. They can be managed using a BPM approach (Sect. 5.1).
- The leaders of organizations that chose to deploy BPM as a management discipline appreciate its value and, therefore, establish BPG. They recognize its importance to topics such as strategy execution, growth, and the integration of mergers and acquisitions, innovation, agility, efficiency, compliance and standardization, or internal alignment of employees toward the market (Sect. 5.1).
- There are three essential components involved in getting BPG started: creating a high-level enterprise process model; the setting of goals and a management plan, including an enterprise architecture (EA) with business and IT aspects; and activating the organizational structure for people involved in BPM activities (Sect. 5.2).
- Enterprises require a set of leadership behaviors that facilitate the development of critical BPG components and contribute directly to the effectiveness of BPM (Sect. 5.2).

- To apply the enterprise process model on a company-wide basis, this model should be the entry point into a structured design of processes on all levels of detail. This is supported by an enterprise architecture (EA) (Sect. 5.2).
- The definition of a BPG approach is influenced by multiple factors, including the enterprise strategy, legal requirements, and "megatrends" (Sect. 5.2).
- Leaders who chose to deploy BPG and BPM recognize the importance of shifting traditional functional thinking at executive, middle management, and operational levels (Sect. 5.2).
- Success in establishing and sustaining BPG, and hence BPM, relies both on leadership attitudes and organizational skills in the deployment of the required management discipline (Sect. 5.3).
- BPG and the BPM-Discipline can be established in a centralized, decentralized, or hybrid approach. This needs to be determined based on the enterprise context—the BPM journey (Sect. 5.3).
- A BPM Center of Excellence (CoE) is required to support the necessary BPG and the execution of the process of process management (Sect. 5.3).
- In order to sustain a BPG approach, the definition of the BPM Center of Excellence needs to be formalized more and more as required by the existing and targeted BPM maturity level (Sect. 5.3).
- The process of process management is the operating model of the BPM organization, including the BPM Center of Excellence (Sect. 5.3).
- In terms of executing and sustaining BPG, digital technology matters tremendously and can be used to enforce and execute BPG guidelines (Sect. 5.3).
- BPG applications (specific software to support BPG) require appropriate implementation approaches (Sect. 5.3).

References

1. Spanyi, A.: Business Process Management is a Team Sport—Play It to Win. Anclote Press, Tampa (2003)
2. Spanyi, A.: More for Less—The Power of Process Management. Meghan-Kiffer, Tampa (2006)
3. Kirchmer, M.: Business Process Governance: Orchestrating the Management of BPM. White paper, Berwyn (2005)
4. Kirchmer, M., Spanyi, A.: Business Process Governance, 2nd rev. edn. White paper, Berwyn (2007)
5. Franz, P., Kirchmer, M.: Value-driven Business Process Management—The Value-Switch for Lasting Competitive Advantage. McGraw-Hill, New York, e.a (2012)
6. Kirchmer, M., Franz, P.: Chief Process Officer—The Value Scout. BPM-D Whitepaper, Philadelphia (2014)
7. Kirchmer, M.: Enabling High Performance Through Digitalization—The BPM-Discipline as Value-Switch. In: CIO Review, 14 Jan 2016.
8. Franz, P., Kirchmer, M.: Process Standardization and Harmonization—Enabling Customer Service in a Digital World. BPM-D Whitepaper, Philadelphia (2016)
9. See Wikipedia, 3/2016
10. Scheer, A.-W.: ARIS—Business Process Modeling, 2nd edn. Springer, Berlin (1998)

11. Kirchmer, M.: Business Process Oriented Implementation of Standard Software—How to Achieve Competitive Advantage Efficiently and Effectively, 2nd edn. Springer, Berlin (1999)
12. Bossidy, L., Charan, R.: Execution: The Discipline of Getting Things Done. Basic Books, New York (2002)
13. Franz, P.: Developing a Process Agenda for Value-driven BPM. Point of View Document. Accenture, London (2011)
14. Kirchmer, M., Franz, P.: Targeting Value in a Digital World. BPM-D Whitepaper, Philadelphia (2014)
15. Porter, M.: What is strategy? Harvard Business Review, November–December (1996)
16. Rummler, G.: Brache, A.: Improving Performance: Managing the White Space on the Organization Chart. Jossey-Bass, San Francisco (1990)
17. Kirchmer, M., Franz, P., von Rosing, H.: The chief process officer: an emerging tope management role. In: von Rosing, M., Scheer, A.-W., von Scheel, H. (eds.) The Complete Business Process Handbook—Body of Knowledge from Process Modeling to BPM, vol. 1, pp. 343–348. Amsterdam, Boston e.a (2015)
18. Scheer, A.-W.: ARIS—Business Process Frameworks, 2nd edn. Springer, Berlin (1998)
19. O'Rourke, C., Fishman, N., Selkow, W.: Enterprise Architecture Using the Zachman Framework. Thomson Course Technology, Boston (2003)
20. Lapkin, A.: The seven fatal mistakes of enterprise architecture. In: Gartner Research Publication, ID-Number: GOO 126144, 22 Feb 2005
21. McGovern, J., Ambler, S.W., Stevens, M.E., Linn, J., Sharan, V., Jo, E.K.: A Practical Guide to Enterprise Architecture. Prentice Hall, Upper Saddle River (2004)
22. IDS Scheer, AG (ed.): ARIS Platform. Product Brochure. IDS Scheer, Saarbruecken (2007)
23. IDS Scheer, AG (ed.): ARIS Design Platform—ARIS Enterprise Architecture Solution. White paper, Saarbruecken (2006)
24. See www.signavio.com (2016)
25. Kirchmer, M.: Knowledge communication empowers SOA for business agility. In: The 11th World Multi-Conference on Systemics, Cybernetics and Informatics, Proceedings, vol. III, pp. 301–307. Orlando, 8–11 July 2007
26. Kirchmer, M., Franz, P.: The Process of Process Management—Strategy Execution in a Digital World. BPM-D Whitepaper, Philadelphia (2015)

Chapter 6
Reference Models: Accelerators and More

Quality and speed of the process design have a significant impact on the management of the business process life cycle through the value-driven BPM-Discipline. The information models produced in the process design lay the basis for the implementation, execution, and controlling of processes. The use of flexible next-generation process execution environments requires an input business process models in high-quality syntactical and semantic formats. Ensuring such modeling is of quality can be very time-consuming. The use of appropriate process-modeling tools and even more importantly leveraging process templates that are adapted to company-specific requirements can help tremendously. The use of appropriate business process templates increases the efficiency and effectiveness of the process design phase. A client I have worked with stated that the use of such predefined templates as a starting point of the process design had reduced the design time by over 50%—while maintaining or even increasing the design quality. The process templates are generally called "business process reference models." Reference models facilitate the achievement of high-quality design while keeping best efficiency.

While working in Japan for IDS Scheer, I started an initiative to develop a reference model for the pharmaceutical industry on the basis of specific documentation and reporting requirements, a model that would also reflect the related capabilities of SAP's enterprise resource planning (ERP) system. We were able to sell the product to clients and could use it ourselves successfully in consulting engagements, which proved that such "content products" were becoming increasingly important in supporting process management initiatives. Accenture, a leading consulting firm I had been working with heading their BPM practice, has built a major reference model repository describing common practices in dozens of industry segments using thousands of process and other information models. This continuously increases the value it offers to their clients. At BPM-D, the company I cofounded, we have developed a patent-pending reference model for the BPM-Discipline itself. This helps to develop a fast and effective company-specific management discipline for people- and technology-based strategy execution.

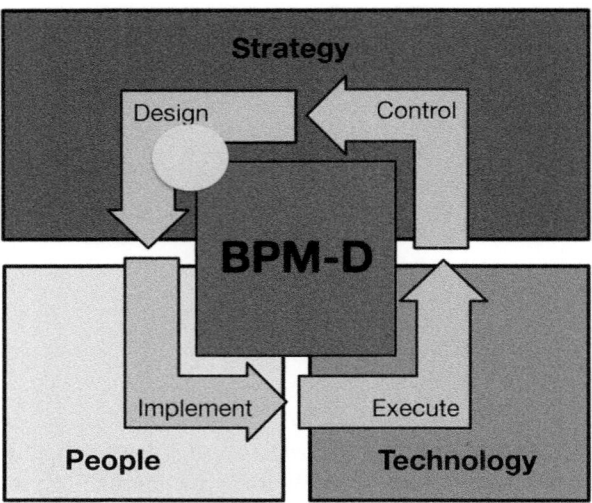

Fig. 6.1 Focus on process design of value-driven BPM

Process reference models truly increase speed and reduce risk of transformation and improvement initiatives.

This chapter will define reference models in general and focus specifically on business process reference models. It discusses how to procure reference models and learn how to use them in practice. The focus of this chapter, the process design of value-driven BPM, is shown in Fig. 6.1.

Process reference models show how process knowledge can be formalized and structured as a step toward "knowledge transfer" into a "product" that can be sold on the market. Just as enterprises today purchase application software, in the future they may procure best and common process practices in the form of reference models.

6.1 What Are Reference Models and Why Should You Use Them?

Let us look at an example. We assume you need to improve your procurement process for office material because it currently performs significantly under industry average: it is too expensive and too slow. This process is not of particular importance, and you do not expect to achieve any competitive advantage through its design. It is a real commodity process. Therefore, it is sufficient to bring it to industry average performance, using common industry practices. But how do you know what those industry common practices are? How can you complete appropriate process models driving the improvement quickly and cost efficiently? This is where reference models help.

6.1 What Are Reference Models and Why Should You Use Them?

Reference models (RMs) are generic conceptual information models that formalize recommended practices for a special domain [1–3]. Therefore, they have the following characteristics [1–5]:

- Representation of common or even best practices: RMs provide the necessary knowledge for conducting business activities in a specific domain at a common or best performance level.
- Universal applicability: RMs deliver business content that can be used well beyond an individual company-specific situation. Hence, they will not only be used in one organization, but a whole set of organizations.
- Reusability and adaptability: RMs are conceptual frameworks that can be easily reused in many related projects. They are structured for easy adaptability to company-specific situations.

This means that RMs deliver common or best practice information that can be used many times, for example, in multiple organizations or for different projects. Their format allows easy adaptability to specific situations in different companies. Therefore, they are, in general, available in digital form, in most cases as files of process-modeling and repository tools. Although the currently available RMs often do not completely fulfill all of those characteristics [4], they at least come close to those requirements.

In the context of value-driven BPM, we will focus on "business process reference models." The RMs consist of "conceptual models" that are relevant for business processes, primarily even process models. Those can be complemented by models for other views on processes, like functions, data, organizational structure, or deliverables. In this chapter, we use RM as a synonym for business process reference models.

In the procurement example explained earlier, one could use an industry common-practice RM that includes a suggestion for the procurement of office material. This enables the simple and efficient use of industry-specific knowledge as required in this situation.

RMs represent content of various domains. According to those domains, one can distinguish different types of RMs. The most important are the following:

- Industry RM: They represent common or best practices of a specific industry sector, like a banking RM, a telecommunication reference model, a pharmaceutical, or a machinery industry reference model.
- Software RM: They describe common-practice processes on the basis of a specific application software system. These could be traditional applications, such as ERP systems or RMs representing the subprocess supported by a service of a service-oriented architecture (SOA).
- Procedural RM: They show best practices of nonindustry-specific domains or of domains that are not part of the daily operational business of an organization, for example, a project management RM, a RM for the BPM-Discipline, or functional RMs, e.g., for human resources or finance.

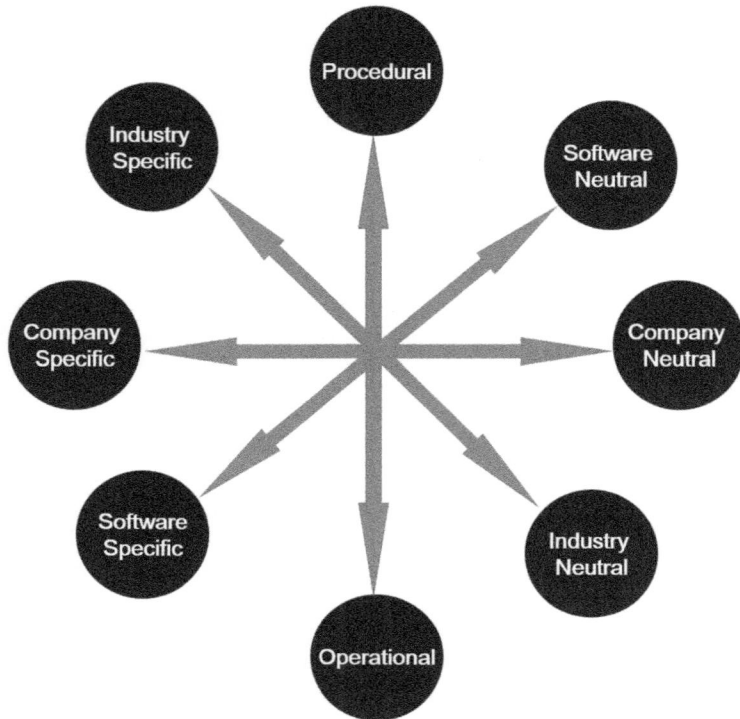

Fig. 6.2 Types of reference models

- Company RM: These models represent common practices within a larger organization or a company group, for example, a common practice for organizing maintenance processes or call center operations—in the specific product, market, and company context. These RMs do not fully meet the criteria of "universal applicability." But in large organizations, those models can be of high importance, for example, for standardization initiatives.

In many cases, RMs represent a combination of two or more model types. For example, the RM could be an ERP-based reference model (e.g., for SAP software) for the consumer packaged goods industry, including special aspects, like a "direct store delivery" process. The different types of RMs are visualized in Fig. 6.2.

The use of RMs provides business benefits in the process design, such as:

- Cost reduction
- Time reduction
- Quality improvement
- Risk reduction
- Transparency
- Common language

6.1 What Are Reference Models and Why Should You Use Them?

- Preparation for benchmarking
- Innovation through transfer of practices between domains

It is much easier to modify an existing process model in order to adapt it to a company-specific context than to develop the entire model from scratch. This is especially true for commodity processes where the goal is to modify as little as possible of the reference model. The result is a significant reduction of design time and with that related cost. Experience has shown that the design time for commodity processes can be reduced by up to 70%. And remember, 80%+ of a company's processes are commodity processes. Design workshops for those processes are mostly about identifying how to adjust the existing organization to the common practice described through the RM.

The anticipated high-quality modeling of RMs can be transferred and used in enterprise-specific process-modeling activities. This is true for syntactical as well as for semantic aspects. The content of RMs is already validated; hence, its application leads to risk reduction. The structure of a RM includes the thinking of various experts and experience from different organizations. The syntax and formal structure can be used as a solid starting point and "best practice" for company-specific process-modeling initiatives. This is especially helpful in defining the different levels of detail an enterprise modeling approach should cover: the levels can be defined in relation to the levels used in the RM [6]. A knowledge domain described by RMs becomes transparent through the clear and easy-to-read structure of the RM. Hence, it is easier to scope projects based on such reference models. A RM defines the terms used in the model, for example, functions or data objects. Hence those definitions can be the basis for a common language for all people involved in related process management. If several enterprises use the same RM as a basis to structure their business processes, this facilitates the benchmarking of those processes later since it is easier to compare "apples with apples" due to the use of the same or similar terms and structure of the processes. RMs can also be used to transfer practices form one industry to another, enabling process innovation. For example, a biotechnology company may use the configuration process of a machinery company by applying a machinery industry reference model.

Summarizing those effects, RMs lead to fast and effective process design and increase with that the agility of an organization. This is visualized in Fig. 6.3.

RMs enable smart decisions and fast execution. They effectively help to link strategy to execution in an organization.

So, where can one find such RMs? Are there specialized vendors?

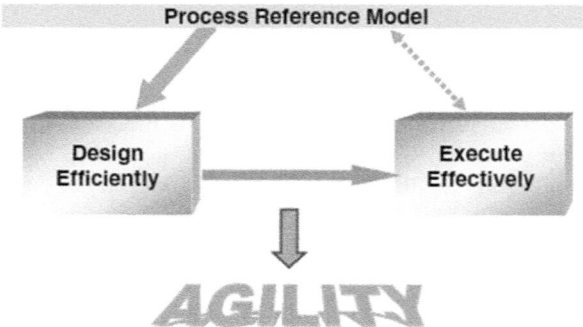

Fig. 6.3 Agility through business process reference models

6.2 How to Obtain Reference Models and How to Evaluate Them?

RMs are basically "products" that you use to build business process models, just as you use other products such as software or hardware. In a broad sense, all of those products can be procured through the information technology market.

Let us review briefly the development of this market of information systems and technology. In the 1970s, the dominating products were hardware—computers. Once the hardware was selected, the software was developed or procured accordingly. This changed in the 1990s with the appearance of software packages, such as ERP systems. Suddenly, the main attention shifted to software products, especially to standard application software packages. Hardware became more or less a commodity. Because the business content of some of those standard software systems was already documented in form of RMs [7], the market for business content in the form of RMs started to develop. I expect that this market will continue to increase in the next few years. Since next-generation software architectures offer organizations increased flexibility, the necessary business content, to manage this flexibility efficiently, has to be procured separately. RMs help to develop the process models necessary to "configure" the next-generation application software. Otherwise, the configuration of major process-oriented software systems may become too cost and time intensive.

Many of the RMs available today are not sold as stand-alone products. They are either provided together with other products, such as software applications or consulting offerings, or they are sold as part of a membership service, for example, of an industry organization. However, I expect that the "productization" of RMs will progress rapidly. Consulting and software companies could have business units delivering RM-based products. Some companies may even decide to only focus on the development and sale of RMs. They may become pure RM vendors.

Today, the main procurement sources for RMs are:

- Software companies
- Consulting companies

6.2 How to Obtain Reference Models and How to Evaluate Them?

- Industry organizations
- Academic organizations

Vendors of ERP systems were forced to make the business content of complex holistic software applications more transparent. For example, SAP documented the business processes enabled by their R/3 software in the form of event-driven process chains (EPCs) [5, 7]. Others, such as PeopleSoft (which has since been acquired by Oracle) followed. Software vendors, especially SAP, have been key drivers in the development of RMs.

Consulting companies were also forced to structure their knowledge in the form of RMs to increase their own productivity: they can use RMs to train consultants and make engagements more efficient and effective. RMs provided by consulting companies can be especially interesting if the companies do not only include common practices but also best and "next" practices or suggestions for process innovations. RMs can include value-related components like capability assessment models, KPI frameworks, or value trees. These components enable an outcome-oriented use of the process reference models increasing the value of those models even more. Using those models, organizations can benefit from a vast business experience in a systematic efficient way. Specifically, utilizing RMs from other industries to support emerging trends and "next practices" in a company's own industry has become a major trend of RMs. However, I also have to mention that most consulting companies combine the use of their RMs with consulting services to make sure those assets are used in the appropriate way.

Models are typically procured indirectly through consulting engagements. PMOLink is one company that already sells RMs as products. They offer a RM for project management, based on the industry standard "PMBOK" [8]. To support usability, the RM is delivered in a database of the process-modeling system ARIS Platform [9]. The structure of the project management model is shown in Fig. 6.4. The size of this RM product is described in Fig. 6.5.

BPM-D, a consulting company focused on establishing and applying a BPM-Discipline that provides value through fast and effective strategy execution, offers a reference model for the underlying process of process management [10]. The reference model consists of over 150 components, many of them linked to job aids and tools providing additional detailed information. It includes process, data, organizational, and value models. The reference model is used to increase speed and reduce risk of establishing a company-specific process management discipline for strategy execution. The RM is visualized in Fig. 6.6.

Industry organizations also deliver knowledge in the form of RMs. For example, the APICS Supply Chain Council offers the supply chain operations reference (SCOR) model [11, 12]. SCOR has been continuously developed for more than 15 years. It is used all over the world and has received great recognition. It is an excellent example for a successful RM. Let us have a closer look at it.

SCOR is a business process reference model that contains all supply chain activities, from supplier's supplier to a customer's customer, including:

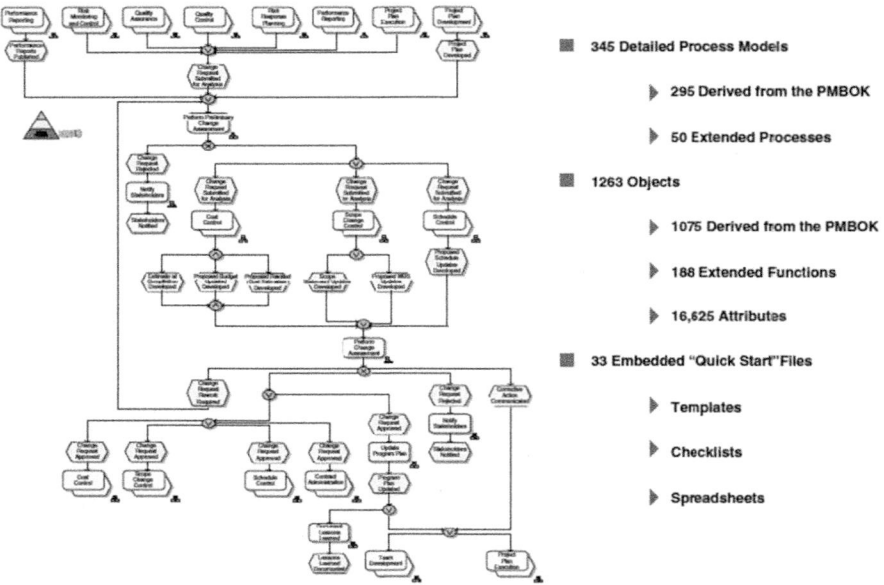

Fig. 6.4 Structure of PMOLink's project management reference model of PMOLink

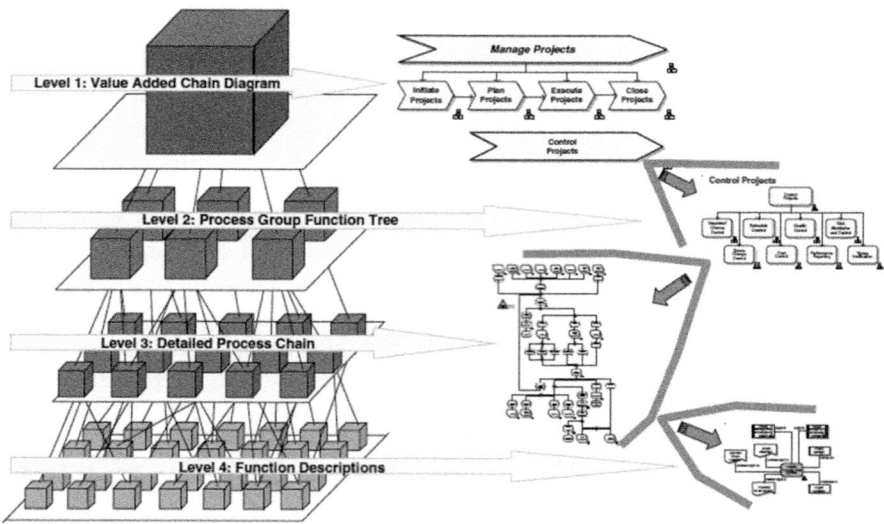

Fig. 6.5 Size of PMOLink's project management reference model

6.2 How to Obtain Reference Models and How to Evaluate Them? 111

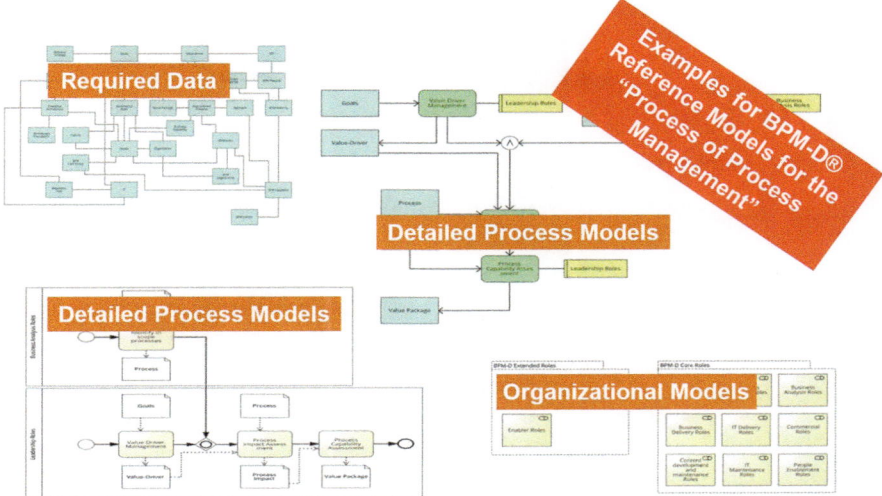

Fig. 6.6 BPM-D® reference model for the BPM-Discipline

- All customer interactions, from order entry through paid invoice
- All product (physical goods, services, etc.) transactions, including equipment, supplies, spare parts, bulk product, software, etc.
- All market interaction, from the understanding of the aggregate demand to the fulfillment of each order

SCOR contains three levels of process detail. The top level (process types) defines the scope and content. It consists of the five top-level processes:

- Plan
- Source
- Make
- Deliver
- Return

The second level of SCOR, the configuration level (process categories), contains more than 30 process categories, such as "make to stock," "make to order," "engineer to order," or "production execution." These process categories can be used to "configure" a company's supply chain. Companies implement their operations strategy through the configuration they choose for their supply chain.

The third SCOR level, the process element level (decomposed processes), is used to fine-tune the operations of a company. It consists of the following:

- Process element definitions
- Process element information inputs and outputs
- Process performance metrics
- Best practices
- System capabilities necessary to support best practices
- Systems/tools to be used

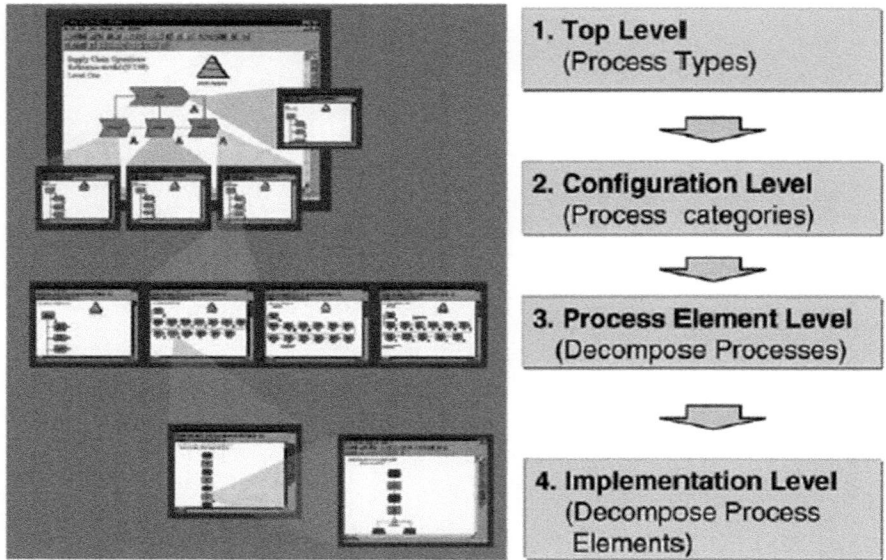

Fig. 6.7 Structure of SCOR

Companies implement their supply chain solution on level four (or even more detailed levels). Level four, or the implementation level (decomposed subprocess), defines practices to achieve competitive advantage and to adapt to changing business conditions. This level is company specific and not in the scope of SCOR. The structure of SCOR is shown in Fig. 6.7.

The American Productivity and Quality Center (APQC) provides high-level reference models in the form of industry-neutral and industry-specific frameworks [13]. These models are, e.g., used to structure processes for benchmarking purposes. RMs are great tools for industry organizations to organize the knowledge of their members and make it available in a useful format.

Academic organizations also deliver reference models. Research in this area is popular in Europe, especially in Germany [4], but it is also evolving in other parts of the world. An example is Scheer's "Y-model," a reference model for industrial enterprises [1, 14] that has been adapted to multiple industry sectors. The top level of the Y-model for discrete manufacturing companies is shown in Fig. 6.8. The left side of the "Y" displays all order-related processes, and the right side shows all product-focused processes. Horizontally, the "Y" structures the processes in execution and planning processes. The support processes are defined above the "Y."

Becker's reference model for retail enterprises [15, 16] is another example of a RM originating in academia. The RM, "retail-H," outlines various aspects of trade information systems, including contracting, order management, goods receipt, invoice auditing, accounts payable, warehousing, marketing, selling, goods issue, billing, and accounts receivable.

6.2 How to Obtain Reference Models and How to Evaluate Them?

Fig. 6.8 "Y-model": reference model for industrial enterprises (after A.-W. Scheer)

As the market for RMs evolves, available models must be evaluated and compared. Just as one selects software, one also has to choose the appropriate RM. The following criteria can be used to support this RM selection process [17]:

- Syntactic criteria
  - Size
  - Correctness and consistency
  - Modularity
  - Structure (hierarchy)
  - Complexity
  - Architecture

- Semantic criteria
  - General applicability
  - Coverage of domain
  - Completeness
  - Efficiency of use
  - Expressiveness
  - Similarity with other models, possible overlaps

- Comprehensibility
- Documentation

• Pragmatic criteria

- Popularity
- Flexibility of use
- Maturity
- Relevance
- Availability
- Cost
- Tool support

Now we know how to find and select reference models. Let us now discuss how to apply those models operationally in a specific company situation to achieve the described benefits.

6.3 How Do You Apply Reference Models?

The basic procedure to apply a RM to support business process design is fairly straightforward. Eliminate parts of the RM that are not relevant for your specific business context and adjust the process logic wherever necessary. If the RM is missing certain elements, for example, a subprocess needed in your company, those elements are added to the model. The result is an enterprise-specific process model, reflecting the design necessary to achieve company-specific goals. This approach is visualized in Fig. 6.9.

Applying reference models in the context of specific business initiatives delivers value based on the specific benefits of RMs discussed before:

- Systematic integration of common and innovative business practices
- Simplification of content discussions through the use of the terminology of the reference model
- Business-driven implementation of application software systems
- Fast and effective scoping of process-related initiatives
- Easier identification of the maturity level of business processes

Reference models deliver available common practices that can be combined systematically with process innovations that fit into the context of a specific organization. They simplify the design of commodity processes and ensure sufficient resources for high-impact processes. The result is a best practice for a company. The RM defines the terminology to be used; hence, it facilitates and simplifies content discussions [18]. This is especially important for initiatives focused on inter-enterprise processes [12], in which members of multiple organizations are involved. Software implementations, such as ERP projects, can be powerful tools to drive process improvements. However, project teams often lose focus on real

6.3 How Do You Apply Reference Models?

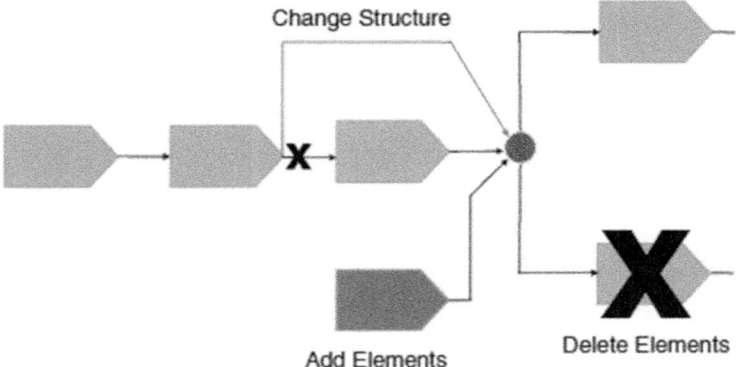

Fig. 6.9 Applying business process reference models

business process topics. The use of RMs avoids that pitfall. The software reference model focuses discussions on the business impacts of the software. It speeds up the process design significantly, especially for the 80%+ commodity processes of an organization. I have worked with clients that stated that the use of RMs in an ERP rollout reduced the design time by over 50% compared to earlier conventional rollouts. A RM also supports the appropriate scoping of an initiative because it describes a business domain in a transparent way. Once several companies have organized their processes, based on the same RM, it becomes easier to benchmark the performance. The performance of supply chain processes, for example, can be compared using the structures delivered by the supply chain operations reference (SCOR) model. As a result, it gets easier to identify the maturity level or processes. This again is key to set up the right improvement and transformation initiatives. These effects of the use of RMs are shown in Fig. 6.10.

Reference models are also in most case not static. New version reflecting new practices are released. This provides the opportunity of further improvements for the areas the RMs are used in. Hence, RMs can become a powerful tool to support a targeted continuous improvement.

A challenge in applying RM is that the models generally do not include any information about what can be modified and how the modifications should look like, so that they really make sense. Is a specific subprocess of a RM optional or do I really need it? Does it make sense to change the sequence of certain functions? These are examples of questions that can be answered by RMs designed as configurable models [19]. These configurable RMs deliver the following advantages [19]:

- Support decisions for the transformation of the model.
- Configuration of all relevant aspects, including data or functions.
- Configuration decisions are classified into mandatory and optional categories.
- Configuration decisions are classified into global (central) and local decision categories.

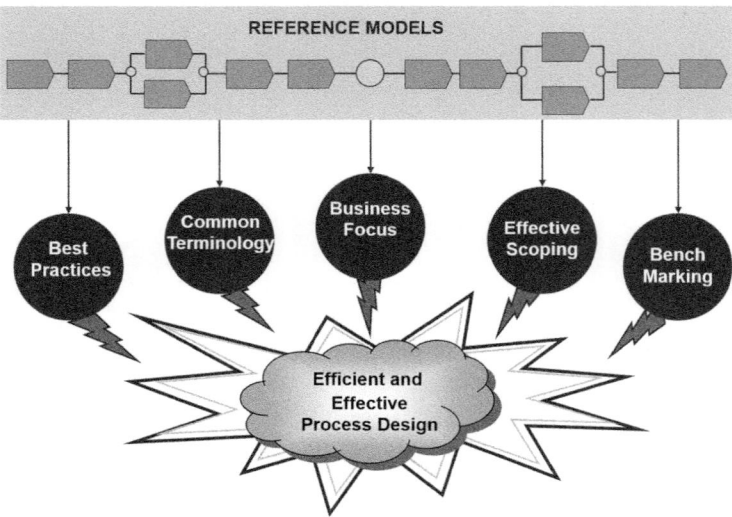

Fig. 6.10 Effects of the use of reference models

- Configuration decisions can be interrelated.
- Relations of decisions must be transparent.
- Guidelines for the use of the models.
- Configurable models are very comprehensive.

Although such configurable models are still not the norm, I am convinced that future RM products will increasingly reflect those requirements to expand the use of the models. This is especially important if those reference models are combined with next-generation process automation systems. The combination of a configurable reference model and the execution engine basically represent a new type of application.

The application of RMs is another accelerator systematically leveraged in value-driven BPM. The process warehouse of the process factory contains all of an enterprise's relevant RMs so that they can be used as components of the process "manufacturing." RMs enable the efficient and effective use of domain know-how around business processes, especially common standards for commodity processes.

6.4 The Bottom Line

- RMs are generic conceptual models, which formalize recommended practices for a special domain. This means RMs deliver common or even best practice information that can be used many times, in multiple organizations. Their format enables easy application in specific situations (Sect. 6.1).

- RMs represent content of various groups of domains, which can be used to distinguish various types of RMs, such as industry or software reference models (Sect. 6.1).
- RMs provide key business benefits for process design, such as cost, time, and risk reduction or the improvement of modeling quality (Sect. 6.1).
- The market for RMs should increase significantly in the next few years, especially due to flexible next-generation software architectures leading to our digital world (Sect. 6.2).
- Today, the main procurement sources for RMs are software companies, consulting firms, industry organizations, and academic organizations (Sect. 6.2).
- Examples of available RMs include the SAP reference models, the BPM-D Framework Reference Model for the Process of Process Management, the PMOLink project management model, the SCOR model, the Y-model, and the retail-H model (Sect. 6.2).
- Criteria for the evaluation and selection of RMs are available (Sect. 6.2).
- The basic procedure to apply RMs to support business process design is fairly straightforward (Sect. 6.3).
- Configurable RMs facilitate the use and transformation of the RM into company-specific process models (Sect. 6.3).
- Reference models are an important accelerator of value-driven business process management.

References

1. Scheer, A.W.: Business Process Engineering—Reference Models of Industrial Enterprises, 2nd edn. Springer, Berlin (1994)
2. Fettke, P., Loos, P.: Classification of reference models: A methodology and its application. Inf. Syst. E-Business Manag. 1(1), 35–53 (2007)
3. Jost, W.: EDV-gestuetzte CIM Rahmenplanung. Gabler, Wiesbaden (1993)
4. Fettke, P., Loos, P.: Perspectives on reference modeling. In: Fettke, P., Loos, P. (eds.) Reference Modeling for Business Systems Analysis, pp. 1–20. Hershey, London (2007)
5. Kirchmer, M.: Business Process Oriented Implementation of Standard Software—How to Achieve Competitive Advantage Efficiently and Effectively, 2nd edn. Springer, Berlin (1999)
6. Scheruhn, H.-J., von Rosing, M., Fallon, R.L.: Information modelling and process modelling. In: von Rosing, M., Scheer, A.-W., von Scheel, H. (eds.) The Complete Business Process Handbook—Body of Knowledge from Process Modelling to BPM, vol. 1. Morgan Kaufmann, Amsterdam (2015)
7. Curran, T., Keller, G.: SAP R/3 Business Blueprint: Business Engineering mit den R/3-Referenzprozessen. Addison-Wesley, Bonn (1999)
8. PMOLink (ed.): Project Management Processes—Based on the PMBOK Guide. PMOLink, New Orleans (2004)
9. IDS Scheer AG (ed.): ARIS Platform. Product Brochure. IDS Scheer, Saarbruecken (2007)
10. Kirchmer, M.: The process of process management—mastering the new normal in a digital world. In: Business Modeling and Software Development (BMSD) Proceedings, July 2015
11. See: http://www.apics.org/sites/apics-supply-chain-council/frameworks/scor

12. Kirchmer, M., Brown, G., Heinzel, H.: Using SCOR and other reference models for E-Business process networks. In: Scheer, A.W., Abolhassan, F., Jost, W., Kirchmer, M. (eds.) Business Process Excellence—ARIS in Practice, pp. 45–64. Springer, Berlin (2002)
13. American Productivity and Quality Center (APQC): Business Process Frameworks. http://www.apqc.org/process-classification-framework (2011)
14. Scheer, A.W., Jost, W., Guengoez, O.: A reference model for industrial enterprises. In: Fettke, P., Loos, P. (eds.) Reference Modeling for Business Systems Analysis, pp. 167–181. Hershey, London (1997)
15. Becker, J., Schuette, R.: Handelsinformationssysteme, 2nd edn. Redline Wirtschaft, Frankfurt (2004)
16. Becker, J., Schuette, R.: A reference model for retail enterprises. In: Fettke, P., Loos, P. (eds.) Reference Modeling for Business Systems Analysis, pp. 182–205. Hershey, London (2007)
17. van Belle, J.: Evaluation of selected enterprise reference models. In: Fettke, P., Loos, P. (eds.) Reference Modeling for Business Systems Analysis, pp. 266–286. Hershey, London (2007)
18. Kirchmer, M., Scheer, A.W.: Change management—key for business process excellence. In: Scheer, A.W., Abolhassan, R., Jost, W., Kirchmer, M. (eds.) Business Process Change Management—ARIS in Practice, pp. 1–14. Springer, Berlin (2003)
19. Recker, J., Rosemann, M., van der Aalst, W., Jansen-Vullers, M., Drelling, A.: Configurable reference modeling languages. In: Fettke, P., Loos, P. (eds.) Reference Modeling for Business Systems Analysis, pp. 22–46. Hershey, London (2007)

Chapter 7
Managing Inter-enterprise Processes

Many organizations still struggle with the management of their internal business processes to overcome functional barriers. However, an increasing number of companies are targeting the integration between organizations or so-called inter-enterprise processes. Successful companies operate in a network with other organizations to leverage their strengths and compensate for their weaknesses. Mutual interdependencies are created and managed to drive additional value and to ensure high performance for the "inter-enterprise organization" as a whole. Companies become "platforms" that integrate customers with various suppliers, as enterprises like Amazon, eBay, or Uber show. Uber, for example, does not own many physical assets like a traditional taxi or limousine company. But they have processes in place linking clients to the owners of cars who are the suppliers of Uber.

These changing management paradigms are reflected in a changing information technology focus. The focus moves from integrated intra-enterprise application packages, such as ERP systems, to Internet-based "e-enabled" and inter-enterprise-focused digital technology, using next-generation automation and integration approaches. The "Internet of things" enables the communication between objects, people, and processes across different organizations. This leads to "e-business processes" which means, inter-enterprise processes supported through Web-enabled digital technology. These processes require a specific approach for BPM [1–4]. The discipline of value-driven BPM has to master these requirements to support a successful strategy execution in a digital world.

This chapter discusses appropriate approaches, methods, and tools to manage inter-enterprise processes enabled through the Internet of things. This is a core capability that vBPM provides. The positioning is visualized in Fig. 7.1.

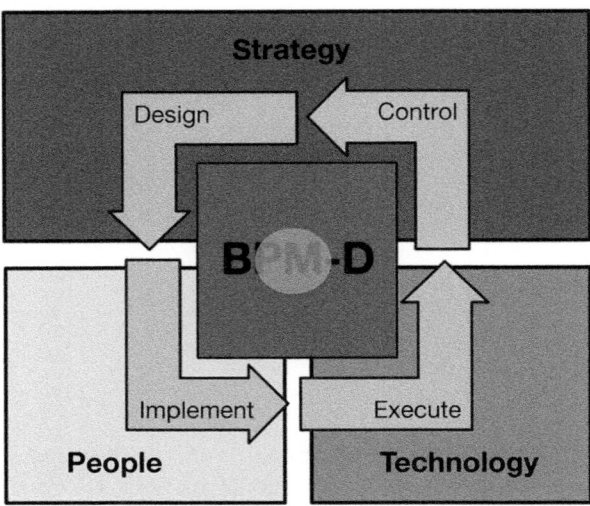

Fig. 7.1 Positioning of the management of inter-enterprise processes

7.1 Why Is the Management of Inter-enterprise Processes So Important?

Inter-enterprise processes are business processes that are distributed across two or more organizations that are independent legal units; thus, there is generally no centralized control. Therefore, the organizational environment of the processes is even more heterogeneous than one of intra-enterprise processes across various organizational units of one and the same company. This results in special integration and coordination requirements regarding people and technologies. The BPM-Discipline needs to handle this special situation to deliver on the overall strategy execution and benefits from a strong integration with market partners. The Internet or even better the Internet of things plays a key role in the management of those processes. Our digital world provides significant improvement opportunities for those inter-enterprise processes which need to be realized through the value-driven BPM-Discipline.

The management requirements in the field of inter-enterprise processes are constantly increasing because companies are more and more often forced to be part of several "enterprise networks" and, with that, participate in multiple inter-enterprise processes. "Platform enterprises," like Uber or Amazon.com, who bring buyer and seller markets together through appropriate processes are especially dependent on managing inter-enterprise processes. Amazon, for example, needs to connect buyers seamlessly with sellers which are parts of other business organizations or private households. The members of inter-enterprise processes are often dispersed around the globe, leading to additional challenges [2]. We will discuss the aspect of globalization in detail later and focus now on inter-enterprise challenges.

7.1 Why Is the Management of Inter-enterprise Processes So Important?

On the technology side, flexible and integrated application architectures and the use of the Internet and the cloud support those inter-enterprise processes. These technologies enable the integration of heterogeneous digital technologies, on the basis of capabilities of the Internet and related standards. This results in Internet-based processes that are often referred to as e-business processes. The organizational integration must be organized through an appropriate process management approach to deliver the overall value proposition of the combined organizations. This also means that the use of the integrated digital technologies based on the Internet of things must be managed in a process-oriented way.

In most cases, an organization's integration in inter-enterprise processes allows the organization to focus on its core competencies, while benefiting from the key strengths of other organizations. For example, in an inter-enterprise scenario, one company may focus on the engineering activities, delivering world-class blueprints for machines. The second enterprise is a leading manufacturing company, producing the machines on the basis of the blueprint from its "supplier." The third organization is a logistics company that specializes in distribution activities. This company ensures the final delivery of the manufactured machine. Every company has one main core process, based on the specific offering. However, for the final customer who buys the machine, only the overall inter-enterprise process and its performance are relevant. If a customer receives the machine too late, it does not matter if the blueprint was not finished in time or if the production was delayed or whether delivery problems occurred. If the final customer is not satisfied, it is an issue for each company involved in the inter-enterprise process. The whole scenario has to be seen and managed as one overall business process. This inter-enterprise process is shown in Fig. 7.2.

Supply chain processes are typical examples for inter-enterprise processes. They integrate suppliers and customers within an overall process [5]. Collaborative engineering processes or maintenance processes are often mentioned examples. In general, inter-enterprise processes enable "enterprise networks" that deliver more value to the end client than single enterprises—when managed accordingly. You can distinguish several different types of enterprise networks [6]:

- Vertical networks
- Horizontal networks
- Regional networks
- Out-of-necessity networks
- Self-promoted networks
- Other networks

Vertical networks, more or less, represent the classic supply chain: one company adds value to a product and passes it onto the next one in the network. In horizontal networks, the involved companies have the same core competencies and all share capacity (e.g., production capacity to avoid bottlenecks). Companies of one region may create a regional network to facilitate close collaboration. For example, this can allow several small organizations to combine their capabilities to fulfill larger orders or demonstrate greater stability. All regional manufacturing companies, for

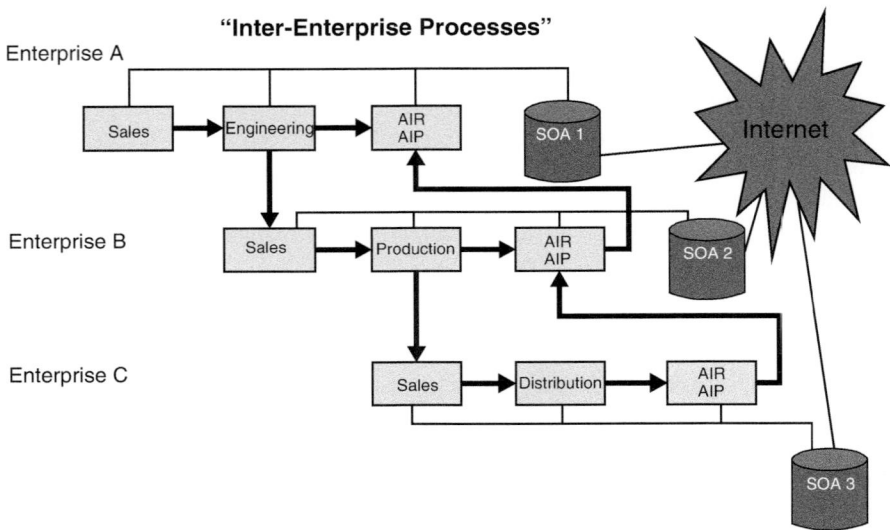

Fig. 7.2 Example of inter-enterprise processes

example, may share one logistics company for their transportation activities. These regional networks are similar to the out-of-necessity networks. For example, if one company cannot pay necessary research and development (R&D) for a new product, it may conduct R&D in an inter-enterprise engineering process together with other organizations. Or a set of companies using similar ingredients for their products form a common laboratory for safety tests of materials they use. A member of a self-promoted network is a company with a core competency that it wants to include in as many networks as possible, independent of the specific final product. Collection companies, e.g., may strive for inclusion in as many inter-enterprise processes as possible and, therefore, form a self-promoted network.

All those networks and the underlying inter-enterprise processes benefit from the easier and more comprehensive integration based on the Internet. This can lead to disruptive innovative business models based on the tight integration of different organizations and their offerings, called "collaboration innovation." General Motors' OnStar system, for example, is based on a tight integration between the offerings of AT&T and GM to deliver directions and supply-related information and provide concierge services. This has been an important competitive advantage of Cadillacs and other GM cars for more than 10 years.

The use of standards, such as best practices, can also lead to the creation of new inter-enterprise processes. For example, if many companies use the same "industry standard process" in a commodity area, this process could be outsourced, resulting in inter-enterprise processes [7].

7.1 Why Is the Management of Inter-enterprise Processes So Important?

The participation in enterprise networks and the related inter-enterprise business processes results in many advantages, such as [6]:

- Synergy: Networks leverage each member's strengths.
- Speed: You can react quickly to a change by adding a new company with new capabilities to the network.
- Flexibility: You can, for example, advance offerings through the capabilities of a new partner or adjust production capacities by leveraging the facilities of a partner.
- Risk reduction: You share risks with other enterprises, reducing your own risk.
- Independence: You are not forced to integrate fully into a larger enterprise group.
- Faster growth and increased profits: You achieve that through the use of the aforementioned synergies.
- Lasting customers: You serve customers over a long time through the broad capabilities of the network.
- Less capital required: This is enabled by the use of mutual capabilities, e.g., shared warehouses.
- Quick failure recognition and feedback: The relationships between the partners of an inter-enterprise process are open enough to provide prompt feedback.
- Increased ability to deal with change: This is due to speed and flexibility achieved through expansion and adjustments of the network.

However, an extensive collaboration in networks and the resulting inter-enterprise processes can also lead to disadvantages, including [6]:

- Too much reliance on one partner in the network and, with that, dependence on the condition of this partner.
- Too much mutual dependence, so that individual survival, for example, in case one partner resigns from the network, is no longer possible.
- Cost and pressure resulting from substantial coordination requirements.
- Lack of overall agility and responsiveness to market changes due to intense cross-company planning requirements.
- Exclusive arrangements between partners of an inter-enterprise process, slowing down innovation and agility. Partners lose the "big picture" view.
- Failure to support a struggling partner of the network in a timely manner due to the overall complexity.
- Risk of missing outsourcing opportunities for support and management processes because everyone focuses on the core inter-enterprise process.
- Ignoring alternative networks or processes.
- Too much or too little mutual trust.
- Neglecting other core competencies currently not present in the network.

An appropriate BPM-Discipline reduces those risks. This management discipline is very important for a systematic strategy execution in this extended business environment. Let's briefly discuss some main aspects of the BPM-Discipline.

In general, the BPM-Discipline discussed earlier, with its approaches, methods, and tools, can also be used for inter-enterprise processes. The views of the ARIS Architecture [8], organizational structure, data, functions, deliverables, and workflow control, are also relevant for those processes across organizations. The structured approach facilitates the comprehensive management of all aspects of inter-enterprise processes. Especially the examination of the "deliverables" of processes in forms of offerings is important. As explained above, the integration of organizations and their individual offerings can provide disruptive new offerings requiring appropriate processes.

Inter-enterprise business processes enable the efficient and effective collaboration between enterprises. In other words, responsibilities are shared between organizational units of the collaborating enterprises. As a consequence, the examination, and sometimes the change, of organizational structures become key for the design and implementation of inter-enterprise processes. This is a key process governance challenge that a BPM-Discipline resolves. The analysis of the "organization view" on an inter-enterprise environment is therefore also of key importance.

The collaboration of different organizations leads to "process-to-process" integration [9]. The coordination of all aspects necessary to achieve this integration is handled as a key aspect through the "control view" of the ARIS Architecture. This topic is again closely related to an appropriate governance approach.

Inter-enterprise processes are subject to even faster change. They are not only influenced through the environment of one company, but through changes relevant for a whole network of enterprises. Therefore, the continuous management and controlling of those processes is especially important and challenging.

We have now identified the importance and key characteristics as well as challenges of the management of inter-enterprise processes. But what does it mean to establish the BPM-Discipline in the different companies? How do the characteristics of inter-enterprise processes influence the design and implementation of business processes? How must the execution and controlling of processes be extended? What does the discipline of value-driven BPM need to deliver to achieve the required performance of inter-enterprise processes?

7.2 What Is Special with the Design and Implementation of Inter-enterprise Processes?

Is the design and implementation of inter-enterprise processes truly different? What has to be changed in comparison to the business processes within an organization? The design of such inter-enterprise processes requires the examination of three key areas [10]:

- A company's business processes, including the current interaction with external players, such as customers, suppliers, or research partners

- The value proposition a company offers to its customers
- The planned degree of collaboration with other organizations in creating shared business processes, harmonized across the inter-enterprise environment

The differences between inter- and intra-enterprise initiatives already begin during the identification of strategic goals and related value drivers that guide process improvement. Contrary to pure intra-enterprise processes, the distribution of benefits between involved organizational units plays an important role. A company's business proposition must improve through the collaboration reflected in an inter-enterprise process. Within one company, the investment of additional resources in one department can be justified through the achievement of additional benefits in other departments. In an inter-enterprise environment, however, the distribution of expected benefits between various involved organizations becomes an important aspect of the definition goals driving the process improvement. All involved organizations should realize benefits. At the very least, organizations involved in an inter-enterprise initiative should not have more disadvantages than benefits. Otherwise, the intended inter-enterprise projects will not be accepted, and the planned process cannot be realized. The identification of a win-win situation is a precondition for establishing sustainable inter-enterprise processes. Defining and targeting win-win situations is a crucial initiative at the beginning of inter-enterprise initiatives.

Strategic goals are defined based on the strategies of the different organizations involved in the inter-enterprise process. This requires that the strategies have to be harmonized as a precondition for proceeding with such collaboration initiatives. Once the strategies are consistent, they can be translated into strategic value drivers using an inter-enterprise "value driver tree." The segmentation of inter-enterprise processes to identify high-impact or commodity areas can then be done using the same approaches applied to intra-enterprise processes [11–13]. This allows the assignment of the right value drivers to the subprocesses of the inter-enterprise network. As a result, the inter-enterprise initiatives systematically target value for all involved organizations [11].

The next important activity in preparing the process design is the definition and extension of each organization's market offerings, consistent with the identified goals. The definition of offerings includes all customer-relevant aspects of the following:

- Physical goods
- Services
- Information
- Rights
- Others

In an inter-enterprise environment, you start with the definition of the "final offering" that is delivered to the end customer. Intermediate offerings of the different organizations involved in the network are adjusted to optimize this final offering. While this process is supported and enabled through the harmonized strategies, it can still be a significant effort. Let's look at an example. A consulting company partners with an application software vendor to deliver automated process solutions to the end customer. Both companies may have to adjust their offerings, e.g., add service components to the consulting offerings or simplify the configuration approach for the software, to come up with an optimal solution for the end client. This is a precondition for the design of successful inter-enterprise processes.

In our digital world, new and often disruptive offerings are mainly created though the following measures:

- The replacement of goods or services through information, for example, the replacement of CDs through digital MP3 files.
- The combination of different products and services from several companies to one new offering, for example, to offer transportation services from different companies through one new "transportation portal."
- The enhancement of existing offerings through new processes, for example, books, accessible through a convenient online store or the custom configuration of snacks that get delivered every month.
- New products leveraging the opportunities of digitalization, for example, deliver information about the stickiness of visitors on a Web page or user-sensitive online marketing packages; aspects like "personalization" and "self-control" of offerings play here often an important role.

It is essential to create new value for the final customer through inter-enterprise networks. Although this can and often does include positive cost effects, the main focus is on additional value creation. A common approach is the development of new service processes around existing offerings, which often becomes an important competitive factor and drives inter-enterprise initiatives. New offerings can be designed and described in product models [14, 15], supporting an analytic approach to the definition of offerings.

Business model and technology innovations are important components of this and the following process design steps [16]. Business process innovation plays a major role. In many instances, inter-enterprise initiatives force organizations to develop process innovations to support new offerings provided by the combination of the different inter-enterprise partners. This can even lead to disruptive new business models for one or several of the involved organizations, for example, through the move of "traditional individual manufacturing" to mass individualization using transponder technologies to coordinate involved production units.

Once the new or modified offerings are defined, you may discover that additional partners are required in the network in order to deliver the final solution. New partners, with new capabilities, can lead to "collaboration innovation." While selecting and adding business partners to a network, it is important to identify the specific strengths of a company and its possible partners to come to the win-win situations [17].

Now, it must be determined how these market partners should be integrated into a collaborative inter-enterprise business process. There may be direct point-to-point integration or a "star integration" through existing or to-be-created, so-called e-marketplaces. These e-marketplaces facilitate the business relations of its members, based on the Internet. The point-to-point integration generally results in an optimized implementation of one relation; the use of an e-marketplace typically ensures increased flexibility to switch among partners. Marketplaces may be industry specific, regional, and/or even focused on the needs of one company trying to optimize its partner network (private marketplace) [18–20]. The discovery of existing e-marketplaces may result in changes in the defined partner network: partners may be added or eliminated, ultimately resulting in the definition of the topology of the partner network.

When the offerings and the partner network topology are defined, the resulting inter-enterprise scenarios can be designed. That means different business processes across multiple organizations are specified. These inter-enterprise processes outline the collaboration between the involved organizations. General business strategies, like collaborative engineering or planning, are defined in this activity. The key here is the knowledge about the organization's current business processes, to know how much they need to change or where it is necessary to harmonize those processes across all partners of a network. Even if the decision is taken to implement completely new processes, for example, to enable a disruptive innovation, knowledge about the existing enterprise environments is important to use benefits from strengths and eliminate current weaknesses where necessary.

It is important to evaluate the current intra-enterprise processes. If they cannot keep up with the required new inter-enterprise capabilities, the targeted results will not occur. On the contrary, the tight integration may reveal the organization's own weaknesses to the other members of the network which can in the worst case lead to a revision of the partner selection.

Each organization plays one or several specific roles in a scenario. The definition of these roles is another important step in the definition of the entire scenario [21]. Partners may play roles, for example, as suppliers, buyers, and facilitators.

The definition of inter-enterprise scenarios and resulting processes is a key deliverable of the process design executed through the projects of a value-driven BPM-Discipline. These scenarios are the guidelines for all following activities.

Related process reference models can be used as a starting point for the definition of such inter-enterprise scenarios. These reference models allow the structured transfer of best practices and experiences within specific business fields. In addition, they are used to establish standards across various organizations, for example, by establishing a common terminology, enabling efficient and effective inter-enterprise process design.

On the basis of the general process scenarios, the detailed inter-enterprise processes can be designed. The analysis of the relevant existing processes ensures a realistic implementation strategy. Processes to be analyzed include inter-enterprise and intra-enterprise processes. Both must fit together to enable appropriate business results. However, a special focus is naturally on the processes or subprocesses responsible for the collaboration of the involved partner organizations.

Companies must decide on three groups of processes to come up with the optimal inter-enterprise processes in your collaboration scenario [10]:

- Processes you perform yourself—mainly intra-enterprise processes
- Processes you perform with others—mainly inter-enterprise processes
- Processes others perform for you ("outsourced processes")

The grouping of processes is the basis for the definition of appropriate process governance across enterprise boundaries. This can be a time-consuming process because all involved enterprises must reach a consensus. Some questions to support that task include [10] the following:

- Of all companies in an inter-enterprise network, which has the best capabilities to manage a process?
- How will the capabilities of the different organizations be used in the inter-enterprise process?
- Have the responsibilities in the processes been clearly assigned?
- How do we determine when one company is not performing sufficiently?
- Do we need governance bodies with members from several involved organizations?
- How can a joint governance body or role influence what happens within one of the involved organizations and drive necessary change?
- How do you integrate inter-enterprise and intra-enterprise process governance?

On the one hand, the analysis focuses on general business approaches, as defined in the inter-enterprise scenarios, for example, to check if a collaborative engineering approach already exists or if it still has to be defined. On the other hand, process inefficiencies are discovered and resolved through the inter-enterprise collaboration.

The "to-be" of the core business processes can be specified on the basis of the defined inter-enterprise scenarios. This includes the assignment of the various governance responsibilities. The specification contains all ARIS information systems views: organizations, functions, data, deliverables (products), and control flow. The different views may be specified in an integrated representation or separately, depending on the complexity of the aspects to be specified. The previously discussed approach of the vBPM process factory is applied again in this design phase.

The structure of the design of inter-enterprise business processes is shown in Fig. 7.3.

On the basis of the business process specifications and the inter-enterprise scenarios, the required digital technologies can be selected. The focus here is on collaborative technologies and the Internet of things, as discussed previously. In this stage, one may even define new online communities for the members of the inter-enterprise processes. This allows members to facilitate the collaboration using techniques, such as blogs or other means of joint content creation.

The process specification is the basis for the realization of the inter-enterprise scenarios, similar to the implementation of intra-enterprise processes. The business

7.2 What Is Special with the Design and Implementation of Inter-enterprise...

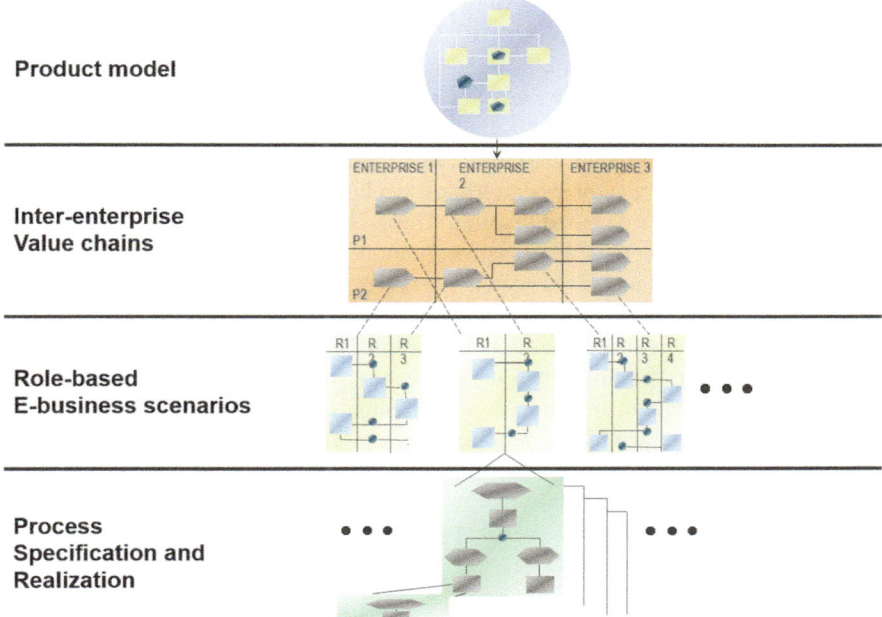

Fig. 7.3 Design of inter-enterprise processes

process models are used as a guideline for the implementation of the selected digital technologies, for example, the application software components. To ensure a fast and effective implementation in an inter-enterprise environment, different subprocesses or functions are realized, according to the capabilities and priorities of the enterprises within the network—based on the common strategic goals and resulting priorities. Since all individual activities refer to the integrated process design (a "master plan" for inter-enterprise scenarios), subprocesses are reassembled step by step to support end-to-end processes across the organization.

The specific realization activities vary greatly, depending on the environments of the involved companies. Therefore, it is impossible to describe all necessary activities in detail. However, a basic structure of the realization measures can be defined, similar to the realization of intra-enterprise processes [22]. The major steps are:

1. Technology-related activities
2. Organizational activities
3. Go live

Contrary to pure intra-enterprise processes, the technology measures of an inter-enterprise process implementation may include more integration work, for example, the use of additional enterprise application integration software, due to heterogeneous IT components of the involved enterprises.

All realization activities can be subject to general company-specific guidelines, for example, from marketing and legal. The development of external Web pages may require a design based on marketing guidelines. The exchange of specific information may be impacted by legal contracts and specifications.

As part of the organizational activates, personnel, process organization, and general infrastructure-related activities can be distinguished. Personnel measures include all change management activities, especially training, but also information and communication, as discussed earlier. These change management activities are all conducted, based on the business process models developed in the design. With regard to process organization-related measures, for example, legal or security aspects of inter-enterprise processes must be resolved.

Once technology and organizational measures are executed, the specified business processes can "go live" based on the new technology and organizational realities. In other words, the process will change according to the design of the inter-enterprise scenarios. This requires appropriate support from the involved organizational units, similar to intra-enterprise projects.

The inter-enterprise processes are now ready to be executed and controlled. This leads to the next question: How do the specifics of the inter-enterprise environment influence those vBPM activities?

7.3 What Is Special with the Execution and Controlling of Inter-enterprise Processes?

The implementation phase begins the process execution, which then requires the management and controlling of the inter-enterprise processes, as explained in the general discussion of vBPM. Continuous process improvement must begin immediately to ensure that the targeted goals are actually achieved and to adapt to changing business environments. Because of the higher rate of change, this is even more important in an inter-enterprise environment. Therefore, the current business situation has to be monitored constantly and compared with the design results. It must be determined whether the defined goals are achieved. If they are not achieved, either smaller improvement steps may be defined and executed in a "kaizen" approach of continuous improvement [23] or a new strategy or design phase must begin to react to a drastically altered environment [24].

In an inter-enterprise environment, the major challenge of this activity is that one company generally cannot make that decision alone. It often requires discussions between members of the involved organizations. This issue can be minimized if clear responsibilities are defined in the design phase. In many cases, there is one "dominating" partner in such an inter-enterprise network. This company can drive the necessary decisions at least in some areas. This situation often occurs in the automotive industry but also in other industry sectors, for example, in the retail area.

7.3 What Is Special with the Execution and Controlling of Inter-enterprise...

To monitor and analyze inter-enterprise business processes means to collect business process performance data and check if the defined goals have been realized, based on the newly implemented processes. Once again, it is most efficient to focus on high-impact processes because they are most relevant for achieving business goals. The analysis determines whether or not the goals are realized. If the goals are not realized, the reasons must be determined, for example, inconsistencies between an actual process and the relevant process design. In addition, the business environment has to be continuously monitored for new developments, such as new products, competitors, business models, or technologies, that may change the basis upon which the inter-enterprise design had been developed.

The collection and analysis of the relevant information is generally very time and work consuming. To execute this step efficiently and effectively, appropriate software tools play a key role. The manual execution of this step must basically be replaced by an application software system. One example of a tool focused on this process performance monitoring is business monitoring and decision software that can be used as "Process Performance Manager" [25]. It can be integrated with application software to collect the necessary process performance, such as cycle times.

Such a process management system can be used specifically to monitor inter-enterprise business processes, as shown in Fig. 7.4. In this case, it is recommended that a third-party service provider host the process management application to ensure that no confidential data is transferred between the involved organizations. This would be part of a process outsourcing offering of a third party.

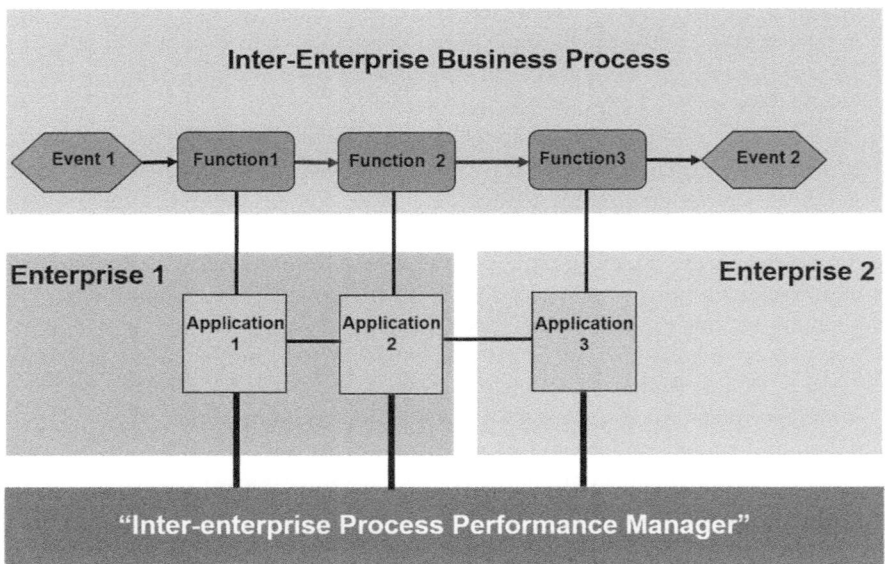

Fig. 7.4 Process performance management applied to inter-enterprise processes

In addition, the general business environment must be continuously evaluated. This can be achieved through the integration of external information sources, as explained previously in the discussion of the new digitalization and collaboration technologies. Membership in various business online communities or the integration of research institutions in the "virtual organization" created through inter-enterprise processes can help to address this situation.

Since the governance of those inter-enterprise processes is challenging, it is recommended to document the key governance rules again in process models, so the governance processes can be managed effectively. An example of such a process is the reaction to certain business environment changes, such as a price increase of raw materials, synchronized across all organizations of an inter-enterprise network.

Communication between the people involved in the process must also be organized, and it is best to include face-to-face meetings to help people "feel good" in the new extended enterprise. This is necessary to bridge various cultural environments in the companies involved in inter-enterprise processes.

The general approach and philosophy of vBPM also fits the requirements of inter-enterprise processes. However, extensions of the general management discipline in key areas like the design and controlling of processes are required.

7.4 Bottom Line

- Inter-enterprise processes are business processes that are distributed across two or more organizations that are independent legal units (Sect. 7.1).
- Inter-enterprise processes require special integration and coordination activities in regard to people, as well as technology aspects as part of the BPM-Discipline so that they enable high performance (Sect. 7.1).
- The Internet of things and the related new digital technologies enable the collaboration along inter-enterprise processes. The organizational integration requires appropriate process governance, addressing all involved organizations (Sect. 7.1).
- In most cases, an organization's integration in inter-enterprise processes allows the organization to focus on its core competencies, while benefiting from key strengths of other organizations (Sect. 7.1).
- An extensive collaboration in networks and the resulting inter-enterprise processes can also lead to disadvantages (Sect. 7.1).
- Inter-enterprise processes are even more subject to change (Sect. 7.1).
- Contrary to pure intra-enterprise processes, the distribution of benefits between involved organizational units plays an important role. Win-win scenarios need to be defined (Sect. 7.2).
- An important activity to prepare the design of inter-enterprise processes is the definition and extension of an organization's market offerings. This can result in disruptive innovation, especially process innovation (Sect. 7.2).

- New partners in inter-enterprise processes can lead to "collaboration innovation," a special form of process innovation (Sect. 7.2).
- Inter-enterprise scenarios, or different business processes across multiple organizations, are specified in collaborative initiatives. It is important to evaluate and, if necessary, adjust the related intra-enterprise processes (Sect. 7.2).
- Each organization of an enterprise network plays a specific role in a specific scenario. The definition of these roles is very important for the definition of the entire scenario (Sect. 7.2).
- Responsibilities must be clearly assigned to the different partners of an enterprise network. This is a new dimension of a process governance approach (Sect. 7.2).
- The specific realization activities for inter-enterprise processes vary heavily, depending on the specific situations in the various organizations involved (Sect. 7.2).
- A continuous process improvement must begin immediately after the "go live" to ensure that targeted mutual goals are actually achieved and to adapt to changing environments. Due to the higher rate of change, this is even more important in an inter-enterprise environment than for intra-enterprise processes (Sect. 7.3).
- The major challenge of continuous improvement activities in an inter-enterprise environment is that there is generally not one company who can make the necessary decisions. Process governance models must be more comprehensive. Tools supporting the process performance management may be run by third-party service providers to avoid conflicts (Sect. 7.3).
- Collaboration technologies can be very valuable to coordinate inter-enterprise processes, for example, through process-related online communities (Sect. 7.3).
- Since the governance of those inter-enterprise processes is challenging, it is recommended to document the key governance rules again in process models (Sect. 7.3).

References

1. Kirchmer, M.: e-Business process improvement (eBPI): Building and managing collaborative e-Business scenarios. In: Callaos, N., Loutfi, M., Justan, M. (eds.) Proceedings of the 6th World Multiconference on Systemics, Cybernetics and Informatics, vol. VIII, pp. 387–396. International Institute of Informatics and Systemics, Orlando (2002)
2. Fingar, P.: Extreme Competition—Innovation and the Great 21st Century Business Reformation. Meghan-Kiffer Press, Tampa (2006)
3. Scheer, A.-W., Habermann, E., Koeppen, A.: Electronic business und knowledge management—Neue Dimensionen fuer den Unternehmenserfolg. In: Scheer, A.-W. (ed.) Electronic Business und Knowledge Management—Neue Dimensionen fuer den Unternehmenserfolg, pp. 3–36. Physica Verlag, Heidelberg (1999)
4. Hammer, M.: The internet and the real economy. Documentation of Sapphire 99, Philadelphia (1999)

5. Kirchmer, M.: E-business process networks—successful value chains through standards. J. Enterp. Manage. **17**(1), 20–30 (2004)
6. McHugh, P., Merli, G., Wheeler, W.: Beyond Business Process Reengineering—Towards the Holistic Enterprise. Wiley, Chichester (1995)
7. Davenport, T.: The coming commoditization of processes. Harv. Bus. Rev. **83**(6), 100–108 (2005)
8. Scheer, A.-W.: ARIS—Business Process Frameworks, 2nd edn. Springer, Berlin (1998)
9. Reilly, B., Hope-Ross, D., Knight, L.: Marketplaces and process mediation—The missing link. In: Gartner Group (ed.) Research Note, COM-11-6855, 19 Sept 2000
10. Champy, J.: X-Engineering the Corporation—Reinventing Your Business in the Digital Age. Warner Books, New York (2002)
11. Kirchmer, M., Franz, P.: Targeting Value in a Digital World. BPM-D Whitepaper, Philadelphia (2014)
12. Franz, P., Kirchmer, M.: Value-Driven Business Process Management—The Value-Switch for Lasting Competitive Advantage. McGraw-Hill, New York, e.a (2012)
13. Kaplan, R.S., Norton, D.P.: The Balanced Scorecard. Harvard Business School Press, Boston (1996)
14. Kirchmer, M.: Market- and product-oriented definition of business processes. In: Elzina, D.J., Gulledge, T.R., Lee, C.Y. (eds.) Business Engineering, pp. 131–144. Kluwer, Norwell (1999)
15. Kirchmer, M., Enginalev, A.: Internationales Informations-management—Aufbau von Informationssystemen im Internationalen Verbund. In: Zentes, J., Swoboda, B. (eds.) Fallstudien zum Internationalen Management, pp. 717–729. Gabler, Wiesbaden (2000)
16. Davila, T., Epstein, M.J., Shelton, R.: Making Innovation Work. Wharton School Publisher, Upper Saddle River (2006)
17. Robinson, M., Kalakota, R.: Offshore Outsourcing—Business Models, ROI and Best Practices. Mivar Press, Alpharetta (2004)
18. Williams, L.: E-Market OS: how BtoB marketplaces are creating a commerce operating system. In: The Yankee Group (ed.) BtoB Commerce & Applications Report, vol. 5, no. 11. The Yankee Group, Boston (June 2000)
19. Williams, L.: Corporate-sponsored vs. independent BtoB exchanges: who will win? In: The Yankee Group (ed.) BtoB Commerce & Applications Report, vol. 5, no. 12. The Yankee Group, Boston (July 2000)
20. Runyan, G.: Logistics marketplaces: shaping the evolution of BtoB commerce. In: The Yankee Group (ed.) BtoB Commerce & Applications Report, vol. 5, no. 13. The Yankee Group, Boston (July 2000)
21. Kalakota, R., Robinson, M.: e-Business Roadmap for Success. Addison Wesley, Berkeley (1999)
22. Kirchmer, M.: Business Process Oriented Implementation of Standard Software: How to Achieve Competitive Advantage Efficiently and Effectively, 2nd edn. Springer, Berlin (1999)
23. Imai, M.: Kaizen—Der Schluessel zum Erfolg der Japaner im Wettbewerb, 8 Auflage. Muenchen (1993)
24. Nolan, T., Goodstein, L., Pfeiffer, J.W.: Plan or Die! 10 Keys to Organizational Success. Pfeiffer, San Diego (1993)
25. See, e.g., http://www.softwareag.com/corporate/products/apama_webmethods/default.asp (2016) or https://www.pega.com/products/pega-7-platform/decision-hub (2016)

Chapter 8
Managing Emergent Processes in a Digital World

The amount of data produced from the beginning of history until 2002 is now produced in about 10 min. By 2020 this amount of data will be produced in less than a second—through over 40 billion interconnected devices in a digital world [1]. But this data is only worth something when it is translated into action. That's where the knowledge worker is active. Routine work is already highly automated. Only the real difficult nonroutine work needs the intervention of a knowledge worker. Knowledge and the people who work with knowledge have become increasingly important for achieving high performance in today's digital world. Knowledge workers are the "emerging heroes" [2]. They know how to take decisions and set actions in an unstructured "chaotic" environment [3].

Knowledge workers are people who "think for a living" [4]. Tom Davenport, a business process and knowledge management thought leader, defines them more precisely as people with a high degree of expertise, education, or experience. The primary purpose of their job involves the creation, distribution, or application of knowledge. Key areas where such knowledge workers are deployed include [4] the following:

- Management
- Business or financial operations
- Digitalization/computers and mathematics
- Architecture and engineering
- Life, physical, and social sciences
- Legal
- Healthcare practices
- Community and social services
- Education, training, and library
- Arts, design, entertainment, sports, and media

Knowledge work is different than other types of work, mainly due to the fact that this type of work is generally less structured. It is typically not very easy to define a process model that describes knowledge work, as we discussed for the process design delivered through the value-driven BPM-Discipline. Special characteristics of knowledge work are [4]:

- Knowledge workers prefer autonomy.
- A detailed specification of knowledge-intensive processes is less valuable and more difficult to define than other types of work.
- You can observe a great deal about knowledge work by just watching it.
- Knowledge workers generally have good reasons for their actions.
- Commitment matters tremendously.
- Knowledge workers value their knowledge and don't share it readily.

Many knowledge-intensive processes, such as those within R&D environments or the management of large projects, cannot be completely defined upfront. These are emergent processes. Design and execution overlap heavily. The upfront definition of process types is replaced through decisions and related rules that define the following steps of a process based on the findings of previous steps [1, 2]. The importance of emergent processes continuously increases for many enterprises; however, their management is typically not addressed with straightforward business process management (BPM) approaches. Case management helps here, but when it is not possible to predefine appropriate decision rules, this management approach is also difficult to apply. Therefore, Majchrzak, Logan, McCurdy, and I conducted research on the management of these emergent processes [5, 6], focusing on defining working approaches and guidelines. This chapter is based on the results of our research.

The chapter focuses all phases of management of the process life cycle through vBPM. It explains how the BPM-Discipline enables the management of emergent processes. The focus of this chapter is visualized in Fig. 8.1.

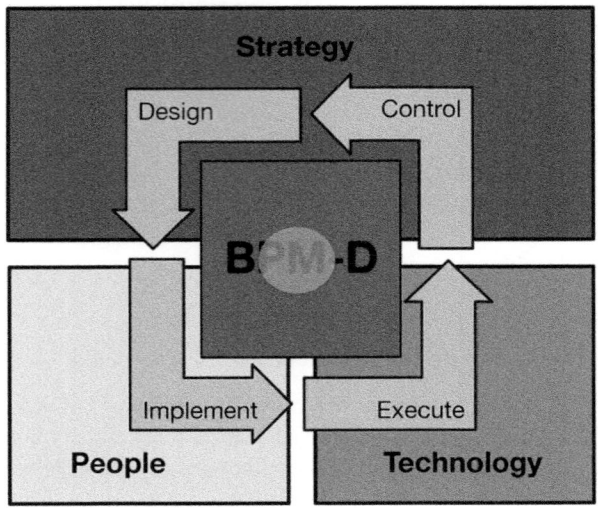

Fig. 8.1 Positioning of the management of emergent processes

The dominating resources needed for this approach are people, the knowledge workers, especially managers who apply vBPM guidelines for managing emergent processes. People play a key role—also and especially in the digital world. Therefore, most of the topics discussed result in suggestions for those knowledge workers, rather than the digital infrastructure needed. However, flexible and collaboration-based digital technologies, for example, automated case management systems, are also useful for the management of emergent processes. Hence, we will address how these opportunities of the digital world can be leveraged.

8.1 What Are Emergent Processes and Why Are They Managed Differently?

Emergent business processes are knowledge-intensive processes for which the outcomes are unpredictable; participants must continuously make sense of their situation and decide, in real time, on the next steps to take. Thus, there is a high overlap between the phases of the process life cycle management. Design, implementation, execution, and controlling of processes are only partly finished when triggering the following phase of the process life cycle. For example, if the first steps of the process are defined, they are directly implemented, executed, and checked before the next steps are designed. This definition of emergent processes is visualized in Fig. 8.2.

New product development, customer service, the testing of materials for specific characteristics, or any knowledge process conducted in a highly dynamic, competitive marketplace must be emergent if a company is to use the unpredictability of the environment for its competitive advantage. Customers often change requirements every day—and they want them fulfilled now. Emergence often happens when least expected. The Red Cross, Wal-Mart, and FedEx, responding to the Hurricane Katrina aftermath, worked together—in an unplanned way—to coordinate the delivery of bottled water to hurricane victims sooner and to more victims than other organizations, such as the City of New Orleans and local churches. Research has repeatedly demonstrated that managers contribute to a company's bottom line when they are able to support their employees in effectively handling

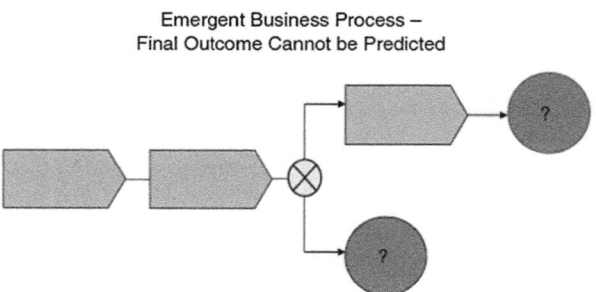

Fig. 8.2 Definition of emergent business processes

unpredictability in the workplace and marketplace—and by so doing turn routine business and work processes into emergent ones. More and more people become knowledge workers since transactional processes get automated in our digital world.

Although managing emergence has been discussed to a great extent, the current literature provides managers with insufficient guidance about activities to undertake while their employees are dealing with the emergence. We are discussing here the process for managing emergence as it is happening. The discipline of vBPM supports that process of managing emergence by combining the build-time process life cycle phases designing/implementation with the run-time phases execute/control of a business process.

Most of the existing advice focuses on enterprises establishing general policies and decision rules for encouraging effective improvisation by workers responsible for emergent work processes, such as:

- Contingency plans must be prepared.
- Alternative future scenarios must be developed.
- The right people must be brought into the workforce.
- The environment must be closely monitored.
- Reward structures encouraging experimentation must be established.

These general activities supporting emergence are clearly critical. But, just as critical—yet much less examined—is what managers should do while knowledge workers carry out their emergent processes. Some questions exploring this topic include:

- Should managers step back and simply enforce the infrastructure?
- Should they continue to encourage their workers to improvise?
- Should they roll up their sleeves and send out experimental probes themselves?

Although it is most likely that managers need to do all three, they also need to do more if their companies are to manage emergence successfully. They must adapt management behavior to the environment. Management becomes part of the emergent business process.

Collectively, Majchrzak, Logan, McCurdy, and I have spent years managing companies and initiatives facing highly uncertain environmental and competitive pressures: leading, listening, and playing in Jazz bands and studying managers whom we consider masters at managing emergence. Our collective experiences have led us to the conclusion that to successfully manage emergence, managers must be actively engaged in the emergent process itself—not simply offer encouragement or ensure that the infrastructure is working. However, if they just take control from employees and conduct the probes themselves, only confident, empowered workers will successfully adapt their processes and knowledge to unpredictable events. Successful managers of emergent processes have their own work process that is unique to managing emergent processes. They execute a special subprocess of the process of process management [7, 8]. The work process and patterns are not the same as for managing employees who are performing transactional routine work.

Successful managers of emergent processes engage in the work process of streaming together "participatory innovative spurts." "Innovative spurts" are the ways in which people continuously innovate in how they do their work, hence in how they design and execute the process they are part of. An engineer who reframes a problem from building a bridge to affecting the flow of traffic is engaged in an innovative spurt. The lead of a laboratory where every research step depends on the results of the previous step is part of an innovative spurt. The Red Cross's redirection during the Katrina disaster from a direct service delivery model to an information broker role is another example of an innovative spurt. In uncertain times, innovative spurts are needed because plans have broken down.

"Participatory" means that anyone may and should be able to take part in these innovative spurts, not simply those who are explicitly tasked with the responsibility to innovate. Subcontractors, customers, insiders, and pundits—all can become engaged in innovative spurts. In the Katrina disaster, individuals and church groups independently posted names of missing persons. None had been tasked with the "responsibility" to find missing persons.

Finally, "streaming spurts together" means that instead of coordinating these spurts in a planned, top-down fashion, managers encourage and guide these innovative spurts to build on one another as they evolve. As Websites and databases listing missing persons from Hurricane Katrina proliferated, the Red Cross stepped in to knit the sites together through links and a search engine—not centralizing the work of others, but rather to innovatively build on the spurts of others. It is something like a coordinated bottom-up approach where the coordination activities are defined based on the results of the different bottom-up activities.

But how does one implement those "participatory innovative spurts"? How can one really manage such emergent processes?

8.2 How Can One Manage Emergent Processes?

To stream together participatory innovative spurts, four key management activities are necessary:

- Continuously engage in discourse with participants and encourage communication.
- Dynamically update knowledge maps to continuously rematch participant responsibilities in a knowledge network.
- Purposely blur boundaries between those who are inside and outside the organization.
- Govern through egocentric reputation networks and changing leadership, not rules.

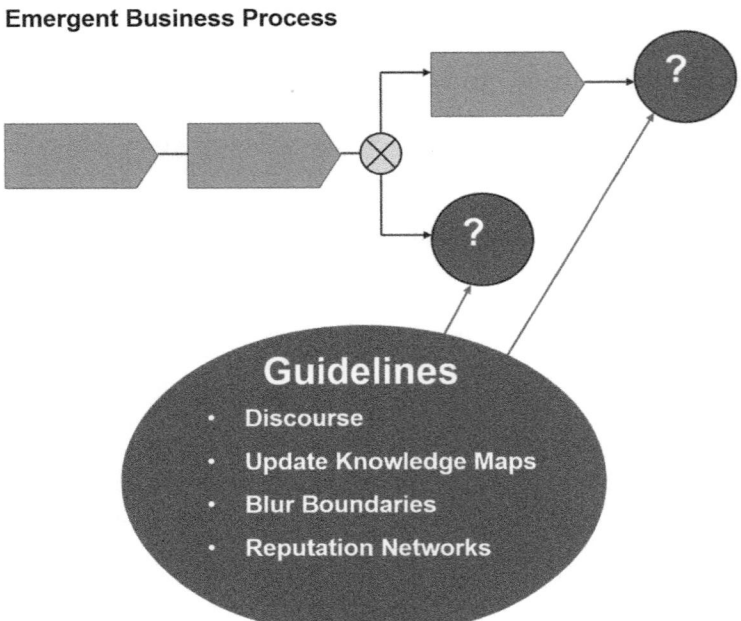

Fig. 8.3 Managing emergent business processes

These guidelines for the management of emergent processes are visualized in Fig. 8.3. They are more general and people oriented than the rules used in classical case management. They are defined to make innovation part of the day-to-day work to deal with emergence successfully. These guidelines help to find out what works instead of trying to develop a top-down plan. They look for quick action as well as clear and direct communication [3]. Considering the amount of available data and its rapid growth in the digital world [1], it is basically impossible to drive emergent processes just through predefined rules and decision patterns. We need a systematic empowerment of people to innovate and act on the spot, just like the musicians in a Jazz band when they play their solo.

What does it mean to engage in continuous discourse with potential participants? In the face of uncertain events, different perspectives are needed to solicit and evaluate alternative interpretations of events, data, and possible solutions. Typically, managers trying to cope with uncertainty will ask employees and consultants to develop white papers, top-down road maps, or market trend reports that are discussed and then used to form the basis for plans to guide employee behaviors. Managing emergence is more than that. Managers may solicit different views in the form of reports and employees may discuss these reports. However, the discussions do not end in a plan; in fact, the discussions do not end at all. The managers organize the work so that the discussion continues as the work is complete.

It is not just continuous discussion that is encouraged, but "discourse." Discourse is a discussion in which data, assumptions, and interpretations are explicitly surfaced, compared with other interpretations, and then challenged in the face of new data and interpretations. Discourse for emergence is the constant sharing and challenging of assumptions about the environment, uncertainties, and possible organizational responses. Why would a manager encourage discourse during work hours even after decisions are made? In uncertain times in a digital world, environmental realities change so rapidly and potentially with such systemic effects that interpretation and assumptions need to be surfaced and challenged frequently to identify the next innovative spurt. Because the business relevant change is continuously happening, the evaluation of potential next steps of emergent processes has to be reconsidered continuously.

Successful discourse is not the normal conversation of an everyday organization. It is different in three ways:

1. For discourse to successfully lead to innovative spurts, participants must be able to freely share and discuss all relevant information, including taboo subjects such as political implications of alternative actions. Common performance metrics for each business unit can help by visibly conveying information on each unit's performance via dashboards, which are then openly discussed.
2. Discourse must intentionally engage alternative perspectives, as when people from many different levels in an organization are engaged in a discourse.
3. Discourse must be focused on actions. Discourses that lead to a lot of pontification will be of limited value; they must affect people's behaviors. In spite of all the change, we have to move continuously toward an organization's goal. Emergent processes must be developed according to that requirement.

So, vBPM for managing emergence means stimulating discourse by walking among workers and asking them questions like the following:

- Have any assumptions changed lately?
- Are you still sure this is the right thing to do?
- Have you thought about other actions we could be taking?

In the discourse, managers purposely include people who have been ignored previously. They share information that might be traditionally hidden. They talk about alternative actions people can take. For example, Novell managers use a process called "dialogic inquiry," in which participants air, openly challenge, and then discuss core assumptions they each hold. Managers have broken from tradition by no longer starting meetings between Novell consultants and software developers with participants presenting proposed actions or decisions. Instead, they begin the meeting with each participant presenting his/her assumptions about emerging market needs and corporate direction. Dialogic inquiry has worked to inspire innovative spurts in both product ideas and marketing campaigns and contributed to a general sense of community and shared understanding.

Dynamically updating knowledge maps to continuously rematch responsibilities means the following: in changing and uncertain times, the knowledge that constituted relevant expertise given a certain set of known conditions may quickly become preempted by new knowledge as those conditions change. The notion of an "expert" is fleeting, highly situation specific, and of limited utility. It is not that people are not experts for a given problem or solution; it is that the set of known conditions continuously redefine what the problem is and, thus, the appropriate solutions and expertise. Expertise is then grounded in the knowledge that can be brought to bear on an issue as it is discussed.

Thus, vBPM managers of emergence do not rely on static expertise directories, yellow pages, or their informal networks of contacts to determine who knows what about something. Instead, they develop—and help others to develop—knowledge maps about what people know about all sorts of unrelated topics and strive to keep these maps updated. Some managers do this by wandering around asking employees about hobbies. This is more than showing an interest in an employee; the hobbies, such as a fascination with Chinese history, may prove helpful in some future Chinese outsourcing deal. Managers may keep knowledge maps updated by sending out e-mails to employees with links to articles about new ways of doing business to see who starts a conversation about the article. Other managers observe posts to corporate blogs to see who is interested in what. Social media and enterprise-specific e-communities as well as the collaboration opportunities of other digital tools, for example, process execution or repository tools, help facilitate this work.

Having adopted the notion of keeping knowledge maps updated to rematch responsibilities, managers of emergence realize that personally updating the knowledge maps for their organization and shifting responsibilities on the fly is too slow for an emergent process. So they create and manage a process in which the workers responsible for the emergent process are able to keep knowledge maps updated to dynamically reshift responsibilities.

In the following true example, Rob and Paul are managers at the New Orleans public utility Entergy. Rob and Paul were responsible for placing the largest transmission cables ever built under the mile-wide Mississippi River. They completed the project on time and below budget. To accomplish this very involved project, Rob and Paul had to rely on contractors to handle each phase of the project—from dirt removal to cable manufacturing and from cable laying to building a shoreline children's park when construction was complete. Because of the size, novelty, and complexity of the project, Rob and Paul knew they would not be able to predefine all of the conditions for handoffs between contractors. So, they created a contractual arrangement in which each contractor was responsible for an effective handoff to the next contractor without specifying details of the handoff. The contractual arrangement effectively encouraged contractors to share their expertise about the site as it evolved with the changing conditions at the site, such as the evolving compaction of the dirt or unexpected underwater hazards. Contractors would negotiate responsibilities on the fly for solving problems as they learned from each other because they were both required to agree that a successful handoff had been completed before payment. In this way, Rob and Paul made it

8.2 How Can One Manage Emergent Processes?

possible for the contractors to do their own knowledge map updating and responsibility shifting.

Purposely blurring boundaries between who is in and outside the organization results in the following behavior: Today, customers are often asked for feedback on product innovations. They are asked to suggest product ideas, to provide financial forecasts and product demand forecasts, and to partner with companies on developing process and product innovations. This behavior puts the company in the center of the communication network, and customers have often been willing to offer help when asked. Managing emergence, however, requires more. Getting solicited feedback from customers is too slow and predictable for an emergent process. Moreover, keeping the company in the center of the communication network means that information will be lost unless it is explicitly routed through the company. Instead, emergent processes require unpredictable input from unpredictable participants.

Suppliers, interested citizens, and employees—as well as customers—need to become more involved. The information they provide should not just be feedback in response to specific requests, but unsolicited information offered out of interest and excitement to become engaged. Ideally, such individuals are not only providing information, but helping to correct inaccurate information offered by others. When someone assumes a constraint on an idea, companies need customers, suppliers, and interested parties to challenge these constraints. Normally, such engagement would be expected only of employees. But emergent work processes cannot afford to miss information from outside the organization. So, managers of emergence blur the boundaries between what company employees do and what external parties do.

Novell has effectively blurred this distinction in its "Birds of a Feather" Forums [5]. At corporate events for its customers, senior developers were traditionally kept out of the customer limelight because marketing employees, not developers, worked with the customer. But this approach changed with the Birds of a Feather Forums. Customers at these events now share their interests and questions about new products or new approaches for existing products. A senior developer with deep knowledge about the specific topic attends the event and discusses the subject matter with the customers, employees, media, and other interested parties. Although some developers may comment on future development activities that are not quite ready for public discussion, the open knowledge-sharing exchange has created relationships and innovative spurts that have inspired both sides. At IDS Scheer the senior development leads participated regularly at customer events to get direct feedback and learn about the thoughts and feelings of the clients while sharing their ideas about future developments. This provided valuable input into the development plans and helped key developers understand why sales and marketing often come up with "strange" requests.

Paul and Rob at Entergy, as employees of a public utility, knew that the public needed to be informed about the public works project if its cost was to be borne by rate increases, rather than Entergy. However, Paul and Rob went beyond simply informing the public; they engaged the public in weekly talk shows, town hall meetings, letters to the editor in the local newspapers, responses to others' letters to the editor, and open houses, at which they did not simply present, but used the time to solicit ideas, discuss unfolding problems in the project, and involve the public in celebrations as the project went through its various phases. This level of customer engagement left the public feeling that they were not simply informed but that they had influenced "their project." The public voted to grant the rate increase.

Another example is the increasing use of social media and related digital concepts, such as wikis, to encourage engagement at all levels inside and outside an organization. At Novell, the Cool Solutions Wiki invites customers to provide solutions for other customers, help developers to understand technical issues, and even cowrite technical white papers with Novell developers.

In the past, managers have been reluctant to share the details of an emergent process with outsiders for fear that others will conclude that the organization is rudderless, blowing in the wind of change. Public projects selectively release information to the public; developers selectively meet with only hand-picked customers; information is gathered from customers but interpreted by the organization behind the firewall. Engaging the external base of interested citizens not by simply providing information but in helping to interpret the information is a level of responsibility given to external parties that blurs the boundaries between internal and external agents.

Govern through dynamic, egocentric reputation networks, not rules. If managers of emergent processes need innovation spurts not only from employees but also external parties, what leverage do managers have to make this happen? The vBPM managers of emergence understand that rules ensure that people will follow specific procedures, but rules will not ensure that people participate in innovation. Instead, managers have created or identified "reputation networks" and used these networks to provide the incentives and the norms for participatory innovation.

Governing by reputation has been found to be useful in the past. Wiki pages indicate the contributor with the greatest number of downloaded pages. Knowledge management systems enable people to rate each other's contributions in terms of how the contribution helps with their immediate problem. eBay rates sellers and buyers. Southern California Edison's Web governance structure for its employee portal governs by reputation. The owners of each port of the portal are publicly known, creating a sort of "United Nations" effort at portal management. The result is a portal that is well managed and kept up to date, in part because reputations are on the line.

However, it's not simply the reputation of individual people that matters if participatory innovation spurts are desired in response to uncertain events. In managing emergence, because problems and events change unpredictably and dynamically, a reputation network for uncertain times is also likely to be dynamic. Thus, instead of a network as a stable community that doles out reputation kudos, a reputation network for emergent processes would be highly unique for each individual party and uniquely adjusted by that party in response to each unique event.

For example, rather than using a general network of security professionals, chief security officers typically selectively draw from their own personal networks to recreate a unique reputation network for each unique security threat they encounter.

Therefore, using these networks for governing requires first identifying them. Then, having identified those networks, the vBPM managers work with the network to affect how reputation within the network is assigned.

For example, Rob and Paul at Entergy knew that they did not have enough leverage to keep their subcontractors on track. So, they learned about the market communities within which each subcontractor worked and then publicly kept that community informed about the subcontractor's progress. In one case, Rob flew to Japan to speak to the subcontractor's customers to explain why working on this subcontract would yield long-term dividends to the customers—a move that gave the subcontractor flexibility to innovatively reschedule production when he encountered problems with the Entergy project.

These four guidelines help managers of emergent processes to react quickly to the uncertainty in unpredictable events—so quickly that it appears from the outside that they are preemptive strategists, prescient soothsayers, excellent predictors of the future, and great planners. Nothing could be further from the truth. What sets them apart from others is neither their planning skills nor their ability to look through a crystal ball. What sets them apart is their continuous discourse, updating knowledge maps, blurring organizational boundaries, and using reputations within egocentric networks among an ever-changing group of participants. By streaming together the participatory innovative spurts that result, managers are able to make an emergent process appear expected.

Although this management behavior is crucial, a certain infrastructure is still necessary. We will now discuss selected digital tools supporting the management of emergent business processes.

8.3 What Tools Support the Management of Emergent Processes?

In our discussion of general aspects for managing emergent business processes, we found out that the use of selected digital, often cloud based, tools can support the management of emergent processes [9]. Wikis or blogs are used to collect and exchange knowledge in an easy and effective way. They support the knowledge worker, especially in the described environment of emergence. The support of an internal and external collaboration through Web 2.0 applications, such as online communities, facilitates all four discussed guidelines. It helps blur company boundaries, create external networks, and define knowledge maps and can even enable the required discourse.

The digital collaboration tools can be combined with a telecommunication environment supporting the necessary intense communication. Certain events may trigger phone calls to mobile phones or start in parallel an "ad hoc blog" related to the same topic. The intense discourse is channeled through various media, bridging even long distances where necessary. Case management systems can trigger necessary actions based on different events in a project and help keeping

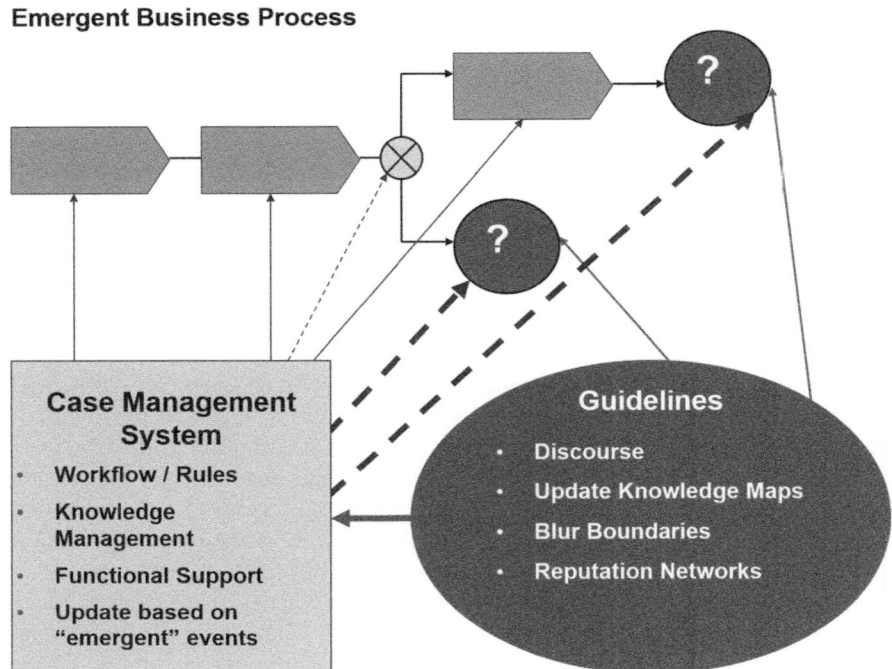

Fig. 8.4 Using case management systems to support the management of emergent processes

the overall process moving forward, even if some business rules of the process have to be defined or modified during the ongoing management of emergence. The use of case management systems is illustrated in Fig. 8.4.

The continuous update and management of knowledge maps can be supported by BPM applications like modeling tools, as discussed previously [10]. They allow an efficient creation of knowledge maps, and the Internet enables updates, independent from specific locations. The maintenance of extensive knowledge assets can be very important while managing emergent processes. To use that knowledge efficiently, it must be structured accordingly. Both can be achieved through BPM modeling and repository tools, especially when they are cloud based and with that easily accessible without creating unnecessary overhead for technology maintenance.

Emergent business processes are also an interesting application area for reference models. Reference models provide knowledge about business processes in a structured, easy-to-apply format [11]. They can be used as the basis for evaluating and defining the next steps of emergent processes, based on the current execution results. They can facilitate the discourse required for the management of emergence. The use of such knowledge components leads to significant advantages because it hastens the discourse and ensures usable transparent results.

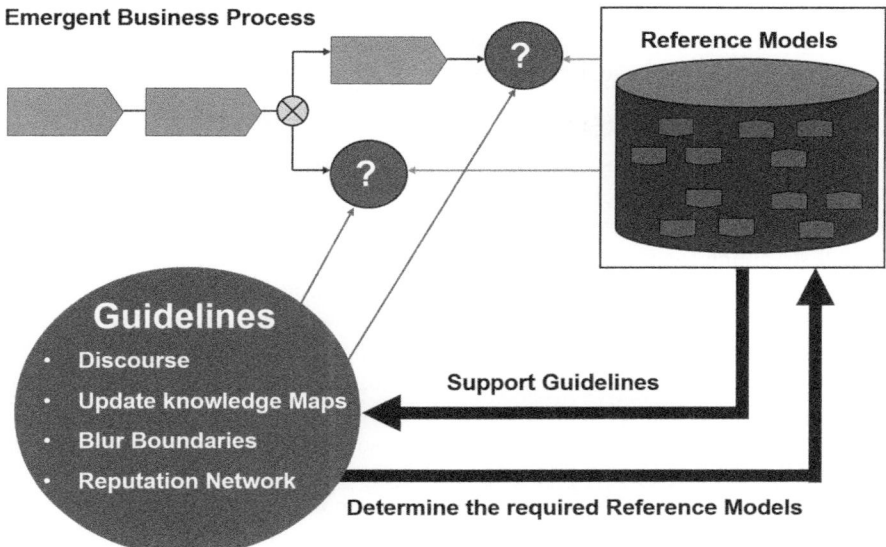

Fig. 8.5 Using reference models to support the management of emergent processes

The use of reference models to support the management of emergent processes in vBPM is visualized in Fig. 8.5.

The use of reference models supports the necessary discourse. On the one hand, the models can be the basis for developing knowledge maps, support the communication and interaction with people outside the organization, and help recognize and verify a special reputation and know-how. On the other hand, the guidelines for managing emergence and the scope of the emergent process also help to select appropriate reference models that can be applied in a specific initiative.

Although management behavior is most important for a successful approach toward emergent processes, the discussed infrastructure delivers key support. It makes the management behavior more efficient and bridges great distances, necessary for work in an international environment.

8.4 The Bottom Line

- Due to the tremendous amount of data produced daily, the management of knowledge-intense processes has become more and more important (Introduction).
- Emergent business processes are knowledge-intensive processes in which the outcomes are unpredictable (Sect. 8.1).
- Participants in emergent processes must continuously make sense of their situation and decide, in real time, on the next steps to take (Sect. 8.1).

- Managers contribute to high performance when they are able to manage their employees to effectively handle unpredictability in the workplace and marketplace—and, by doing so, turn routine business and processes into emergent ones (Sect. 8.1).
- An infrastructure supporting emergence is clearly important. But even more critical is what managers should do while workers are carrying out their emergent processes (Sect. 8.1).
- The work process in which managers of emergent processes engage is what we call streaming together "participatory innovative spurts" (Sect. 8.1).
- Four key management activities (guidelines) are necessary to manage emergent processes: continuously engage in discourse with participants; dynamically update knowledge maps to continuously rematch participant responsibilities; purposely blur boundaries between who is inside and outside the organization; and govern through egocentric reputation networks, not rules (Sect. 8.2).
- The activities of managing emergent processes require changes and extensions in traditional managerial work (Sect. 8.2).
- The use of digital tools, such as social media applications or case management systems, helps to implement and enable the application of those guidelines to manage emergent processes (Sect. 8.3).
- BPM modeling and repository tools as well as process reference models are used to create the necessary transparency to make the management of emergent processes more efficient (Sect. 8.3).

References

1. Palmer, N.: Case management in industry 4.0: ACM and IoT. In: Fisher, L. (ed.) Innovation in Adaptive Case Management—Best Practices for Knowledge Workers, pp. 17–24. Future Strategies, Lighthouse Point, FL (2016)
2. Sinur, J.: Knowledge workers are the emergent heroes of the digital world. In: Fisher, L. (ed.) Innovation in Adaptive Case Management—Best Practices for Knowledge Workers, pp. 25–38. Future Strategies, Lighthouse Point, FL (2016)
3. Snowden, D.J., Boone, M.E.: A Leader's Fraemework for Decision Making. Harvard Busienss Review, pp. 69–77, Nov 2007
4. Davenport, T.: Thinking for a Living—How to Get Better Performance and Results from Knowledge Workers. Harvard Business School Press, Boston (2005)
5. Majchrzak, A., Logan, D., McCurdy, R., Kirchmer, M.: Four keys to managing emergence. MIT Sloan Manag. Rev. **47**, 14–18 (2006)
6. Majchrzak, A., Logan, D., McCurdy, R., Kirchmer, M.: What business leaders can learn from Jazz musicians about emergent processes. In: Scheer, A.-W., Kruppke, H., Jost, W., Kindermann, H. (eds.) Agility by ARIS Business Process Management. Springer, Berlin (2006)
7. Kirchmer, M.: The process of process management—mastering the new normal in a digital world. In: Business Modeling and Software Development (BMSD) Proceedings, July 2015
8. Franz, P., Kirchmer, M.: Value-Driven Business Process Management—The Value-Switch for Lasting Competitive Advantage. McGraw-Hill, New York, e.a. (2012)

9. Chow, L., Conner, C., Comes, S., Mei, J.-L., Bullotta, T.: Cloud-enabled ACM for the age of the customer. In: Fisher, L. (ed.) Innovation in Adaptive Case Management—Best Practices for Knowledge Workers, pp. 57–76. Future Strategies, Lighthouse Point, FL (2016)
10. IDS Scheer AG. (ed.): ARIS Platform Product Brochure. IDS Scheer, Saarbruecken (2007)
11. Fettke, P., Loos, P.: Perspectives on reference modeling. In: Fettke, P., Loos, P. (eds.) Reference Modeling for Business Systems Analysis, pp. 1–20. Idea Group, Hershey (2007)

Chapter 9
Globalization Requires Value-Driven BPM

Globalization is a megatrend that influences the business environment tremendously. Although the world was once dominated by the economies of Europe, North America, and Japan, there are now new and important players emerging like China and India. There is no doubt that globalization is changing the world in which we do business. Most successful enterprises work with customers, suppliers, and other market partners in multiple countries around the world. They often have subsidiaries with operations in various countries on different continents. As Friedman says, "the world has become flat" [1]. For example, a midsized manufacturer of highly sophisticated machinery tools focused on the Canadian and US markets. Step by step, the company began to follow its customers and prospects to Europe and opened a plant in Germany, then on to Brazil, and China. Thus, the company became a player in the global market. The markets are linked through the Internet of things and an all-present digitalization so that most transactions can be executed all over the world, essentially in real time.

There are many factors that bring the world closer together, such as [1]:

- The opening of Eastern Europe
- The rise of the World Wide Web and the Internet of things
- New Web-based software, such as social networks, connecting the world
- Powerful communities, like Open Source Initiatives, to develop software
- Outsourcing, or the execution of processes or subprocesses of an enterprise by service providers located in another countries
- Offshoring, or the transition of entire enterprise units, such as a production unit, into another country
- International supply chain processes as a source of competitive advantage
- Insourcing to deliver holistic services, for example, complete logistics services
- Informing, referring to search engines like Google or BING, which provide information in seconds
- Digitalization in general, mobility, personalization, and virtualization

All of these factors encourage, or even force, enterprises to work across the boundaries of continents and countries as they strive for high performance. Consequently, they must develop business processes suited for a global business environment.

On a strategic level, Bartlett and Ghoshal distinguish four types of companies that work across country borders [2]:

- Multinational companies
- International companies
- Global companies
- Transnational companies

In multinational companies, the subsidiaries are more or less independent units that are only required by headquarters to have a certain financial performance. Subsidiaries are typically run as self-sufficient enterprises. In international companies, the transfer of knowledge from headquarters to the subsidiaries is more important; the controls are better developed. Global organizations are even more centralized; the subsidiaries are tightly controlled. In a centralized organizational structure, the world is seen as a single economic entity. Transnational companies consist of networks of interdependent specialized units in various countries. Subsidiaries have different roles. Knowledge is developed jointly and shared internationally.

Although the transnational enterprise seems to be the most efficient and effective, the other forms of internationalization are also valid in specific phases of the life cycle of an organization, depending on company-specific strategies [3]. A start-up company that wants to quickly enter international markets may choose to do so as a multinational or international organization and then gradually become a global and then a transnational enterprise. At IDS Scheer, I was part of a team transforming a national company into a multinational enterprise with subsidiaries around the world and eventually into a global company. Accenture, where I have been working as the global lead for BPM, is clearly a transnational company, with knowledge centers around the world. BPM-D was founded with the goal of creating a transnational company with specialized units in North America, Europe, and Asia, closely connected through governance processes that focus the units on local as well as global goals.

All of those enterprise structures require the appropriate business processes to be implemented successfully across locations in different countries. The discipline of value-driven BPM is the key to managing those processes. But what are specific influence factors of the global business environment? Do they result in any particular vBPM tasks or special infrastructure? These questions are discussed in this chapter, which focuses on all aspects of the BPM-Discipline and the entire lifecycle of a business process which are visualized in Fig. 9.1. The design and implementation of processes in a global environment is specifically discussed since these phases of the process lifecycle are most impacted; execution and control activities build on the modified design and implementation. Key measures for overcoming challenges through globalization are taken during design and implementation.

Fig. 9.1 Positioning of value-driven BPM for globalization

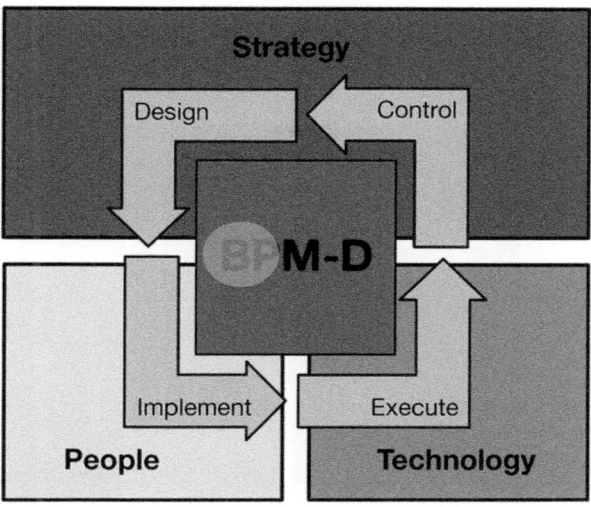

9.1 Some Personal Impressions

During my time at IDS Scheer (now Software AG), I was able to gain quite a bit of international management experience. IDS Scheer was a German software and consulting company with subsidiaries in more than 20 countries around the world. While working for more than 6 years in Europe, mostly in Germany but also in France and other countries, I managed consulting units. After that, I lived in the United States for more than 10 years, holding several different management responsibilities, mostly executive management as head of the region. In between, I worked in Japan for a year and assumed responsibility for overall business in the country for 5 years. Working for Accenture as managing director and global lead for BPM, I continued to have an international focus with BPM consulting units in more than 10 countries. I also had very close interaction with the India team since most of the asset development and maintenance was handled there. BPM-D has offices in the United States, the United Kingdom, and India. Here we have applied many of my past experiences.

I found the differences between working in the United States and Japan extremely interesting and learned a lot "on the job." I would like to discuss some of those experiences because I believe they may help others learn what it means to manage business processes in an international environment. Since I was born and raised in Germany, I will also share my observations from a German perspective—although I have lived in the United States for over 20 years now.

Most US offices in typical companies are composed of cubicles, as shown in Fig. 9.2. The cubicles offer employees a certain degree of privacy—everyone has her or his own little kingdom. In most cases, executives have offices, of which location and size show the importance of the position, as indicated on top in Fig. 9.2.

A Japanese office looks very different, as you can see in Fig. 9.3. People sit in rows, one person next to another. People are courteous, so as not to disturb one

Fig. 9.2 Office in the United States

Fig. 9.3 Office in Japan

another. Employees feel like they are part of a "family." Even executives are typically integrated into that environment. Their desks are often in the same room, just positioned separately to oversee their employees. That does not mean a loss of respect—in contrary. Even those slight differences say a lot in Japanese context.

This first impression I share indicates some major differences regarding the behavior of employees in the work environment. In the United States, everyone behaves as an entrepreneur, primarily focusing on their own interests and goals. Employees are moved in the company direction through appropriately structured compensation and formal measures, such as job descriptions, policies, and procedures, hence a formal governance approach. Company policies play an important role, ensuring employee rights, but also protecting the employer company on a legal level. People in the United States are often accustomed or at least open to multicultural work environments. Companies can assemble teams with members from multiple countries and enable them to move the company forward, using the strengths of each individual. However, in most US states, employment is "at will." In other words, people can leave on any given day—a situation that is legally impossible in many European countries, for example, in Germany where employees have to give notice well in advance. Therefore, employers must manage people accordingly, on the one hand, motivating them to encourage them to stay with the company and, on the other hand, always preparing for a situation where a key employee leaves. People in a US work environment seem to be very open and direct; however, you often have to read between the lines to understand what they really mean. If someone calls a presentation "great," it does not necessarily mean that he really liked it. A follow-up invitation says much more. People are generally self-confident and convinced of the superior quality of their capabilities. A "we are the best" mentality is common. Therefore, it is often not easy for a foreigner to criticize someone in a way that would not upset the person. One must criticize positively, so people learn quickly and support necessary actions.

In a Japanese work environment, the situation is quite different. People smile often and appear friendly—all the time. This goes so far that it is generally considered impolite to answer a question with "no." But "yes" does not always mean "yes." I remember when I asked a Japanese colleague if he had sent out a specific letter and he answered "yes—but not yet." At the time I was very surprised, but now I understand that he just wanted to be polite. Conflicts that would require a "no" are often carried out "undercover," for example, through e-mails. In Japan, people typically pay close attention to detail. You may receive a schedule with an elaborate color code—but this also takes time. Do not expect a high-speed environment. However, people finish what they start, so you can expect results. People in Japan are accustomed to very long working hours. Some of my colleagues started the day between 9 and 10 a.m., but they rarely went home before 10 or 11 PM. And their commute involved a 1–2 h train ride. In general, I found it difficult to encourage creativity and the development of new ideas. In most cases, some external input was required. Once you have hired an employee in Japan, you can count on loyalty. People do not leave their jobs easily.

Although globalization brings the behaviors of employees closer together, it is still important to know about country-specific behaviors when designing and implementing business processes. This is especially the case for manually executed processes and subprocesses or necessary teamwork activities.

Country-specific differences are not only observed within the office but also in customer-facing behavior and the habits around business transactions. In the United States, there is generally a very high customer focus. The customer is just as important as the product. The quality and performance of a product are demonstrated through the customers using it. This is a big difference from many German enterprises, where people love their products and think in terms of functions and features. In the United States, the characteristic of "invented here" is very important. The aforementioned self-confidence and pride often make it difficult for foreign companies with foreign products to enter the market. In general, the created perception of a company and its offerings is very important. Perception is often considered reality; therefore, marketing is extremely important in the promotion of offerings. For the IT market, industry analysts, including The Gartner Group, Forrester, or IDC, play an important role. In many cases, customers rely on analyst research to support their buying decisions. Change and speed are very common in the United States. Executives switch companies, sometimes even on a quarterly basis, projects start and stop quickly, contact persons change. Change is the only stable part of business, which often leads to short-term viewpoints. In many cases, it is difficult to sell solutions with long-term impacts. "Why should I care what happens next quarter or even next year?" is a common attitude.

The attitude is very different in Japan and continuity is important to many people. Although globalization has already changed many things, people still try to reduce the speed of change and keep a well-controlled pace. They are very careful. You will often have the same contact person at a client over many years. Executives stick with their companies and you can count on their commitments. The characteristic of "invented here" is not nearly as important as it is in the United States. On the contrary, American and European products are well accepted. Trust is the key in business life. It counts more than contracts, which can cause conflicts with Western accounting requirements for formal paperwork. Business decisions are often heavily influenced by personal relations and less by general perception. Business meals are very important in Japan. True negotiations often occur during dinner, in a very casual atmosphere. The formal negotiations are simply a means to revisit the arguments and conclusions discussed previously.

These customer- and market-related behaviors are again important for the design and implementation of business processes. It is essential to be aware of those particulars when a company standard business process is defined and rolled out in a specific country.

The following are some general lessons I learned while working and living in Germany, France, the United States, and Japan. They can be applied to the management of processes in an international environment:

- Listen, listen, and listen: Do not think you already know everything. Hear what the local employees have to say.
- Even in an unfamiliar environment, always look on the bright side of things: This keeps you in a good mood with a positive attitude. Your co-workers feel and appreciate that.
- Accept differences wherever possible: Different countries have different habits—in most cases, it is best to accept that as fact and work with it, not against it.
- Communicate clearly what you do not accept: When you intentionally do not want to support certain habits, it is important for the people around you to know that so that they can actively adjust.
- Show that you are interested in being integrated: Generally, local people are proud to make you part of their community, but you have to show that you are willing to accept and support that integration.
- Clarify and explain the value you bring to the table: People have to know why you are in another country and what the benefits are to them personally.
- Share your interests and introduce yourself as a "private person," not just a "business person": People work with and accept people, not just positions or roles.

These were some of my personal impressions about global business and what it means for managers and the processes for which they are responsible. So, what are the key influence factors of globalization on business processes and how do they impact processes? How does globalization change processes?

9.2 Globalization Changes Processes

Globalization leads to processes carried out in several countries or regions and influences business processes in two or more geographic areas. Therefore, different country-specific factors influence those processes. Important influence factors are the following:

- Legal system
- Geography
- Culture
- Education
- Language

The legal system provides country-specific regulations that must be reflected in processes. For example, tax regulations influence finance processes, but can also lead to modifications in the supply chain. Human resource (HR) administrative processes, such as in the payroll area, are another example of processes often influenced by legal regulations. The geography of a country can also affect processes, such as the transportation planning and management of goods in transit. Specific cultural aspects also influence processes. The focus on details in Japan may

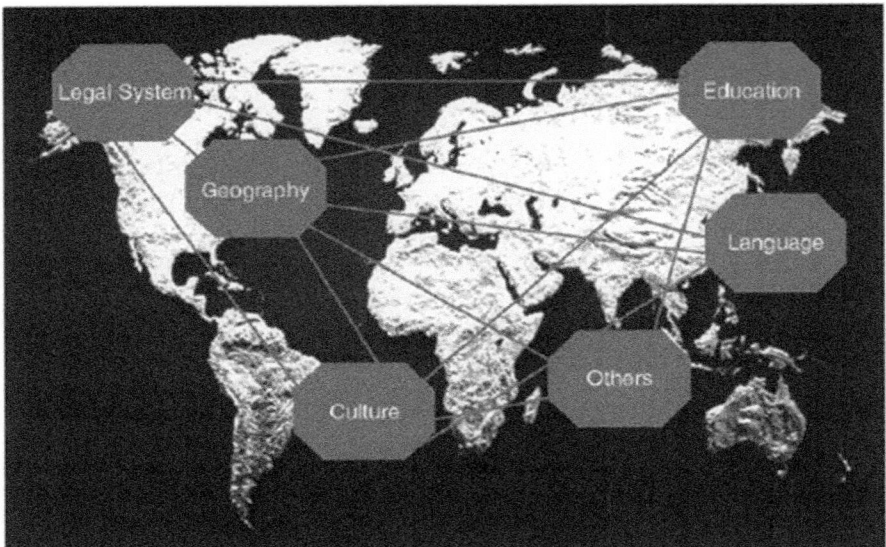

Fig. 9.4 Country-specific influence factors on processes

necessitate a modified process design in comparison with the design in Western countries, where too much detail may be perceived as having a negative impact on the personal work environment and the degree of freedom people need. A country's average level of education can influence process design and implementation. Highly automated processes in countries with little expertise may not make sense. Even the languages spoken in different countries can influence processes: you may not be able to use certain software systems for the process execution because they do not support specific languages. This has often been a challenge for Asian languages. Besides those main influence factors, there are many others, like the international experience of a consulting company that determines if the firm gets included in the request for proposal of a global potential client. The county-specific influence factors are shown in Fig. 9.4.

Such influence factors impact business processes and typically lead to country-specific or regional variants of processes that can be carried out in subsidiaries or in a central headquarters location.

Such factors also influence the BPM-Discipline and the business process management approach in and of itself, the "process of process management." vBPM must address the impacts of the global business environment and develop appropriate capabilities. This situation is visualized in Fig. 9.5.

The factors can either influence the business processes directly or indirectly through offering or product variants. Country-specific requirements may lead, for example, to modified products that necessitate additional engineering activities, leading to new production and logistics processes. This can then result in new or modified processes in various areas of an organization. The direct and indirect influences of country-specific factors are illustrated in Fig. 9.6.

9.2 Globalization Changes Processes

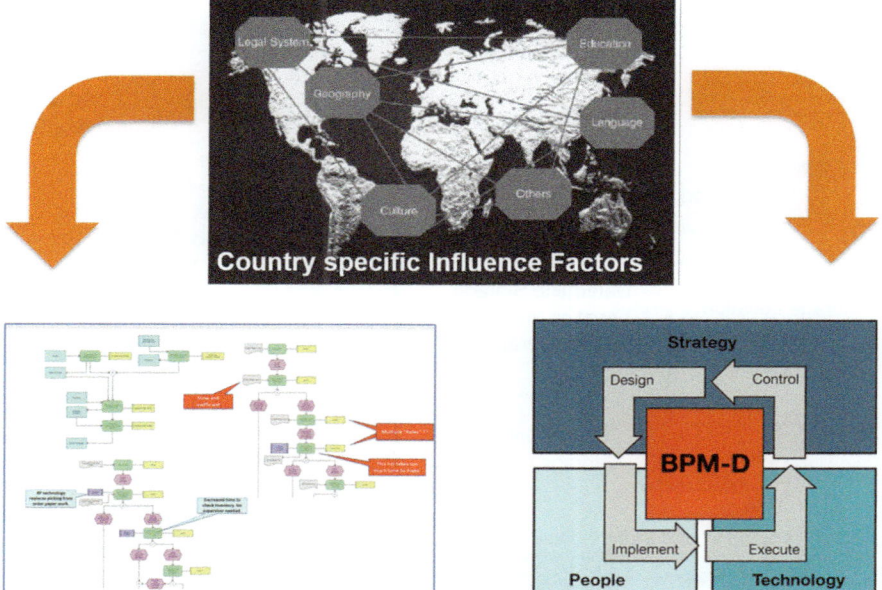

Fig. 9.5 Impacts of country-specific influence factors

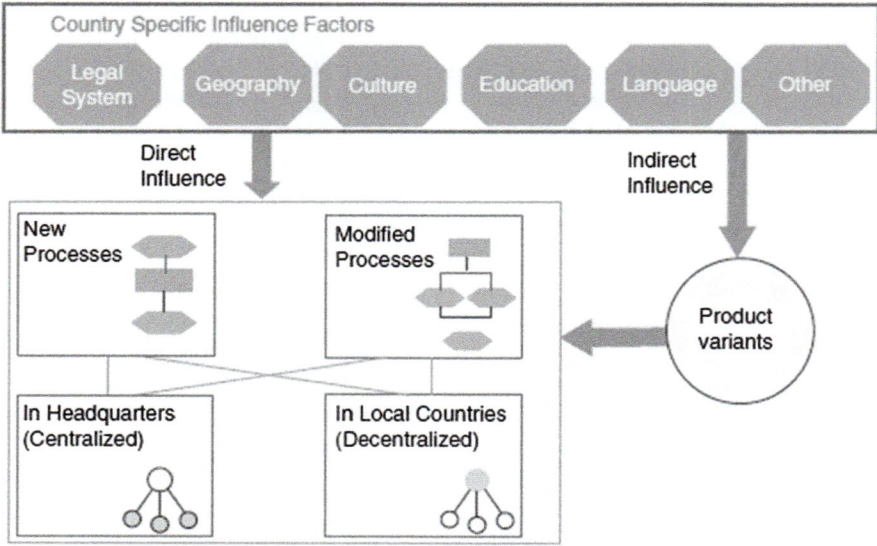

Fig. 9.6 Direct and indirect influence of country-specific factors on processes

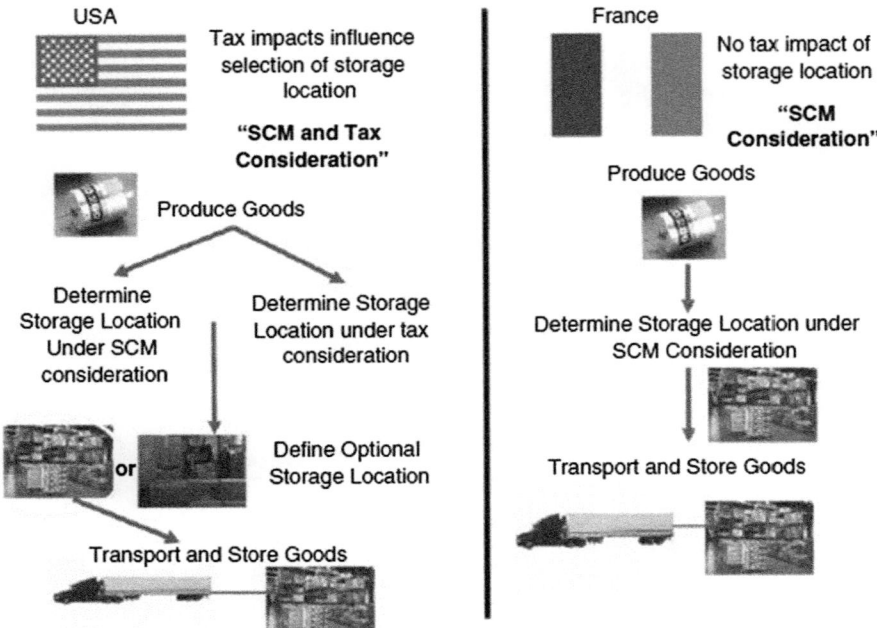

Fig. 9.7 Example: legal regulations influence processes

We have previously discussed one example of country-specific processes. In a Japanese environment, the focus on quality can lead to planned redundancies of quality control activities. This may not be acceptable in Western organizations focused on cost and time efficiency. Transforming the Japanese processes to comply with Western efficiency standards will be much more challenging than optimizing the processes of an underperforming western organization. Introducing highest-quality standards with planned redundancies to reduce risk of errors may lead to questions in a Western environment.

Country-specific tax regulations can impact logistics processes. For example, in the United States, you can select storage locations for specific goods on the basis of state tax regulations. In France, where taxes are the same across the entire country, this selection criterion does not need to be applied. The related logistics process is simplified, as visualized in Fig. 9.7.

In a vast country like the United States, it has become increasingly difficult to conduct face-to-face meetings—especially due to increasing cost and time requirements for air travel. Therefore, the use of Web-based remote presentations and meetings is extremely important and part of many sales processes. In a geographically smaller country, such as Germany, this may not be as important. Most of the cities are close enough to be reached by car or train. Focusing in the United States on one or few neighboring states may lead to a similar situation. This influence of country-specific factors on processes is shown in Fig. 9.8.

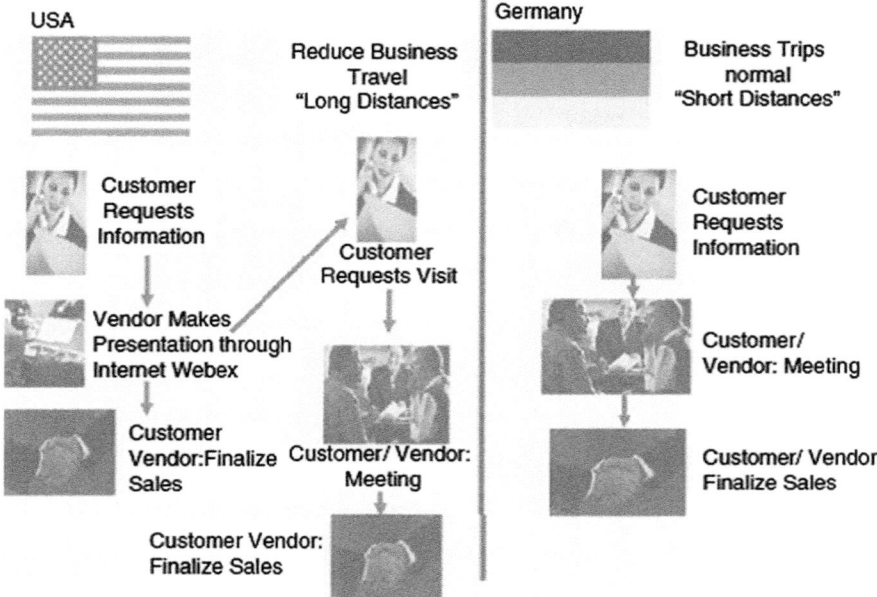

Fig. 9.8 Example: geography influences processes

Even the language of a country can influence processes. For example, Japanese or Chinese language characters require specific printing capabilities. But there may be a requirement for certain documents, such as invoices, to be printed in a language that can be checked by centralized global departments. Therefore, the same document may need to be printed a second time in a Western language, resulting in process variants, as shown in Fig. 9.9.

There are many other country-specific influence factors. Therefore, a company should evaluate the specific influence factors of countries where it has subsidiaries or market partners involved in a business process. An example is the difference in the voltage between US and European countries. A company producing electric motors in the United States must develop country variants of its products to deliver its offerings to Europe. These product variants lead in general to new or additional activities in the entire organization and ultimately to modified processes. Additional product variants must be designed, handled throughout the logistics processes, and reflected in marketing and sales processes. This situation is explained in Fig. 9.10.

The global business environment directly or indirectly influences the design of business processes, their implementation, and ultimately also the execution and controlling of the resulting processes. In most cases, customer-facing processes, subprocesses, and offerings are localized. Support processes or back-office activities can typically be standardized and carried out in a central location, for example, as a shared services organization. That's why people refer to current trends as

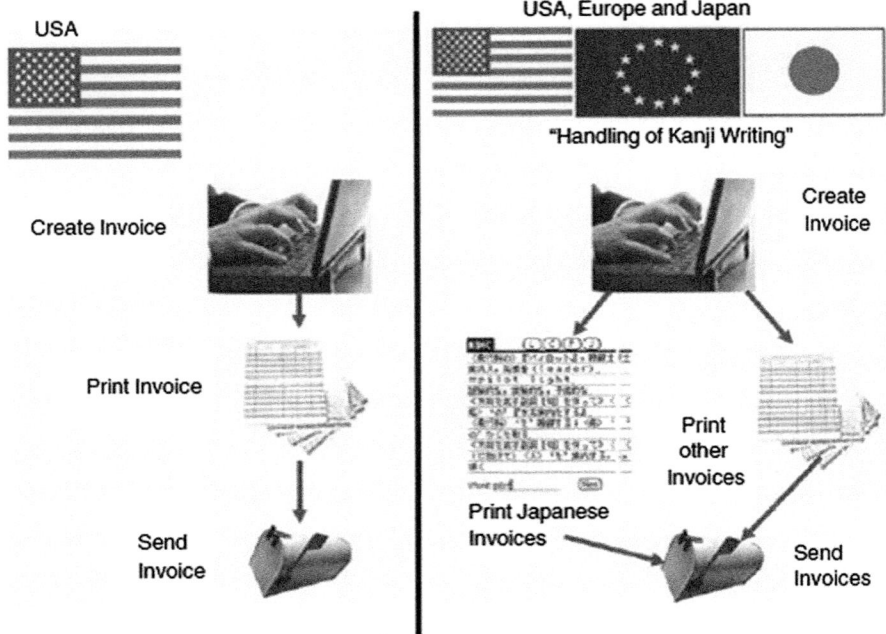

Fig. 9.9 Example: languages influence processes

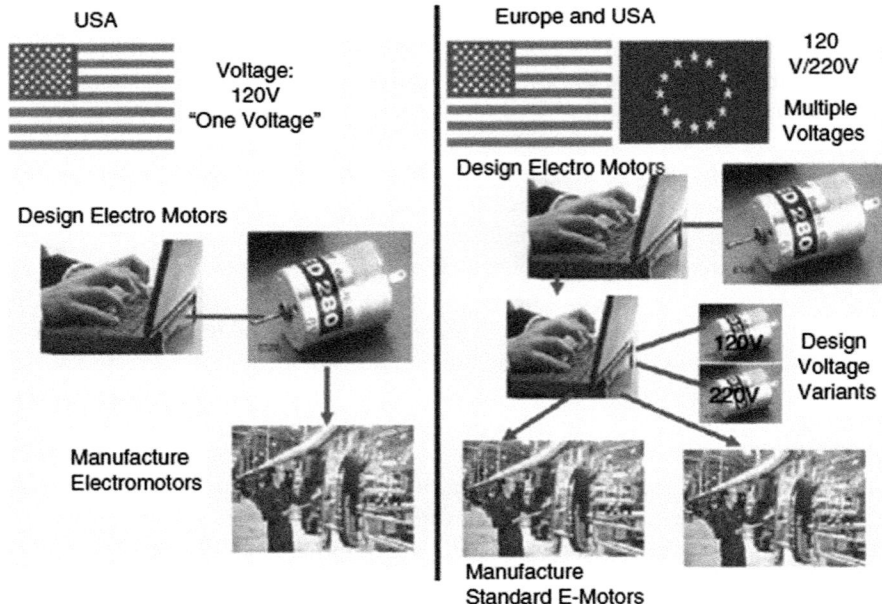

Fig. 9.10 Example: other country-specific factors influence processes

"going glocal" [4]. The influence of globalization must be reflected in the value-driven BPM-Discipline.

9.3 How Can Value-Driven BPM Help?

On the basis of the discussion thus far, we can identify necessary capabilities of the value-driven BPM-Discipline to handle global business environments:

- Identify the degrees of centralization and decentralization of business processes according to a globalization strategy.
- Define country-specific influence factors, especially for customer-facing processes and offerings.
- Identify the impact of those factors on the value-driven management of business processes.
- Modify the process management approach recognizing the country impacts.

The centralization and decentralization of processes reflects the general strategy, leading to international, multinational, global, or transnational organizations, as explained. The positioning of the innovation process is very important in today's volatile digital world. To benefit from the international input, this process must be integrated in corporate and subsidiary activities, for example, to support idea finding. The integration of international third parties, such as customers, universities, or research institutions, can also support the global environment.

Country-specific influence factors can be defined on the basis of the reference list discussed previously. Additional factors must be added and those that are not relevant should be deleted. Then, the business impact of those country-specifics is defined, as presented in the aforementioned examples. The closer the processes are to local customers or local production facilities, the stronger the localization requirements [4, 5]. General activities and support processes can often be centralized, or at least standardized, across countries in shared services organizations. The influence of country-specific factors is often smaller. The business impacts of country-specific influence factors are incorporated in the design of the business processes and drive from there the entire process lifecycle.

The right standardization and harmonization of business processes is key in global organizations [6]. In the process design within a globally active organization, one "master process" can be used to develop one or several process variants for decentralized country-specific processes. Therefore, one must manage process variants over the entire business process life cycle and continuously update the design. Changes in the business environment can relate to one or several of the process variants. They may be triggered globally through a change in the master process or locally through changes in the country-specific business environment. This activity must be organized through the process governance and is generally supported by process modeling and repository tools as well as process execution systems. The management of process variants is visualized in Fig. 9.11.

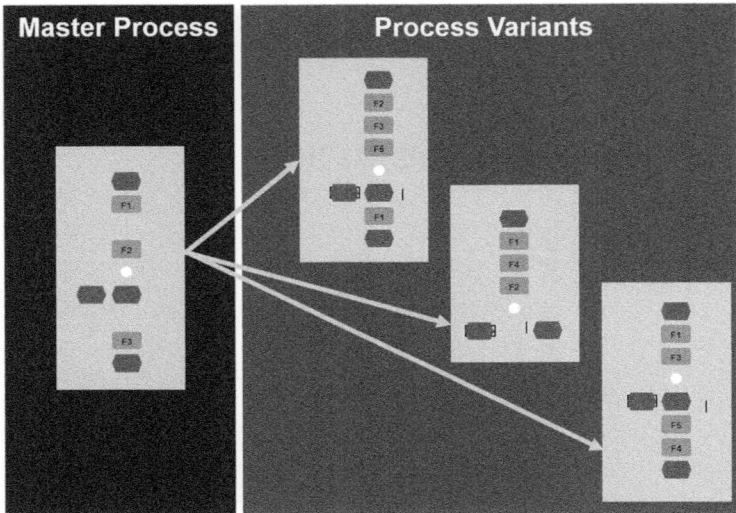

Fig. 9.11 Management of process variants

The discussed reference models can deliver initial solutions to those processes. They must now be modified according to country requirements. With the increasing importance of global business aspects for nearly every organization, the development of reference models with country-specific content will also become highly relevant. Content providers may progressively move toward this direction and offer reference models related to such topics of globalization.

In general, the management of the right degree of process standardization and harmonization requires a high maturity level of selected process management capabilities. Working with organizations of different sizes and industries, my Co-CEO, Peter Franz, and I have identified five important core enabling BPM capabilities [6]:

- Process and data governance
- Process knowledge management in the form of a comprehensive enterprise architecture
- People enablement, hence change management and community management
- BPM Tools and Technologies
- Value realization through metrics and their monitoring.

These core capabilities to manage the standardization and harmonization of business processes is visualized in the BPM-D Process Framework for the "process of process management" [7] in Fig. 9.12.

The utilization of standard application software systems or software components developed for global use simplifies the implementation of processes in a globally

9.3 How Can Value-Driven BPM Help?

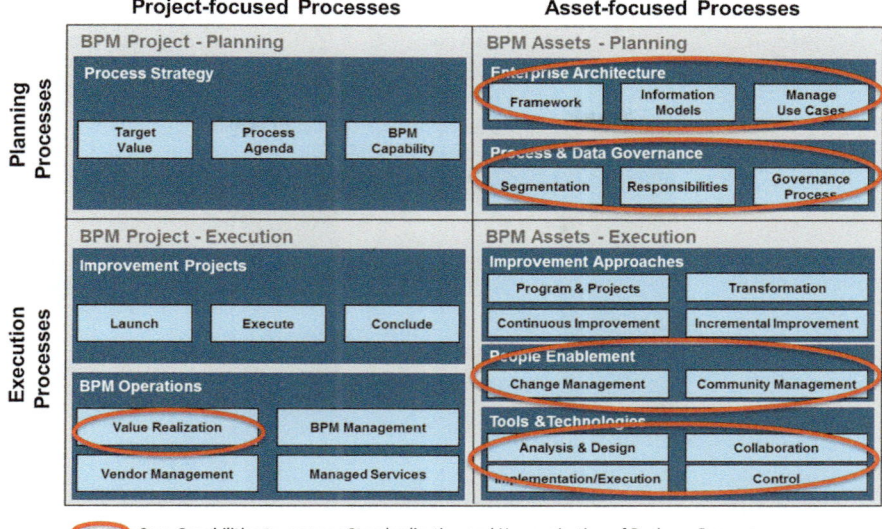

Fig. 9.12 Core capabilities for the harmonization of processes in the BPM-D framework

acting organization. Standard software typically supports the following aspects, which are important for the realization of country-specific processes:

- Multiple currencies
- Multiple languages
- Multiple units of measurement
- Various legal standards
- International documentation
- International rollout strategies
- International hotline/support

This is visualized in Fig. 9.13.

In many cases specific functionality of the supporting software or at least the related workflow is required. This is where BPM execution systems can be used and combined with traditional standard software packages like ERP systems. What's important here is to use BPM solutions with little to no programming requirements to keep implementation and maintenance cost low [8].

Change management activities must be adapted to the countries involved in the implementation of a business process. This may include multiple ways of representing process models: in some environments more abstract representations work, while in others little specific pictures that represent roles or functions may be better received. Information, communication, and training must be adapted to the country-specific habits.

The advantages of BPM modeling and repository tools can be especially well applied in global business environments because the data volume to be handled

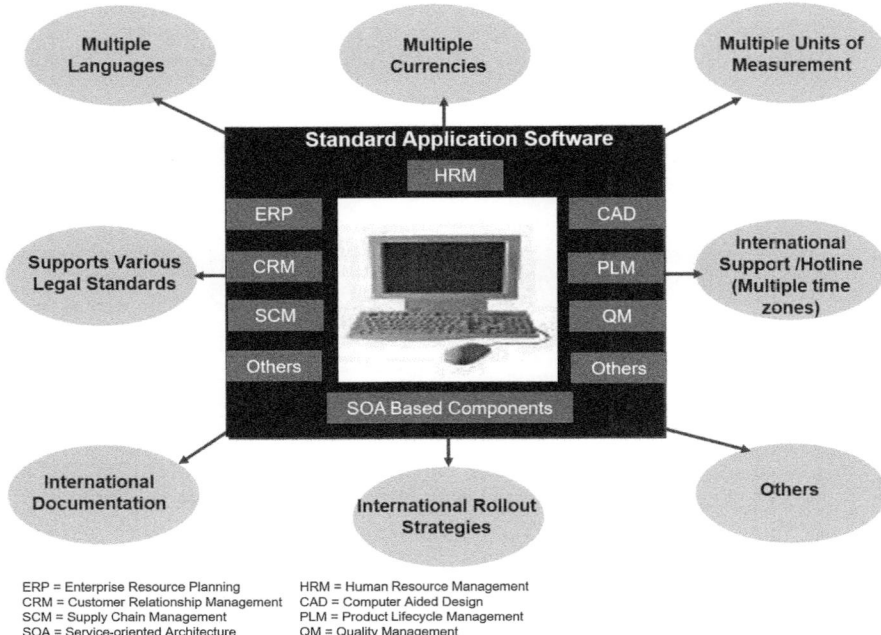

Fig. 9.13 Standard software supports internationalization/globalization

increases and the remote work with process models becomes more and more important. The probability of changes in the business environment also increases, resulting in higher maintenance frequencies for the business process models and other information models in the process warehouse.

The discipline of value-driven BPM delivers the appropriate capabilities to handle the challenges of a global business environment and enable high performance across the distributed enterprise. It has become a key enabler of international business operations.

9.4 The Bottom Line

- It is especially important to know about country-specific influences on process management in cases of manually executed processes and or necessary teamwork activities (Sect. 9.1).
- Country-specific behaviors of employees and customers are important influence factors for the management of business processes (Sect. 9.1).
- Simple lessons learned can be used as guidelines for the management of processes in a global environment (Sect. 9.1).

- Globalization leads to processes carried out in several countries or influencing business processes in one or more countries. Therefore, country-specific factors influence those processes and the way they are managed along the process lifecycle (Sect. 9.2).
- Those country-specific influence factors impact business processes, especially customer-facing processes and processes related to the design and production of offerings. In most cases, this impact leads to country-specific variants of processes (Sect. 9.2).
- Country-specific support processes are often centralized in a shared-service organization where different country process variants need to be managed (Sect. 9.2).
- The country-specific influence factors also influence the business process management (BPM) approach itself, the "process of process management." The discipline of value-driven BPM must reflect that (Sect. 9.2).
- The country-specific factors can either influence the business processes directly or indirectly through product (offering) variants (Sect. 9.2).
- The BPM-Discipline includes necessary steps to handle international business environments (Sect. 9.3).
- In the process design within an international organization, one "master process" is often used to develop one or several country-specific process variants for decentralized processes carried out in different countries (Sect. 9.3).
- There are key capabilities within the "process of process management" for managing standardization and harmonization of processes. These can be well applied in international environments to deal with country-variants of processes (Sect. 9.3).
- The utilization of standard application software systems developed for global use simplifies the implementation of processes in an internationally acting organization. Also flexible BPM Execution Engines are helpful in the management of country variants of processes (Sect. 9.3).
- The value-driven BPM-Discipline delivers the appropriate capabilities to handle the challenges of an international business environment (Sect. 9.3).

References

1. Friedman, T.L.: The World Is Flat—A Brief History of the Twenty-First Century. Farrar, Straus and Giroux, New York (2005)
2. Bartlett, C.A., Ghoshal, S.: Managing Across Borders—The Transnational Solution. Harvard Business School Press, Boston (2002)
3. Scheer, A.-W.: Start-ups Are Easy, But. . ... Springer, Berlin/New York (2001)
4. Franz, P., Kirchmer, M.: Value-driven Business Process Management—The Value-switch for Lasting Competitive Advantage. McGraw-Hill, New York (2012)
5. Kirchmer, M.: Business Process Oriented Implementation of Standard Software—How to Achieve Competitive Advantage Efficiently and Effectively, 2nd edn. Springer, Berlin (1999)

6. Franz, P., Kirchmer, M.: Process Standardization and Harmonization—Agile Customer Service in a Digital World. BPM-D Whitepaper, London/Philadelphia (2016)
7. Kirchmer, M.: The Process of Process Management—Mastering the New Normal in a Digital World. In: Business Modeling and Software Development (BMSD) Proceedings, July 2015
8. Appian (ed.): Low-code Tools: Fueling Business Transformation at Digital Speed. Whitepaper, Washington (2016)

Chapter 10
Small and Medium Enterprises Need Value-Driven BPM

Small and medium enterprises (SMEs) are playing an important role in the global business environment. More than 90% of all firms in the European Union are considered as SMEs [1]. The Kauffman Index 2016 for Startup Activities in the United States reports currently over 500,000 new business owners per month [2]. Also, larger companies often organize their divisions as small enterprises that conduct business like mid-market firms.

An increasing number of software and consulting companies focus a segment of their offerings on SMEs. The mid-market is not only considered to be dynamic but also has a growing demand for enterprise-wide solutions. SMEs have become interesting customers for many suppliers in the digital market.

During my time at IDS Scheer, I worked with some colleagues to launch several mid-market initiatives to bring business process management (BPM) to SMEs. In addition, I managed IDS Scheer subsidiaries in the Americas and Asia for more than 10 years—subsidiaries that were typical SMEs themselves. At Accenture, I was part of the team that was building a business unit around process excellence topics, just as one might launch a start-up company. And most recently I co-founded BPM-D together with my Co-CEO Peter Franz—a company that has been ranked by Insights Success as one of the 50 most valuable technology start-ups in the United States [3]. This chapter is based on a combination of experiences in both fields: working at a service and software provider for SMEs and managing such small- and midsized organizations myself.

In this chapter, the definition of SMEs is discussed briefly, and some key characteristics of mid-market organizations are presented. Why are SMEs special? Are their BPM requirements really different than large organizations? What does that mean for the discipline of value-driven BPM? Do SMEs need vBPM too?

The discussion of value-driven process management in an SME context is relevant for the entire BPM-Discipline, as shown in Fig. 10.1.

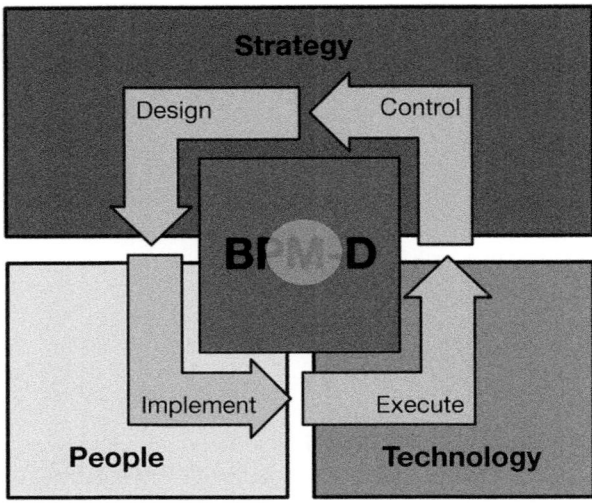

Fig. 10.1 Positioning of value-driven BPM for small and medium enterprises

10.1 Definition and Characteristics of SMEs

If you look through literature for a clear and globally valid definition of SMEs, you will not find one. Also, the criteria to define this market used by vendors to mid-market businesses are not consistent, often showing significant differences. However, there are certain commonalities. In most publications, enterprises are defined as SMEs, based on two major criteria:

- Revenue
- Number of employees

One or both of these criteria must fall under a certain limit. However, the limits are generally defined differently in different countries or by different organizations. For example, a company with less than 500 people is considered an SME in Germany; but that limit could be 100 employees in Belgium [1]. Companies considered SMEs in the United States may already be viewed as large businesses in some European countries. For the purposes of this book, we will introduce a general definition for SMEs that I believe can be applied across country boundaries.

In the United States, solution vendors often consider organizations with revenue up to $1 billion as medium companies. This is most likely the broadest SME definition, including all companies that could be somehow considered SMEs. However, this broad definition produces a very heterogeneous group of companies that is difficult to characterize. In most cases, a company with $1 billion in revenue will have different requirements and characteristics than a company with $10 million in revenue. Such a broad definition does not help to define a targeted BPM approach for SMEs.

In general, the characteristics discussed in this chapter best apply to companies with $20–500 million in revenue and approximately 50–1000 employees. This definition includes organizations with one or several locations in one or multiple countries. A small or medium enterprise can be an independent organization or a subsidiary of a larger company that is essentially operated as a self-sufficient unit. This is the type of company we will discuss in this chapter and call here SMEs.

Most mid-market organizations have characteristics that challenge the implementation of BPM approaches. This is especially true for the execution of business processes, based on enterprise resource planning (ERP) systems or more flexible process execution engines. However, SMEs also have attributes that simplify the rollout of a BPM-Discipline. We will now discuss both types of characteristics.

In looking at the group of characteristics that create challenges in applying a BPM-Discipline to achieve high performance, the following SMEs attributes stand out [4]:

- Cost pressure
- Time pressure
- Human resource capacity
- Multiple roles of employees
- Skill level

SMEs are often under tremendous cost pressure. They may be funded through venture capital or smaller, private budgets. In many cases, the owner of the company has invested his or her own money in the company. Therefore, the cost of BPM approaches and related infrastructure play a key role. Often, SMEs simply cannot afford investments even if they see and understand the potential benefits. Other times, they just do not want to take the risk of bringing in additional money or new investors for such an operational investment.

The low number of employees in smaller organizations precludes them from staffing projects over a long time period, resulting in a great time pressure for any initiative. There is no budget to increase the number of people—the resource capacity. People must focus on vital, day-to-day operations. Time for BPM initiatives, which have to be started as projects, is very limited. Project team members are normally only available on a part-time basis. Even small changes in the business environment can have major resource impacts relative to the overall company size.

Once processes must be executed, the personnel restrictions again come into play. Employees often play multiple roles. BPM approaches need to blend into that environment. There is little or no time for additional tasks. In many cases, hiring new employees is impossible, due to the previously discussed budget restrictions. BPM has to be implemented in a manner that is well integrated with the other multiple tasks of SME employees. It must be clear that additional effort in one area truly leads to less work in others or that the resulting benefits, e.g., in improved customer experience, definitively justify the investment and lead to an appropriate return. There is not much room for experiments.

Mid-market organizations generally have no well-developed IT or organizational departments. They often consider those fields to be pure overhead that must be kept to a minimum level. Therefore, SMEs are lacking sufficient technology skills as well as method and tool know-how necessary to build and run a BPM infrastructure which benefits from the opportunities of our digital world. The development of the talent and capabilities needed to start and manage even a simple process management capability can be a challenge.

However, SMEs also have characteristics that simplify the rollout of a value-driven BPM-Discipline. These characteristics contribute directly to the success of BPM and truly support the company in achieving high performance [4]:

- Fast decision making
- Integration of activities
- Necessity to implement and modify new business models
- Employee work ethic and style

Most mid-market organizations can ensure fast decisions on critical topics. In many cases, the company owner himself or herself decides, without many meetings or discussions. Even if there is a more collaborative decision-making process in place, the number of involved people is considerably lower than in large organizations. There are also not as many politics involved as in larger organizations. The result is increased speed in launching initiatives once they are accepted by top management. It also helps once the BPM-Discipline is in place: decisions on necessary process adjustments can be made quickly resulting in an agile and highly effective process of process management. This natural agility of SMEs overcompensates for the many resource restrictions discussed before.

The fact that people are in short supply also has positive side effects: SMEs are truly forced to focus on the important key capabilities of BPM and make them happen quickly and effectively—all of which is driven by rapid top management decisions.

The small size of the organizations leads to a "natural" integration of business activities. People are accustomed to working in a business process-oriented manner and understand how things fit together. This is the positive side of people playing multiple roles. In many cases, this integration even crosses company boundaries. SMEs know their customers and suppliers as well as their other market partners often better than large organizations since many people, especially management, interact with those organizations on a regular basis.

Sometimes, a few very dominating clients will deliver input about the way inter-enterprise processes should be organized. Intra- and inter-enterprise business processes are not distributed over many organizational units in SMEs because their organizational structure is generally much simpler than that of a large organization, which has to build more complex structures to get their large numbers of employees focused on specific tasks. For large organizations to leverage size, their employees are often specialized on single tasks, ultimately challenging their integration and management in one business process. SME employees performing multiple tasks of a process can be more easily organized into a process-based structure. Change management efforts are significantly reduced.

Many small companies, especially start-ups, need to implement a new business model or at least modify an existing one. This forces them to think about their value proposition and the targeted markets but also about the processes to make the new business model happen. We have discussed that in the previous chapter about innovation. A focus on establishing and managing business processes is crucial for those organizations [5]. This paves the way to the appropriate top management attention to the BPM-Discipline. It makes it a "must-have" capability that needs to be established and applied in the organization.

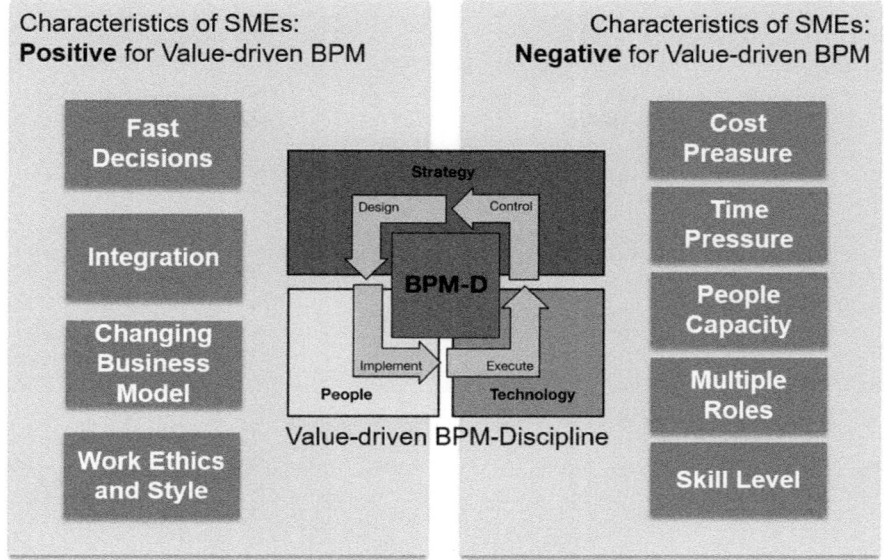

Fig. 10.2 Characteristics of small and medium enterprises impacting the BPM-Discipline

In many cases, SME employees have a proactive and result-oriented work attitude. They are accustomed to recognizing, analyzing, and resolving upcoming challenges. They do not have many guidelines, policies, and standard-operating procedures on which to rely. People must act—quickly and effectively—in order to be successful. The company depends on them figuring out the best possible actions. This simplifies the implementation and application of value-driven process management and the related activities. The process governance model can be simpler and rely on the employees' solution-oriented working style.

The key characteristics of SMEs are shown in Fig. 10.2. Although this list is surely not complete, it highlights the most important aspects to be considered. These characteristics define the basis for an efficient and effective approach to a value-driven BPM-Discipline in SMEs. They help to identify specific requirements for a BPM-Discipline established in a mid-market organization.

But why do SMEs need a BPM-Discipline? Is that not a management discipline more suitable for large organizations?

10.2 Why Do Small and Medium Enterprises Need BPM?

In principle SMEs benefit from the same values BPM delivers as large organizations: quality and efficiency, ability and compliance, external integration into networks and internal alignment, as well as innovation and conservation [6]. However, some of those effects of BPM are even more important for mid-market

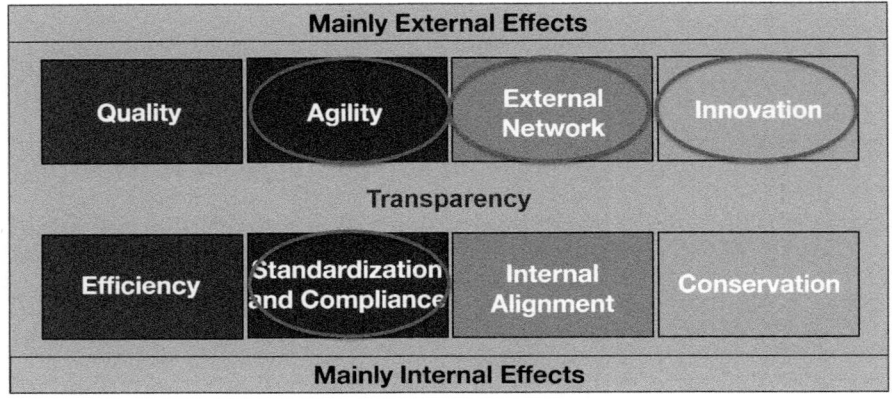

Fig. 10.3 Core reasons for the importance of value-driven BPM for SMEs

organizations. To be successful in our dynamic competitive business environments, SMEs have to be faster, more agile, and more innovative than large organizations. Since they do not have any significant economy of scale, attributes like speed, agility, and innovation are preconditions to survive. SMEs often must be focused on innovation to justify their existence. While large organizations can just follow trends in the business environment and leverage their size to be successful, SMEs do not have that lever. They are generally built on innovative business ideas that make them unique. More and more often, business process innovation plays a key role, as we have discussed previously. If SMEs want to grow, they also need to start standardizing processes to achieve the necessary scalability. This is a step start-up companies often struggle with. Value-driven BPM can help here to find the right balance between standardization and agility. The core reasons for the importance of value-driven process management for SMEs are shown in Fig. 10.3

According to *Fortune* magazine, only one out of ten start-ups succeeded [7]. Many of the reasons for the failure of those companies can be addressed through the BPM-Discipline. It helps to bring the necessary structure to be able to scale, and it focuses everybody on the clients and the value the company delivers to them. BPM helps to identify the processes that really matter for an organization and its business model so that the enterprise can focus on them. BPM transfers processes into assets which is helpful to acquire necessary funding. These are just a few reasons why even start-ups should have a BPM-Discipline.

In general, the BPM-Discipline helps mid-market organizations to be successful in their current business environment and support a targeted growth into a large organization through the appropriate structure and strategy execution. BPM enables mid-market companies to move successfully to the next level of performance required for their short- and long-term success. It eliminates repetitive work and inefficiencies typical for fast-growing small organizations.

10.3 How Do SME Characteristics Impact Business Process Management?

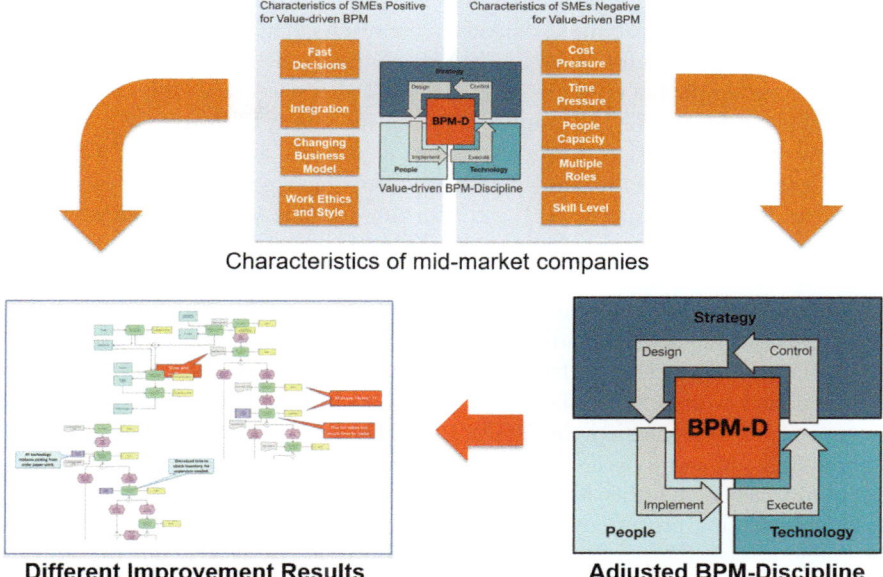

Fig. 10.4 Impact of SMEs characteristics on business process management

The next logical question is what should a BPM-Discipline for SMEs look like. How can an organization meet the presented challenges of mid-market companies and utilize the SME-specific strengths? What does it mean to manage business processes in an SME environment to enable high performance and move quickly from strategy to execution in the digital world we are living in?

10.3 How Do SME Characteristics Impact Business Process Management?

The discussed characteristics of mid-market organizations have direct impacts on establishing and applying a BPM-Discipline in SMEs. They deliver the context that a BPM-Discipline needs to address to be really successful in a mid-market environment. Value-driven BPM in SMEs has to fulfill resulting requirements to realize its full potential. This means the BPM-Discipline itself is adjusted to those requirements but also the outcomes it delivers. The improved SME processes are often less sophisticated, for example, less automated, than processes of larger organizations. The use of digitalization has to be examined even more carefully. The overall impact of the characteristics of SMEs on process management is shown in Fig. 10.4. We concentrate in this chapter on the analysis of the necessary adjustments of the BPM-Discipline in SMEs.

The cost pressure in an SME environment requires that a BPM-Discipline is established and applied in a very efficient manner. The request for fixed price proposals to deliver BPM-related services and products is common. SMEs have to focus on core BPM capabilities, delivering the results that are most important. It is key to "target value" with any activity. Nice-to-have capabilities are generally not affordable; a simple but effective approach to BPM is necessary. This can often be best achieved by defining solutions, covering the entire life cycle of a business process, including design, implementation, execution, and process controlling. Using a reference model for the process of process management, as the previously described BPM-D Framework [6], and adjusting it to the specific organization are very beneficial to save time and cost. The combination of building process management capabilities while applying them to existing issues is crucial to achieve a fast return on the BPM-related investment.

As a consequence of the time constraints, BPM initiatives must be executed in short projects of weeks or a few months, not several months or years. This goes hand in hand with the described definition of a clear BPM focus on what really matters for the organization. Successful BPM initiatives within SMEs require easy-to-use methods and tools to keep change management activities to a minimum, again ultimately saving cost and time while enabling the efficient use of existing resources. During process execution and controlling, related BPM activities must be integrated seamlessly into the day-to-day work, ensuring again the highest efficiency, avoiding or least minimizing the need for additional resources.

Since employees play multiple roles, they require a process execution that allows for the combination of many different tasks. Appropriate "process components" of an entire end-to-end process must be defined so they can be handled by one person. The BPM capabilities must support this structure of process execution, so that high performance can be achieved with the same or a similar number of employees. Traditional, function-oriented activities must be replaced through logically connected process-oriented work steps targeting value for the client at the end of entire business process.

To accommodate the skill level in SMEs, the BPM-Discipline must be built and run using a minimum of specialized skills. Those need to be developed best in a "learning-by-doing" approach during the setup of the BPM-Discipline and its initial application to the organization. Again, easy-to-use and straightforward approaches to establishing and applying process management capabilities are preferred to very sophisticated procedures. SMEs typically cannot afford to increase their skill levels in many areas to the level of which large organizations are accustomed to. Combining key BPM capabilities that are developed and applied simultaneously to achieve fast results while developing a lasting BPM capability is again important. Outsourcing some of the infrastructure or procuring it through the cloud can be another helpful initiative.

Fast decisions enable handling the time constraints in BPM initiatives. They reduce cost for lengthy analyses and studies often required by large organizations to prepare for a more sophisticated and complex decision-making process. They support the necessary agility during the execution and controlling of business processes. Fast decisions are a key enabler for many of the values that BPM can deliver, especially agility and innovation. They help drive strategies quickly into execution. The BPM governance to be established must ensure that this SMEs advantage is applied effectively. Simple governance concepts are required that actively use the advantage of that rapid decision making.

Due to the natural integration of functions in SMEs, people have multiple roles and already have good knowledge about subprocesses of end-to-end business processes; they can therefore easily understand and appreciate the process thinking necessary to ensure the best results for the final customer of a business process. This people skill must be utilized systematically. It simplifies the analysis of the existing business situation as well as the design and implementation phase of process initiatives. In addition, it reduces the change management requirements, especially in regard to business-related training. The tight collaboration with customers and suppliers enables the inclusion of inter-enterprise processes in the early phases of a BPM initiative. This is often crucial for SMEs because they have to focus on their specific role in a network of different companies. The active use of the natural integration in SMEs is a key success factor for mid-market BPM initiatives. This supports a simple but still effective governance approach. It is easier to combine roles like process owner with other more conventional functional roles. Governance processes can be simple and in general don't require a sophisticated design approach.

The fact that especially start-up companies are focused on establishing a new business model, realized through appropriate processes, creates more opportunities that can be used to realize the full potential of a BPM-Discipline. The business model is implemented through appropriate processes; hence processes need to be treated as assets from the beginning. The BPM-Discipline makes that happen and is therefore considered a core capability which justifies appropriate top management attention, a crucial precondition for successful BPM initiatives. The BPM-Discipline becomes even more important once the start-up decided to scale and adjust its processes accordingly. BPM strategy, governance, people enablement, and methods and tools need to reflect this.

The positive "can-do" work attitude simplifies the implementation of BPM as a new approach to managing an organization and executing strategy. Successful BPM initiatives in SMEs must take advantage of the fact that employees are in most cases accustomed to dealing with new situations and change, especially if they work for a start-up company. In older mid-market companies, this may be a bit different, but people are still used to taking larger responsibilities than in bigger organizations. A BPM initiative needs to help them understand the value process management delivers to the organization. Then they quickly become active drivers of the initiative. Early knowledge transfer ensures that employees can quickly become leaders in the BPM effort. This can lead to dramatic reductions of the change management efforts and is a key success factor for a lasting BPM-Discipline.

10.4 Examples for Mid-market Business Process Management Offerings

BPM consulting and software companies reflect SME-specific requirements through appropriate solutions and related offerings. Let's discuss a few examples to make things more tangible.

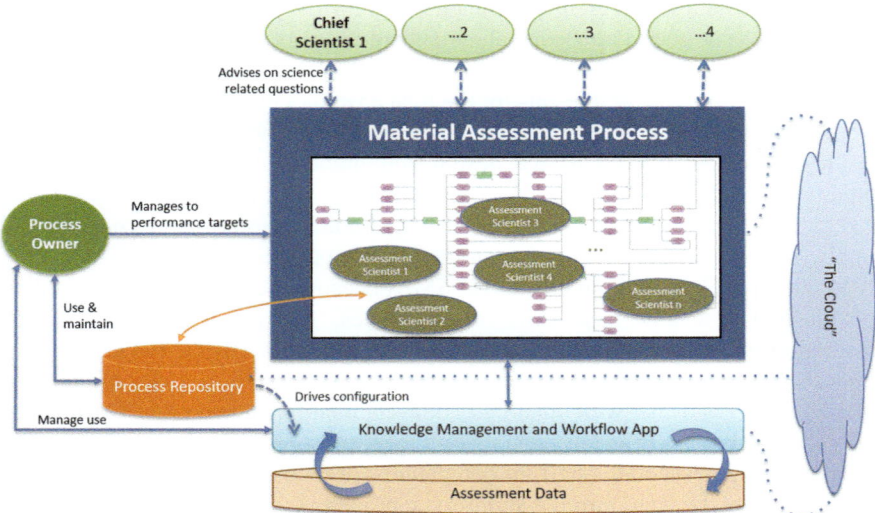

Fig. 10.5 BPM-D process performance factory—example

The BPM-D approach to focus on addressing specific issues while simultaneously building a lasting BPM-Discipline [6] is in general a good fit for the mid-market. In SMEs this approach is additionally adjusted through the use of accelerators, like the BPM-D Rapid Improvement approach, and the BPM-Discipline is in many cases kept on a low maturity level. It often addresses the identification of high-impact processes, creating transparency through a simple enterprise architecture and process repository capability, a straightforward governance, and an easy-to-use improvement approach. Applied tools and technologies also reflect this lower level of sophistication.

In small or very immature organizations, an even more focused approach has shown to be successful: the BPM-D Process Performance Factory, defined based on the patent-pending BPM-D Framework. The BPM-Discipline is built and applied to only one or two core processes that the enterprise needs to get right. The name refers to the fact that a structured "factory approach" is used to produce performance regarding the defined goals systematically. An example for such a solution is shown in Fig. 10.5. The material testing process of a research organization is executed through assessment scientists. Experienced chief scientists support this work and ensure the appropriate quality. The process owner is not a scientist. Their role is responsible to design, implement, and control the high-performing testing and assessment processes using a simple cloud-based repository for the design and a small number of metrics to control performance. A simple knowledge management and workflow application help to keep the process execution efficient and on the appropriate quality level. Such process performance factories can achieve significant benefits in a very short time [8].

10.4 Examples for Mid-market Business Process Management Offerings

Fig. 10.6 ARIS SmartPath—solution architecture

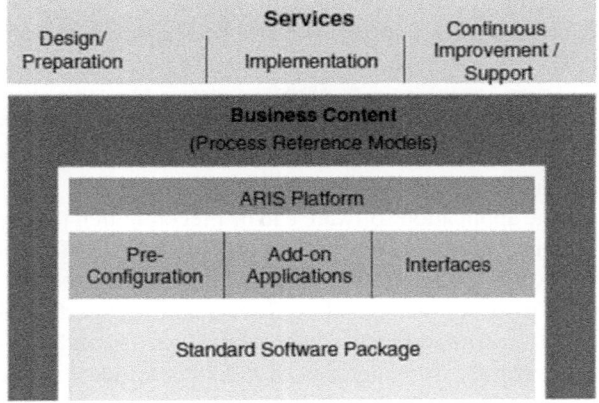

Another example is IDS Scheer's (acquired by Software AG) industry-specific ARIS SmartPath solutions [4]. I was also part of the team developing this process management solution for SMEs which includes specific software products, hence goes a step further than the approach we have chosen at BPM-D. The advantage is that this avoids any tool selection activities and allows a pre-configuration of applications. The disadvantage is less flexibility and a certain dependence on the involved tool vendors. ARIS SmartPath is similar to the BPM-D Process Performance Factory but less flexible due to the preselected software components and is intended to be a company-wide solution enabled through a process-led ERP solution.

The ARIS SmartPath overall architecture is based on ARIS, the previously described process architecture for the efficient and effective design of business processes [9, 10]. The solution leads organizations on a "smart path" to master future business challenges. It helps to design, implement, execute, and control processes in an efficient and effective manner. During the implementation, a "smart path" for rapid and cost-efficient project success is chosen.

ARIS SmartPath consists of three major components:

- Application software, such as ERP, customer relationship management (CRM), and supply chain management (SCM) systems (based on SAP) [11]
- Business content in the form of reference models in the ARIS Tool
- Consulting services to establish the to-be processes as well as the BPM-Discipline, but could also be ERP from other vendors, for example Oracle or Microsoft [12, 13].

These components are consolidated into one solution package that can be offered at a fixed price and delivered in an efficient and effective way to meet SMEs cost and time requirements. It also includes an early knowledge transfer and the definition of an appropriate process governance approach. The solution architecture of ARIS SmartPath [4] is shown in Fig. 10.6.

At the core of the solution is a standard application software product, which is enhanced by an industry-specific pre-configuration and add-on software components, as well as standard interfaces. This application software is combined with the design and performance management component of the ARIS Platform [14]. The ARIS Platform contains the necessary business content in the form of business process reference models. On the basis of this content, the pre-implementation, implementation, and post-implementation services are provided in a process-oriented approach. The standard application software ensures the future execution of the processes.

The application software can be preconfigured to support the processes (e.g., of a specific industry). Add-on applications and interfaces for the applicable standard application software are developed in customer-specific projects or purchased from third-party software vendors. This enables support of additional business scenarios (e.g., inter-enterprise business processes). The industry-specific pre-configurations are generally more detailed than standard industry solutions delivered from standard software vendors [15]. These pre-configured software solutions are another way to save time and increase resource efficiency during the implementation. Business content is delivered in the form of business process reference models. These reference models support effective process design, based on best practices. Services are offered for general project work, the definition of the required process governance model and other components of the BPM-Discipline, as well as hotline and helpdesk support during process execution and controlling. These services ensure the smooth transition from design to execution and support continuous improvement. It also applies the principle of simultaneous improvement and capability building activities.

So, what are the conclusions for the BPM-Discipline in SMEs? What does value-driven BPM mean for mid-market organizations?

10.5 What Does It All Mean for Value-Driven BPM in the Mid-market?

The value a BPM-Discipline delivers is also required by small and medium organizations. This is especially true for agility and innovation which are mission critical values for many SMEs. Start-ups also benefit through the ability of BPM to establish the necessary structure to scale. Hence BPM is also needed in mid-market companies.

However, the approach to establish and apply a BPM-Discipline in the midmarket has to be adjusted to the specific characteristics of such organizations. We have discussed general characteristics but those have to be completed with company specific aspects in a specific case. There is no "one fits it all" solution for vBPM.

Consulting and software companies offer specific solutions for mid-market organizations. These can be seen as starting points for the development of a company-specific process management discipline.

The discipline of value-driven BPM enables the development of SME-specific strengths, helps mitigate the weaknesses, and facilitates the achievement of high performance. It transfers also in mid-market organizations processes into valuable assets of the organization.

10.6 The Bottom Line

- SMEs are generally defined on the basis of two criteria: revenue and number of employees. One or both criteria must fall under a certain limit (Sect. 10.1).
- SMEs are typically defined in a country-specific manner; for this book, a general definition is applied (Sect. 10.1).
- Although most mid-market organizations have characteristics that challenge the implementation of a BPM-Discipline, they also have attributes that simplify the implementation application of such a management discipline (Sect. 10.1).
- SMEs need a BPM-Discipline in general for the same reasons as large organizations. However, agility and compliance as well as the ability to scale are often even more important in an SME environment (Sect. 10.2).
- The described characteristics of SMEs have direct impacts on a BPM-Discipline established in small businesses (Sect. 10.3).
- BPM consulting and software vendors reflect those requirements in holistic solution packages and offerings (Sect. 10.4).
- The BPM-Discipline needs to be established and applied simultaneously to meet SMEs requirements (Sect. 10.4).
- BPM capabilities are in general on a lower maturity level than in large organizations (Sect. 10.4).
- BPM tools and technologies can be less sophisticated in SMEs than in large organizations; outsourcing or the procurement through the cloud often plays an important role (Sects. 10.4 and 10.5).
- The discipline of value-driven BPM enables the development of SME-specific strengths, helps mitigate the weaknesses, and facilitates the achievement of high performance (Sect. 10.5).

References

1. Wikipedia (ed.): Small and Medium Enterprise. wikipedia.org (2007)
2. Fairlie, R.W., Reedy, E.J., Morelix, A., Russel, J.: The Kauffman Indx 2016 for Startup Activity—National Trends, Research Report by the Ewing Marion Kauffman Foundation, August 2016
3. InsightsSuccess. (ed.): BPM-D—Enabling the Next Generation Enterprise. In: IS Top 50 Most Valuable Tech Companies, December 2015

4. Kirchmer, M.: ARIS SmartPath—From process design to execution in mid-market organizations. In: Scheer, A.-W., Jost, W., Wagner, K. (eds.) Von Prozessmodellen zu lauffaehigen Anwendungen—ARIS in der Praxis, pp. 87–98. Springer, Berlin/Heidelberg (2005)
5. Lueg, R., Malinauskaite, L., Marinova, I.: The vital role of business processes for a business model: the case of a startup company. In: Problems and Perspectives in Management, vol. 12, Issue 4, pp. 213–220 (2014)
6. Kirchmer, M., Franz, P.: The Process of Process Management—Strategy Execution in a Digital World. BPM-D Whitepaper, Philadelphia, London (2015)
7. Griffin, E.: Why Start Ups Fail, According to Their Founders. In: Fortune Magazine, September 25, 2014. Online
8. BPM-D, RIFM. (ed.): Research Institute for Fragrancy Materials (RIFM) Moves the Safety Assessment Process ot the Next Performance Level Using the BPM-D Framework—"Assessment Factory" will Increase Capacity and Throughput by Over 300%. Joint BPM-D/RIFM Press Release, Philadelphia/Woodcliff Lake, February 2016
9. Scheer, A.-W.: ARIS—Business Process Frameworks, 2nd edn. Springer, Berlin (1998)
10. Scheer, A.-W.: ARIS—Business Process Modeling, 2nd edn. Springer, Berlin (1998)
11. SAP AG (ed.): http://www.sap.com/usa/solutions/sme/index.epx (2007)
12. Oracle Inc. (ed.): http://www.oracle.com/applications/jdedwards-enter-prise-one.html (2007)
13. Microsoft Inc. (ed.): http://www.microsoft.com/dynamics/default.mspx (2007)
14. IDS Scheer AG. (ed.): ARIS Platform. Product Brochure. IDS Scheer, Saarbruecken (2007)
15. Kagermann, H., Keller, G.: mySAP.com Industry Solutions. SAP Press/Addison-Wesley, London/New York (2000)

Chapter 11
What Has Jazz to Do with BPM?

Jazz and BPM have more in common than you may realize. Jazz and its inherent improvisation can be used as a metaphor that helps business process engineers deal with the continuous change and dynamic of today's business environment as they help their organizations pursue high performance in our digital world. Business process engineers can learn a lot from Jazz musicians.

While working closely with August-Wilhelm Scheer, founder of IDS Scheer, and many other companies, for more than 10 years, I learned a lot more than just business processes from this renowned BPM thought leader. He also introduced me to the world of Jazz and how it relates to business, which had a major impact on me, my thinking, and the way I work on business processes for strategy execution. Jazz became my number one hobby. I started to learn to play Jazz on the piano so that I could understand some of the challenges and great skills of professional Jazz musicians. Whenever possible, I listen to live Jazz, at famous clubs like Blue Note, Birdland, Iridium, Smoke or Village Vanguard in New York City, Jazz Showcase in Chicago, the Jazz Bakery in Los Angeles, or Snug Harbor in New Orleans. But I also like to go to smaller, lesser-known Jazz clubs, such as the former Vincent's in West Chester or Chris' Jazz Cafe in Philadelphia which is on its way to becoming a major club. For some time, I had even been co-owner of a Jazz club.

The collaboration with Scheer also resulted in a few CDs—unfortunately, my musical skills are not sufficient to play with the renowned musicians featured on those CDs. However, I acted as the executive producer, organizing the development of all arrangements, bringing the musicians together, booking a recording studio, and seeing the project through to the completion of the engineering work. The CDs are named "Bebop Process Excellence"—Volumes 1 and 2, referring both to "Bebop," an important core Jazz style, and to the notion of process excellence.

This title refers to the close relationship between Jazz and BPM. A band playing a Jazz tune can be interpreted as a process execution, delivering a result of value for the audience, the customers. They enjoy the tune and pay a cover charge for the music. The sheet music used can be compared to the process models, the "design" of the process of music. The Jazz band recording "Bebop Process Excellence—Volume 1"

Fig. 11.1 Playing a tune is a process; the sheet music is the process model (photos published with CD)

is shown in Fig. 11.1. The band included August-Wilhelm Scheer; Cecil Payne, the famous baritone saxophone player who passed away in December 2007; Mickey Roker, who played in the Dizzy Gillespie Band; Gunnar Mossblad, the musical director of the Dave Liebman Big Band; John Swana; and Mike Boone. Mossblad also arranged the tunes. For the recording of Bebop Volume 2, even Jimmy Cobb, the legendary drummer of the Miles Davis Group that recorded the "Kind of Blue" CD which was released in 1959, joined the performing musicians.

A few years later, I organized another interesting recoding project with Scheer where we added Randy Brecker, one of the finest Jazz trumpet players, to the band to play Monk tunes—again all arranged by Gunnar Mossblad. Also at BPM-D we continue to support Jazz and recently sponsored the production of Gunnar Mossblad's CD R.S.V.P that includes a tune he has written for me, "Calypso for Mathias", as well as one for my partner Peter Franz, "Sail on, Peter" [1].

The relation between Jazz and business has numerous facets [2]. An increasing number of professionals use the comparison of Jazz and business for management education in general [3, 4]. This chapter will focus on aspects of Jazz important for value-driven BPM. Learning about the principles of Jazz can help to organize the

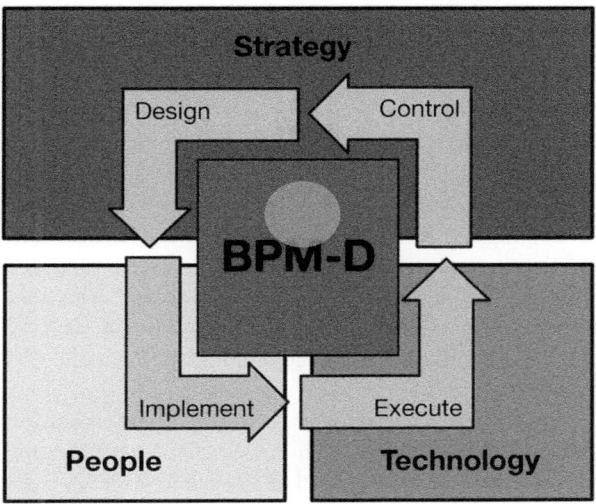

Fig. 11.2 Positioning of what Jazz has to do with BPM

discipline of vBPM and establish the right process culture. In working toward particular concepts, such as digitalization or the agile organization, the dynamics and characteristics of a Jazz band and Jazz music become very relevant.

Gold, a musician and educator, distinguishes five key behaviors of Jazz musicians that are relevant for business [3]:

- Autonomy: self-governing, independent, and adaptable, but still supporting a larger organization (the band)
- Passion: commitment and energy to pursue excellence
- Risk: ability to take chances and explore new things and to support others in doing so
- Innovation: creating new solutions by finding new ways to recombine existing things
- Listening: ability to really hear and feel the communication of others

We explore these aspects in the following discussions about Jazz and BPM. This chapter focuses on all aspects of the value-driven BPM-Discipline, as shown in Fig. 11.2. It closes the loop from Chap. 1, which introduced the concept of vBPM. The principles of Jazz help to establish the overall thinking and culture for this successful management discipline that moves strategy into people- and technology-based execution—at pace with certainty.

11.1 Teamwork with Continuously Changing Roles

Each musician of a successful and well-performing Jazz band is individually very skilled. This is the basis for the musician's certain level of autonomy. However, to be really successful, the band must work together as a team, toward a joint goal. The melody of a tune is presented by one of the lead instruments and supported by the others. Then, each musician plays a solo, an "improvisation," supported by the rest of the band. After the solo, the musician steps back and supports the next musician in his improvisation. Everyone leads and follows during a Jazz performance. Naturally, there is a band leader who decides which tunes are played and organizes the band. But during the "process of playing," everyone must lead, support, and follow.

This behavior is coordinated by a very intense informal communication. Brief looks, nods, or other signs enable the band members to exchange information very efficiently and effectively. Musicians listen to one another, so their playing is inspired by the playing of fellow musicians. This results in a very agile team, in which every musician uses their own particular skills to move the entire band—the team—forward to reach its goal of high performance. The band adapts to the overall atmosphere and to the audience.

Traditional companies are still organized like a symphony orchestra. The conductor hands out the sheet music that everyone must play. Then he leads the performance and ensures that everyone follows the plan as defined. All of the other orchestra musicians follow—all the time. They also deliver a result of value to the audience—but through a "standard product" in a standardized process—depending all on the conductor. The Jazz band delivers "individualized products" that can be adjusted quickly to the audience's mood and requests, using agile processes created through the creativity of the individual musicians. Top management of a traditional company can be compared with the conductor and the employees with the musicians of the orchestra.

A modern organization which is successful in our business environment of continuous change must work like a Jazz band to deal with the fast pace of new developments, for example, the opportunities and threats digitalization brings. Everyone has to lead efforts in his or her areas of expertise and follow in other initiatives, supporting another leader. This results in high levels of agility and a climate of innovation. The resulting dynamic is especially important for emergent processes, as described previously [2, 5].

Modern organizations are increasingly replacing static organizational structures through the changing roles employees play. The BPM-Discipline provides the framework for the required intense communication and the use of team members' individual skills to achieve overall goals. BPM delivers the basic alignment and environment in which the agile business team can truly produce value for clients and enable the organization to become a high-performance business.

Continuous change management is supported by ongoing intense communication. Every member of a modern company learns from colleagues and provides others with new ideas and know-how, just like musicians in a Jazz band. Change becomes part of the day-to-day routine. This is the business environment targeted by value-driven BPM and ultimately makes BPM a team sport [6].

The changing roles in Jazz bands and enterprises are visualized in Fig. 11.3. In both areas an intense informal communication is required.

Fig. 11.3 Leading and supporting—continuously changing roles

11.2 Find the Right Degree of Freedom

People who are not accustomed to listening to Jazz and its improvisations may think that a musician can just do what he wants during improvisation. But that is not the case. A Jazz tune sets certain parameters, which guide the improvisation. The musician must consider the key in which the tune is written, the form, the harmony defined through the chord changes, the rhythm, and the melody.

These parameters define a musician's degree of freedom. If you listen to the classical New Orleans style of Jazz for a few hours, it may become boring. The reason is that the musicians have very little freedom to improvise; the creativity has narrow boundaries. If you listen to Free Jazz for an hour, you may end up with a headache because you do not recognize any structure at all. The musicians have a great degree of freedom—but not much direction. The most interesting and, in my opinion, best-to-listen-to Jazz sets the degree of freedom somewhere in the middle, such as the Bebop style. In this style, musicians have enough freedom to really improvise and be creative while still maintaining harmony, form, and other parameters that makes listening easier and more pleasurable. They have a framework in which they work. They follow a direction that ensures they deliver a result of value to their audience, their customers.

An organization using BPM also must find the right degree of freedom for employees. If every working step is defined in detail through highly refined process models, human creativity is lost, and innovation and agility are difficult to achieve. If there are no rules or guidelines, the organization becomes chaotic without direction and is not focused on the company goals and the clients. In some areas, for example, in finance, you may even intentionally not want to give people too much freedom for creativity. It is more about being compliant with standards and legal requirements. Therefore, companies must set the right degree of freedom when defining business process governance guidelines.

Organizations define the degree of detail to which the business processes should be modeled and, with that, the degree of freedom of the people who must apply and execute them. This can even vary from process to process, e.g., depending on the form of execution—automated or manual. The process governance and related guidelines provided by the BPM-Discipline organize this degree of freedom. One consequence is process models reflecting the different degrees of freedom for specific processes or subprocesses. Value-driven BPM sets enough direction to reach the defined goals by moving the enterprise strategy into execution and leaves enough freedom to use all the potential of the involved people. BPM delivers the framework and basic structure for success—while enabling innovation and agility through the right degree of freedom.

The definition of the right degree of freedom in Jazz and business is described in Fig. 11.4.

11.3 Use a Common Language

When a Jazz musician plays a solo, this improvisation is "invented" on the spot. The musician is an "ad hoc composer." However, not everything is invented from scratch. Musicians practice music patterns, or licks, and voicings of chords, e.g., for piano players, which they use during their performances. A lick consists of a certain set of notes that fit well together. Licks are combined to "produce" the improvisation. They can be transferred from one scale to another and from one tune

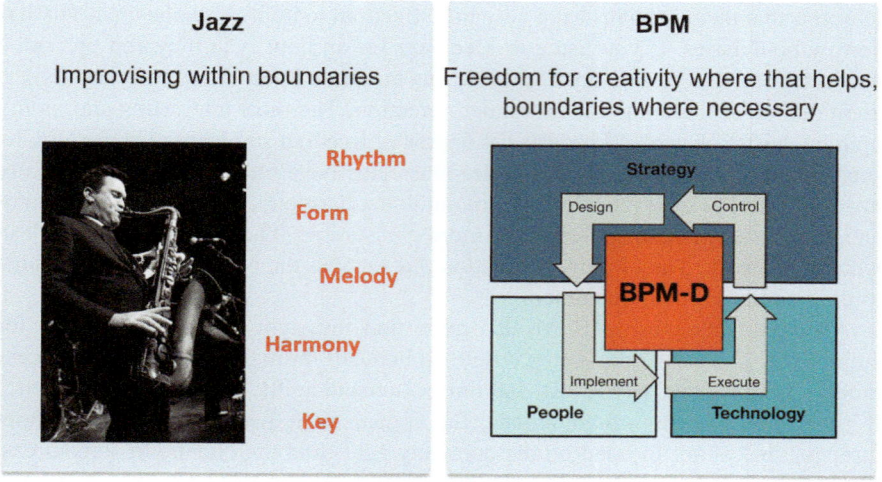

Fig. 11.4 Defining the right degree of freedom

to the next. Every Jazz musician develops a "vocabulary" of music and communicates the tune based on that "language" during the performance. New musicians start with a limited vocabulary, which they increase over time. They read the sheet music that visualizes licks and listen to their colleagues to learn the licks.

It is key to use this language of music at the right time during a performance. A Jazz tune has a rhythmical element called "swing" that creates a certain tension. This timing is a main characteristic of Jazz tunes. Every "music communication" must follow that timing. If the tune does not swing during the performance, it is not really Jazz. Jazz musicians communicate and deliver their music under strict time considerations.

Business process engineers also use a specific language. Aforementioned information modeling methods, e.g., event-driven process chains or the business process-modeling language, describe processes. Such methods can be used as the basic language of BPM that can be compared to the notes on sheet music for a tune. This language drives process automation and supports change management activities—information, communication, and training. Reference models can be compared to the licks Jazz musicians use. They are predefined components that are used to design entire business processes. The overall BPM-Discipline provides the guidelines for the communication and the targeted use of language. This supports the agility required in today's business environment because it ensures an efficient and effective communication based on a common language. New employees can learn from the structured documentation of process, data, functions, organizations and delivered value. They increase their "language knowledge" step by step until they can understand the entire processes in which they are involved and master the subprocesses they actively work on.

The timing of process initiatives and related communication is also very important. Enterprises must react quickly, preferably in real time, to changes in the business environment. Digitalization and analytics are all about providing timely information. The "real-time enterprise," which is enabled through the BPM-Discipline, has to keep the right "swing" using the common "language of BPM," just like a Jazz band. The factor time, combined with effective communication, is just as important for BPM as it is for a Jazz tune.

The use of a common language is visualized in Fig. 11.5.

11.4 Continuous Innovation

During an improvisation, Jazz musicians "invent" new music. As discussed previously, they use existing patterns in the form of licks to put together a new improvisation. This is done in such a way that the audience appreciates the music, and so it is not only something new, but new music that is successfully positioned "on the market." It is a short-term innovation.

In addition, most of the very successful Jazz musicians also contribute to entirely new styles of Jazz. For example, Dizzy Gillespie and Thelonious Monk were at the

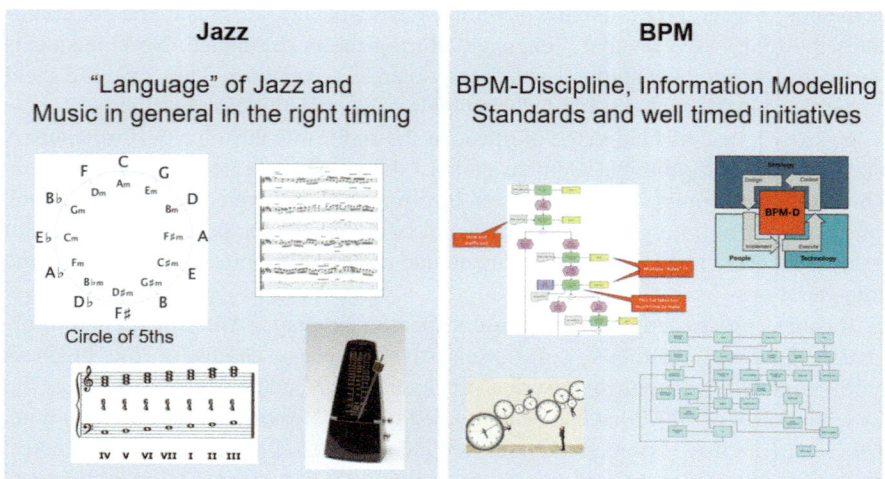

Fig. 11.5 Use of a common language

forefront of Bebop and made this Jazz style a reality [7, 8]. Miles Davis not only heavily influenced Bebop, but was also a driver of Modal Jazz and later Jazz Rock or Fusion Jazz [9]. Based on their improvisations and strong commitment to discovering new musical dimensions, Jazz musicians initiate continuous innovation. In this situation, it is a long-term innovation with a transformational character.

To innovate, Jazz musicians take risks—controlled risks. If someone plays a wrong note, that is generally not a major concern. One can repeat the "mistake" several times and, therefore, make it part of an interesting improvisation, of an innovation, if you will or one can correct the situation quickly by playing a neighboring note that resolves the initial "mistake". The high degree of creativity and innovation is possible based on the general acceptance of taking the necessary risk and defined approaches to manage risk.

This strong focus on innovation is also a key aspect of the discipline of value-driven BPM. Innovation and agility are among the main values it delivers. Therefore, BPM encourages that people act like Jazz musicians. They must be excited about doing things in a new and better way, about improving processes and inventing new ones to transform the organization. Driving a process from manual execution to semiautomated, then automated, and finally to a flexible, adaptive process can be the key for an organization's success. Business model innovation based on new processes is crucial for many enterprises. BPM needs the Jazz spirit to ensure short-term innovation, as well as long-term innovation and transformation effects. That is not something that one can plan and execute in detail. Every employee must practice the appropriate basic behavioral patterns. Everyone must behave and act like a successful Jazz musician, delivering first-class, short-term improvisations and supporting more and more long-term transformational changes.

An organization must create an environment that encourages taking risks in order to be successful. Innovative companies encourage creativity, even if it increases the risk of controlled mistakes. Tools, methods, and approaches provided by BPM, such as the approach to managing emergence or the use of simulation and process-modeling approaches to create transparency, allow organizations to manage and mitigate risk so they can encourage their employee's creativity.

This also means the organizational structures in a company must be flexible enough to encourage such innovative behavior. The next-generation enterprise has to be organized like a Jazz band, not like a symphony orchestra. Larger companies may have characteristics of a Jazz Big Band, requiring additional structure, but still offering individuals the freedom to be creative and innovative.

Continuous innovation for short-term step-by-step improvements or longer-term transformational improvements is illustrated in Fig. 11.6.

11.5 Having Fun Is Important, Too

When you listen to live Jazz performances, you can generally feel the excitement and passion of the musicians. You often see that they really have fun doing what they do—improvising, being creative, and taking risks to come up with new, unique ideas. In many cases, this becomes especially obvious in the last set of an evening, when the musicians demonstrate all their talents while feeling good about finalizing a successful performance. "Having fun" is an important basis for delivering good music and for giving the audience the best "result of value." "Having fun" while delivering the "process of music" is a significant aspect of the work of a successful Jazz musician.

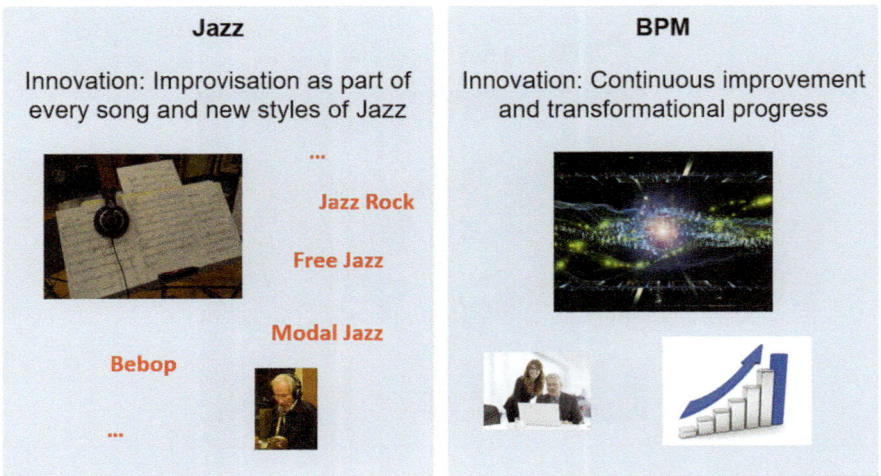

Fig. 11.6 Continuous innovation

That does not mean that playing Jazz music does not require a lot of hard work. Even professional, experienced musicians often practice eight or more hours per day. Having real fun at a performance requires significant effort on the front end. For instance, while learning very basic piano skills, I began to realize how many times I had to practice simple techniques before I could really have fun playing an entire tune.

When I moved from Germany to the United States, an American friend told me that there were two key aspects for being successful in the United States: "funny" and "money." Successful processes should contribute to revenue and profit, but it must also be fun to design, implement, execute, and control those processes. Business process engineers and all of the people involved in working on business processes should like their jobs and have fun during their work—at least most of the time. They must have a passion for processes and their particularities—and have fun while managing a process toward high performance to execute the business strategy. The BPM-Discipline needs to address this aspect to realize its full potential.

This does not mean that there is no hard work involved here, too. Process engineers have to learn the basic capabilities to work on processes and be productive and successful member of the BPM-Discipline community. Then they can really have fun making things happen, transferring strategy in to execution—fast and at low risk.

"Having fun" and "passion" enables creativity and innovation. BPM needs people to have fun with their work—and who can transfer that to their colleagues. Then the BPM-Discipline is on its best way to enable high performance and deliver value through systematic strategy execution, "Funny and Money."

This concept is visualized in Fig. 11.7.

Fig. 11.7 Having fun is important, too

11.6 The Bottom Line

- A successful Jazz band must work together as a team. The members continuously change roles. Everyone leads and follows. This dynamic is also required by the BPM-Discipline, especially for the management of emergent processes (Sect. 11.1).
- Jazz musicians must have enough freedom to really improvise and be creative while still maintaining harmony, form, and other parameters of a tune to make listening easier and more pleasurable. The discipline of value-driven BPM also has to deliver the right degree of freedom to an organization, especially through the appropriate business process governance and the appropriate design of processes (Sect. 11.2).
- Every Jazz musician develops a "vocabulary" of music, a common language. Based on this language, the music must be delivered in the right timing. BPM uses process and other information models as a language. Reference models and their components are "words" and "sentences" that are re-used. The language of process management drives related actions. Those must also be executed in the appropriate timing (Sect. 11.3).
- Based on their improvisations and the strong commitment to discovering new aspects of their music, Jazz musicians initiate continuous innovation, short term and long term. This is also essential for value-driven BPM: short-term improvements and longer-term transformational changes are critical for high-performance organizations (Sect. 11.4).
- Having fun and true passion is a significant part of the work of a successful Jazz musician. It is also essential for BPM and the involved people. It is important to create a culture of innovation and high performance both in Jazz and business environments (Sect. 11.5).

References

1. BPM-D. (ed.): BPM-D's Corporate Social Responsibility Initiative supports Jazz Project—Production and Release of Gunnar Mossblad's CD R.S.V.P. Press Release, Philadelphia (2015)
2. Scheer, A.W.: Epilog: Jazz Improvisation and Management. In: Scheer, A.W., Abolhassan, R., Jost, W., Kirchmer, M. (eds.) Business Process Change Management—ARIS in Practice, pp. 270–286. Springer, Berlin (2003)
3. Gold, M.: Negotiating Change—Jazz Impact—Business Lecture Series. http://www.jazz-impact.com/about.shtml (2007)
4. Wheatland, T.: Jazz in Business. http://www.jazzinbusiness.com/engelse%20versie/indexen.htm (2007)
5. Majchrzak, A., Logan, D., McCurdy, R., Kirchmer, M.: What business leaders can learn from Jazz musicians about emergent processes. In: Scheer, A.W., Kruppke, H., Jost, W., Kindermann, H. (eds.) Agility by ARIS Business Process Management. Springer, Berlin (2006)
6. Spanyi, A.: Business Process Management Is a Team Sport—Play it to Win! Anclote Press, Tampa (2003)

7. Maggin, D.: The Life and Times of John Birks Gillespie. Harper Entertainment, New York (2004)
8. De Wilde, L.: Monk. Marlowe, New York (1996)
9. Troupe, Q.: Miles and Me. University of California Press, Berkeley/Los Angeles (2000)

Chapter 12
The Discipline of Value-Driven BPM in Practice: A Case Example

Several readers of the past editions of this book have asked for an integrated case study. That is why I have added this chapter describing the case of a consumer goods company that needs to address, on one hand, urgent business issues using process-led approaches and wants, on the other hand, to establish BPM as a management discipline that supports the ongoing systematic execution of the business strategy.

The case covers many aspects we have discussed in past chapters—but of course not all. The discussion of this case is intended to help one understand the overall idea of value-driven BPM as a management discipline and how it can also deliver short-term value toward strategy execution. The case study covers all dimensions of the value-driven BPM-Discipline as shown in Fig. 12.1.

12.1 Company and Situation Faced

In this chapter we will discuss the case of a North American subsidiary of a leading consumer goods food company [1]. Let's refer here to "FoodCo." While FoodCo is part of a large international enterprise group, it is still run as a typical mid-market company. The organization had been very successful by focusing on a niche market with one major product line. Inefficiencies were mainly compensated through price increases ensuring a solid profitable growth.

However, about 2 years ago the first competitors entered the market segment offering similar products at lower prices. This development required an adjustment of the business strategy. The chief executive officer (CEO) of FoodCo and his leadership team decided to move from a focus on one product line and one market segment to a multiproduct line and multi-market segment approach. The price for the core products in the core market segment had to be reduced to stay competitive in this business-to-consumer market. The growth and profitability had to be met through the expansion into new markets with new products. This strategy required a

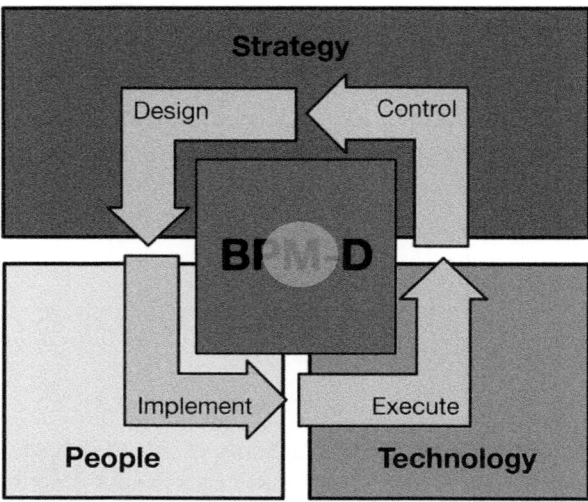

Fig. 12.1 Positioning of the consumer goods case study

cost reduction to be able to reduce the price of the core product line and the fast introduction of new products to the market. Since the CEO of FoodCo expects more frequent strategy adjustments in the future, he also requested the establishment of a management discipline enhancing the ability to deliver the required changes and enabling the execution of new or revised strategies.

FoodCo decided to meet those challenges through appropriate process management initiatives that needed to deliver fast results to implement the new strategy while building a value-driven BPM-Discipline to execute future strategy adjustments which will be increasingly influenced through digitalization opportunities. The company expected BPM to enable the targeted profitable growth. Therefore, the chief executive of FoodCo sponsored the BPM journey personally.

12.2 BPM Actions Taken

The resulting process management project was structured into three main initiatives to deliver the desired outcomes:

- Rapid Improvement Initiative
- Import Capability Initiative
- BPM-Discipline Initiative

The Rapid Improvement Initiative focused on cost reduction measures, while the Import Capability Initiative set up a new business unit to import products from other countries, mainly from vendors who are part of the same enterprise group as FoodCo. The BPM-Discipline Initiative was about establishing a lasting process management capability to enable ongoing strategy execution. All three initiatives

12.2 BPM Actions Taken

were executed in parallel. Capabilities developed in the BPM-Discipline work stream were applied right away in the other initiatives. The project was executed by a team of up to four consultants and appropriate part-time members of FoodCo.

The process improvement activities were based on BPM-D's rapid process improvement, a combination of a pragmatic process-modeling approach with design thinking methods to identify improvement potentials [2, 3]. The basic approach has been consistent with the process factory approach discussed before. For process modeling in a repository, the cloud-based Signavio tool was selected [4]. FoodCo's supply chain and logistics processes were in scope as well as the finance and controlling areas. In those areas 139 potential improvements were discovered. They were translated into 183 creative and pragmatic ideas to address those potential improvements and to drive the to-be design of processes to meet the defined business goals.

A typical potential improvement found in many processes was the misalignment between the actual work procedures and the supporting SAP enterprise resource planning (ERP) software [5]. Many employees kept their manual processes in place while doing, at least a part of the work, a second time using SAP. This resulted in significant time and cost impacts. The solution to this issue was, in many cases, pretty straightforward: adapting the processes to the common practices suggested through the business software [6]. An example for this improvement approach is shown in Fig. 12.2: currently nine activities are executed in the approval process, and after the improvement it will be only four. Most of these improvements could be executed as "quick wins" without defining additional implementation projects.

Other potential improvements required more sophisticated process adjustments that would take more time and effort to implement. Those were transferred into

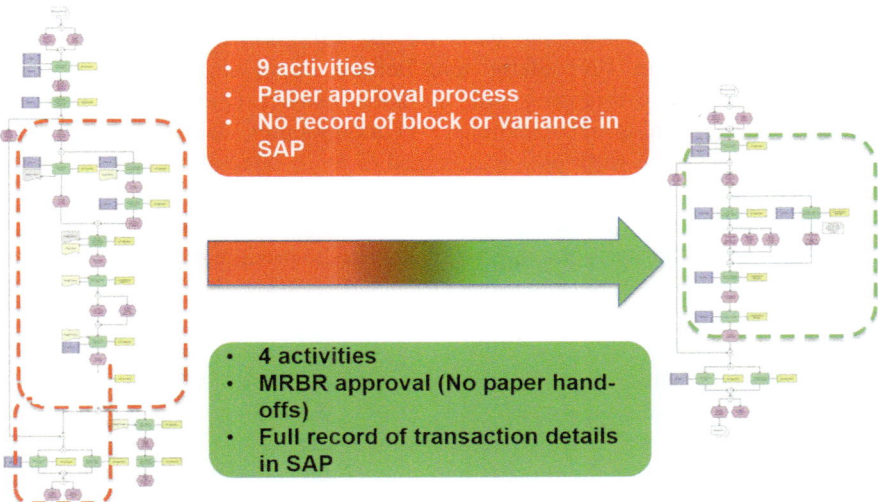

Fig. 12.2 Process improvement through adaption of common practices (example)

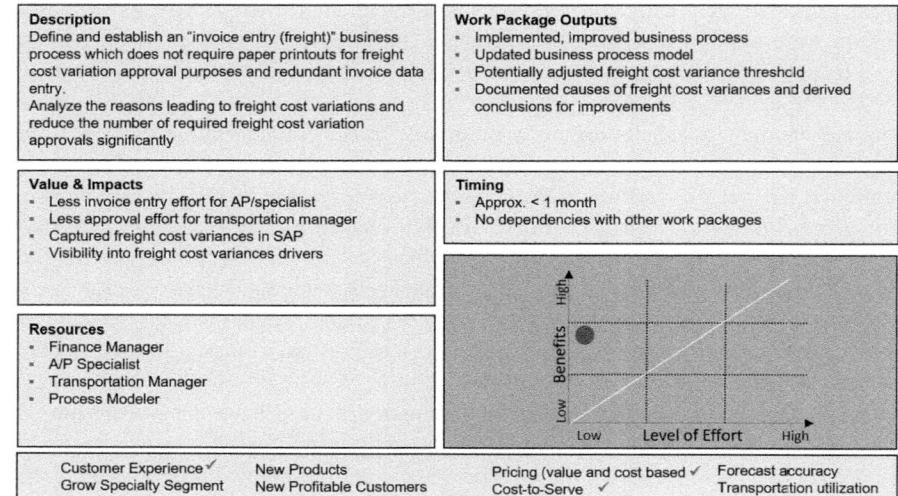

Fig. 12.3 Work package for process improvement execution (example)

work packages that basically define small projects of 3–6 months of duration. The definition of a work package included information like affected business processes, expected outcomes of the mini-project, expected value, relation to strategic value drivers, a rough cost-benefit estimation, preconditions for executing the work package, and a high-level guidance regarding the required people for its execution. Those work packages allowed FoodCo to decide which improvement work to execute internally and where to request additional external consulting or coaching support. An example of such a work package is shown in Fig. 12.3.

The work packages were the basis for the definition of a phased process improvement roadmap. Five of the nine defined improvement packages were started immediately, overlapping with the initial project. One of those required limited external coaching and operational execution support, mainly due to a lack of internal resources. The work packages helped to focus internal activities on what matters to achieve the strategic goals of FoodCo. It enabled the alignment of existing resources with the requirements of the strategy execution.

The new import business unit with its capabilities to procure products from other international members of the enterprise group and occasionally also from external suppliers was established using the existing SAP software as digital enabler. The basis for this initiative was the BPM-D approach for process-led SAP [6, 7], focusing on the business impacts of such a software implementation. A number of technical SAP experts were added to the project team to address specific software configuration topics. Business requirements were translated into process models which were used to drive the process implementation and software configuration. Process design and implementation were tightly integrated. The digital integration

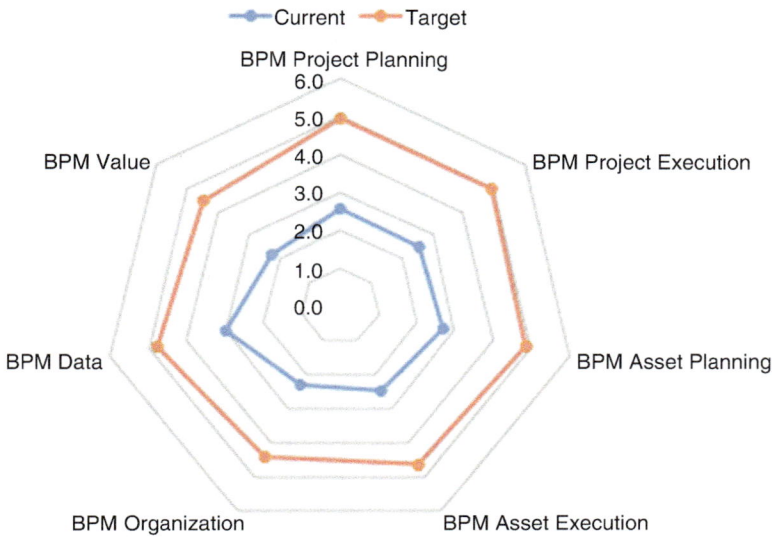

Fig. 12.4 Summary of results of BPM capability assessment (example)

of external market partners providing warehouse space was established to support an efficient overall planning and supply chain management approach.

The third initiative focused on establishing a simple FoodCo-specific BPM-Discipline. The standards and guidelines developed here, such as modeling guidelines or responsibilities of the process owners, were quickly applied through the other initiatives. The setup of the right process management discipline was prepared through a BPM capability assessment. The basis for this assessment was mainly the BPM-D Process Framework but also the BPM-D Value, Organization, and Data Frameworks [2]. The frameworks are entrance points to an underlying reference model for a comprehensive "process of process management." At FoodCo it enabled at a company-specific assessment that only checked process management areas relevant for the strategy execution in this specific organization. Figure 12.4 summarizes the results of the BPM maturity assessment at FoodCo.

Resulting key activities to establish the BPM-Discipline at FoodCo were the identification of high-impact processes in regard to FoodCo's strategy, the design of a simple governance organization, as well as the setup of the FoodCo repository in Signavio for current and future use. Knowledge transfer during the application of those capability components of the BPM-Discipline as well as training on the job helped to establish the necessary process management know-how in a "digestible" step-by-step approach.

An important topic addressed was the identification of FoodCo's high-impact business processes. A company competes with less than 20% of its processes. Those are the ones the organization needs to get right to make the strategy happen [8]. For FoodCo it is important to check in at every change of the market or the strategy for changes regarding those high-impact processes: "Are there now different processes

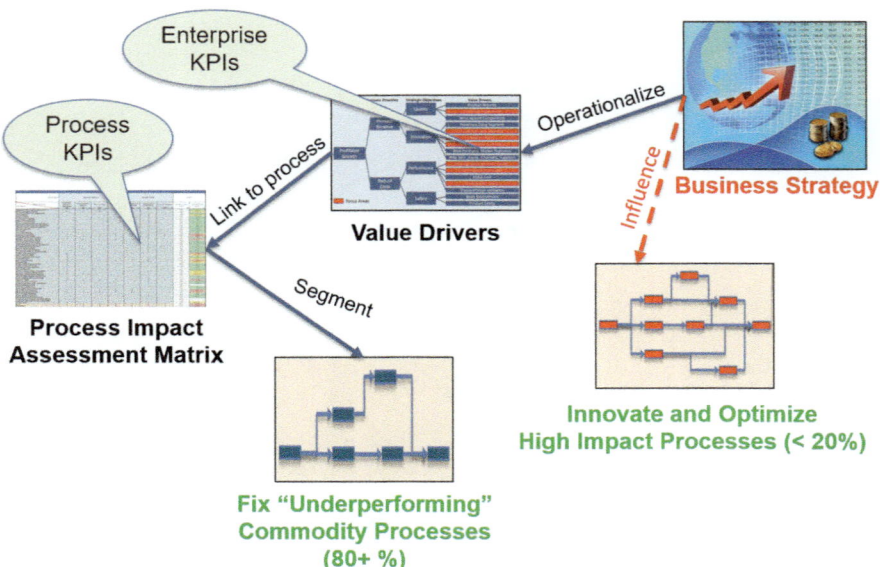

Fig. 12.5 BPM-D targeting value approach for process segmentation

in this high-impact segment?" and "How do processes have to be adjusted?" are typical questions to be answered. This identification of the relevant processes was achieved through the BPM-D targeting value approach [9]. This approach operationalizes the business strategy through value driver trees. The key value drivers are linked to processes through a Process Impact Assessment Matrix. This matrix allows the identification of high-impact and commodity processes as well as related key performance indicators (KPIs).

At FoodCo we identified less than 10% of the processes as high impact based on their influence on eight main value drivers, such as New Product Introduction or Reduce Cost-to-Serve. The process segmentation approach applied at FoodCo is shown in Fig. 12.5. In a second step, we identified, with the leadership team, the most important value drivers that the company needs to get right to make the new strategy happen. They were used as the basis to identify relevant process improvement suggestions, in the improvement initiative. We also discovered a third group of processes that are in a "gray" area between "high impact" and "commodity." We decided on a case-to-case basis how to treat those processes. The development of the Process Impact Assessment Matrix at FoodCo was challenging, from a facilitation point of view, since the involved top executives had different views and opinions regarding the impact of different processes on the defined value drivers and the importance of the value drivers. However, the result was a set of jointly agreed upon priorities in the form of high-impact processes which justified this effort. This allowed us to launch more sophisticated improvement activities at FoodCo in the high-impact areas and to copy common practices for the commodity processes. On an ongoing basis, high-impact processes are the ones that will receive highest attention.

Key roles defined for the governance organizations were the chief process owner (CPO) to lead the ongoing BPM initiative, the process owners to manage key end-to-end processes, as well as a small core team to maintain the process repository. The business-focused chief information officer (CIO) of FoodCo took over the role as CPO as an additional responsibility because it provides huge synergies with his original role. Selected functional leads became process owners as additional roles. Since the process repository is cloud based, it does not require a lot of maintenance. It was structured using a simple business architecture which requires minimal ongoing work to keep the content up to date. This has been handled by a two-person core team. All as-is and to-be process models of the rapid improvement and the import initiatives were captured as process models in the repository.

Activities to establish a full BPM-Discipline that require more effort were again defined through the previously described work packages. We defined six of such enabling work packages. An example is the work package to address the definition and measurement of process KPIs for the high-impact processes.

12.3 Business Results Achieved

All three process management initiatives delivered significant impact and value to FoodCo. In less than 3 months, the Rapid Improvement Initiative resulted in cost and time reductions based on "quick wins." In the next 6 months, more significant cost reductions, but also customer experience improvements, were achieved through the execution of first work packages. The results were, for example, a better alignment between finished goods stock, customer requirements, and transportation capabilities. This led to a reduction of transportation cost since trucks are better filled, less waste of finished products, and, last but not least, higher customer satisfaction by receiving the right products at the right quality at the right time.

Work packages that still have to be executed were segmented based on cost, benefits, and urgency, so that they could be included in a phased execution plan for the next 12–15 months. This represents the way forward regarding FoodCo's strategy execution. In case of short-term strategy or market changes, those packages and the impacted processes may need to be adjusted as part of the "targeting value" approach. Figure 12.6 shows the roadmap developed based on this segmentation: the realization of the remaining work packages and their grouping into "execution waves."

The import unit was fully functional after approximately 6 months. Appropriate business processes and supporting SAP software are in place. This has been the basis to import new products and introduce them into the market. The resulting revenue is sufficient to offset the revenue decline in the former core market segment. The strategy change has been executed and delivered the expected results.

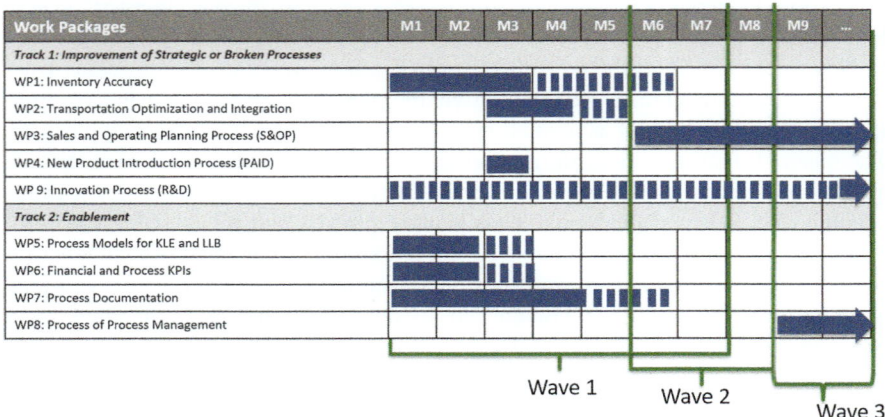

Fig. 12.6 Roadmap based on segmentation of work packages

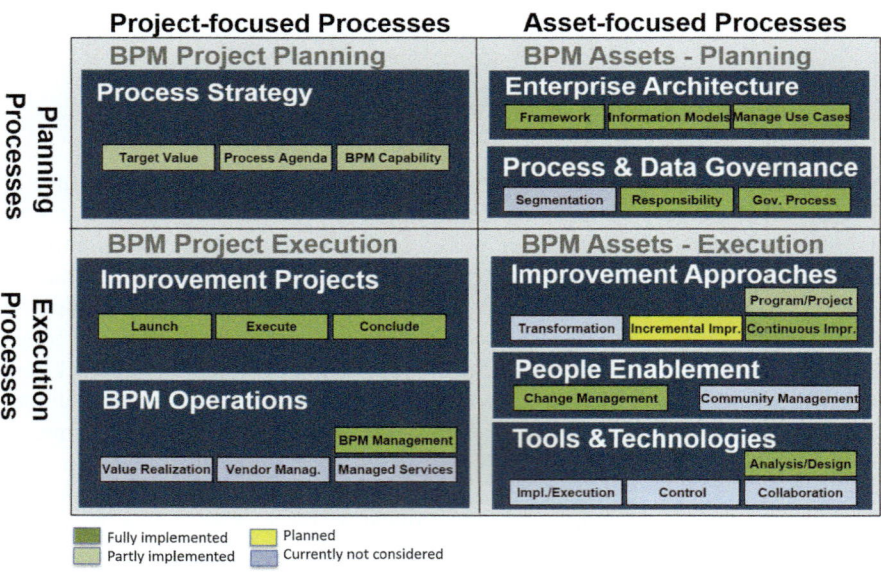

Fig. 12.7 BPM capabilities shown in BPM-D process framework (example)

The BPM-Discipline is up and running in key areas. High-impact processes are identified, and the process to adjust to new strategies and market situations is defined. The process management core team and the most important process owners are in place and have started to grow into their roles. The enabling work packages are included in the execution plan and will be realized as part of the overall improvement program. Figure 12.7 shows the current coverage of the "process of process management" at FoodCo using the BPM-D Process Framework [2].

FoodCo now has a BPM-Discipline in place that enables a systematic strategy execution. The integration of the process management discipline with a business-driven information technology unit enables the targeted realization of value from digitalization opportunities.

12.4 Some Lessons Learned

The start of the process management project at FoodCo had been challenging. In spite of the support of the chief executive, there was a lot of skepticism regarding BPM in general due to negative experience in the past. It was perceived as a complicated set of tools that costs a lot of time and effort without providing much value. With the help of the CEO, the leadership of the CIO, and the focused use of BPM-D assets and consultants, we could overcome those hurdles and deliver fast and sustainable results together. People had been motivated, showed a positive attitude, and still drive the initiatives forward.

Here are some key lessons learned from this value-driven BPM initiative for strategy execution at FoodCo:

- Get top management support. Having the CEO as sponsor of the initiative at FoodCo has been the key to true success. Establishing and applying a value-driven BPM-Discipline requires top-down support. To achieve fast and sustainable results through the BPM-Discipline, top executive and their team need to understand and support the strategy execution through process management.
- Deliver fast benefits while building required and lasting BPM capabilities. At FoodCo the visibility of the rapid operational improvements paved the way to a broader acceptance of the BPM-Discipline in general.
- Set clear priorities; don't try to "boil the ocean." The initial BPM maturity level of FoodCo was relatively low. Fixing and changing everything at once would overwhelm people—in spite of top management support. It was key at FoodCo to see what the organization can digest and how much people can contribute besides their regular jobs.
- Keep things simple, "less is often more." This is especially true for the use of tools and technologies. At FoodCo we replaced a complex process repository tool with very rich functionality through a simple cloud-based solution that people can use and maintain without too much expert knowledge. Once the maturity level increases, the switch to a more sophisticated solution can still be done—if the additional value justifies this.
- Encourage innovation and creativity instead of punishing people for making mistakes. Empathy and the transfer of solutions from other areas of experience have been important to come up with solutions to address the improvement potentials. People at FoodCo started to see BPM as something that helps them to move forward on a different and better path. This was the basis for ongoing motivation.

- A value-driven BPM-Discipline is an enabler of growth and strategic agility, not just a cost reduction engine. It has been sometimes challenging to keep the project at FoodCo focused on all dimensions of strategy execution—which was very important for the overall success. Cost cutting alone is not a strategy.
- People are key for success. You need to treat them accordingly. The FoodCo success is mainly due to the motivation and commitment of the involved people.
- A value-driven BPM-Discipline and its leadership recognize the potential business value of technology and digitalization and make it transparent to the organization. It enables real business outcomes from digital initiatives. At FoodCo people started to understand better the value of their SAP software and how it helps them in their day-to-day jobs. It prepared them for more sophisticated technology solutions, for example, in the transportation planning and the integration with main customers.

The patent-pending BPM-D Framework [2] and the approaches based on it have been important assets for the success of this project at FoodCo. It allowed them to benefit systematically from vast experience in other organizations and newest academic research resulting in time savings and a risk reduction.

At FoodCo BPM has become a value-driven management discipline that transfers strategy into people- and technology-based execution—at pace with certainty. This management discipline is implemented through the process of process management. It enables FoodCo to execute its business strategy systematically in a digital world.

12.5 The Bottom Line

- The launch of a value-driven BPM-Discipline has in most cases two goals: address immediate business challenges and build a management discipline for ongoing strategy execution (Sect. 12.1).
- The establishment of a value-driven BPM-Discipline is a top management topic (Sect. 12.1).
- Actions necessary to establish and apply a BPM-Discipline are company specific. Typically, they include the application of an improvement or transformation approach to achieve quick business results and the development of simple process management capabilities, especially around identification of high-impact processes—setup of a process repository and implementation of a basic process governance (Sect. 12.2).
- Some actions can be executed immediately to achieve rapid results. Others have to be defined in work packages and executed as part of the process management journey (Sect. 12.2).
- A value-driven BPM-Discipline and its immediate application bring significant short- and long-term business benefits (Sect. 12.3).

- Some lessons learned during this specific initiative can be used as input into BPM-Discipline initiatives in other organizations (Sect. 12.4).

References

1. Kirchmer, M.: Strategy execution in a consumer goods company: achieving immediate benefits while building lasting process capabilities for our digital world. In: Proceedings of BPM 2016, Rio de Janeiro, Brazil, 18–22 September 2016
2. Kirchmer, M., Franz, P.: The Process of Process Management—Strategy Execution in a Digital World. BPM-D Whitepaper, Philadelphia, USA; London, UK
3. Kirchmer, M.: Value-driven Design and Implementation of Business Processes—From Strategy to Execution at Pace with Certainty. In: Proceedings of the 4th International Symposium on Business Modelling and Software Design, Luxembourg, 24–26 June 2014, pp. 297–392
4. Signavio (ed.): The Business Transformation Platform—Signavio Process Editor. In: http://www.signavio.com/products/business-transformation-platform/
5. SAP: "Explore the SAP Portfolio". In: http://go.sap.com/solution.html (2016)
6. Kirchmer, M.: Business Process Oriented Implementation of Standard Software—How to Achieve Competitive Advantage Efficiently and Effectively, 2nd edn. Springer, Berlin (1999)
7. Scheer, A.-W.: Business Process Engineering—Reference Models for Industrial Enterprises, 2nd edn. Springer, Berlin (1995)
8. Franz, P., Kirchmer, M.: Value-driven business Process Management—The Value-Switch for Lasting Competitive Advantage. McGraw-Hill, New York (2012)
9. Kirchmer, M., Franz, P.: Targeting Value in a Digital World. BPM-D Whitepaper, Philadelphia, London (2014)

Epilogue: Business Process Management Is Becoming Popular in the Digital World

The notion of "business process" and the discipline of managing business processes is nowadays considered a mainstream topic with top management relevance. Today, in almost every organization, every manager has to deal with business processes, with the value-driven management of such processes to achieve a systematic strategy execution and benefit from the opportunities of digitalization. "Business process" has become part of today's mass culture of business in our digital world.

Consequently, the concept of "business process" should start to get interesting for artists dealing with topics and images of mass culture. Why should the value-driven BPM not become a topic for pop art? We have discussed the relation between Jazz and process management; let us finish this book with some thoughts about pop art and process excellence.

Pop art generally involves the use of existing images from mass culture that are already represented in two dimensions, for example, in advertisements, photographs, comic strips, or other mass media sources. Pop art paintings are often emphasizing a flat frontal representation of those popular images and day-to-day life objects. Artists mostly use strong unmixed colors bound by hard edges and suggest a depersonalized approach of mass production. Pop art targets the popular taste sometimes even close to kitsch that was previously considered outside the limits of fine art [1].

You may have heard about well-known pop artists like Andy Warhol, Roy Lichtenstein, Robert Rauschenberg, James Rosenquist, Jasper Johns, Claes Oldenburg, Tom Wesselmann, and Keith Haring [1]. But there are also many more emerging and, in the meantime, more and more accepted artists dedicated to pop art, such as Jeff Schaller, Romero Britto, Burton Morris, Peter Mars, Robert Mars, and Steve Kaufman [2]. These artists are confronted with a new reality of mass culture.

An important component of the discipline of value-driven BPM is the transfer of business reality into business process and other information models. These models and the digital technology supporting their development and execution have made process management a real mass phenomenon—that even requires a new leadership position: the Chief Process Officer. The depiction of complex business environments in such models and their focused digitalization provide a link to pop art by delivering the images that can be picked up by interested artists.

When I discussed this development with Jeff Schaller [3], one of the important emerging pop artists [4], he got interested in the topic. The result was the painting shown in Fig. E1. It is entitled *Performance Process* and shows the human element

Fig. E1 "Performance Process" by Jeff Schaller

of processes as well as the technology aspects—and in the background the key business motivation: to make money through the appropriate strategy execution and the right digitalization approach. Typical for many pop art pieces is that he even includes a kind of description in the painting. Jeff has really shown that business process management has become popular (Fig. E1).

I hope you enjoy the painting and get interested in learning more about business process management for strategy execution in a digital world and pop art.

References

1. Livingstone, M.: Pop Art—A Continuous History. Thames and Hudson, London (2000)
2. McKenzie, M.: Images We Love—Popular Art in America. (2003)
3. Schaller, J.: Biography. In: http://www.pinkcowstudio.com/about/bio.html (2016)
4. Lee, A., Rooney, E.A.: Encaustic Art of the 20th Century. Schiffer Publishing, Atglen (2016)

Appraisals to the Previous Editions

Process Excellence is not optional, but a necessity for companies competing in the new global economy. This book is an important contribution to the field and will help managers harness the power of process excellence to drive better performance.
Dr. Michael Hammer, Author of Reengineering the Corporation, Boston, USA

Managing an organization's business processes distinctively well can be a fundamental source of competitive advantage in today's fast growing global economy. Doing so, however, requires a unique cohesion between strategic vision, operational execution, and information technology sophistication. Dr. Kirchmer's wide experience in helping organization's Manage Business Process Excellence is succintly captured in this well thought-out book.
Thomas Kurian, Senior Vice President, Oracle Corporation, Redwood Shores, USA

Business process management helps you to really understand your business and manage essential process innovation opening new ways to growth. Based on his profound experience in this area, Dr. Kirchmer presents a clear vision how to do this best.
Falko Lameter, CIO, Kaeser Compressors, Coburg, Germany

Kirchmer's book takes the concept of process excellence into the 21st century. He explains how processes evolve, how process management encourages innovation, and why high growth starts with the foundation of world-class processes.
Bill McDermott, CEO, SAP Deutschland, Walldorf, Germany

Companies that lack an integrated business process management structure cannot fully leverage the advantages inherent in current released versions of enterprise software. This gap in effective business process management (BPM) practice places these businesses in a position of competitive disadvantage. Dr. Kirchmer's book outlines a clear, straightforward path for any organization to move to BPM and improve to process excellence.

Steve Tieman, Vice President, Technical Integration Lead, Strategic Modernization Initiative, Estee Lauder Companies, New York, USA

Kirchmer's book outlines how business process management delivers real value to an organization. It shows how companies can achieve competitive advantage by moving more effectively from business strategy to people and IT-based execution. The book is an important contribution to establishing business process management as a high impact management discipline.
Sander van't Noordende, Group Chief Executive Officer, Accenture, New York, USA

Bibliography

Abolhassan, F. (ed.): Was treibt die Digitalisierung? Warum an der Cloud kein Weg vorbeifuehrt, SpringerGabler, Wiesbaden (2016)

American Productivity and Quality Center (APQC): Business process frameworks. On: http://www.apqc.org/process-classification-framework (2011)

Appian (ed.): Low-code tools: Fueling Business Transformation at Digital Speed. Whitepaper, Washington (2016)

Bartlett, C.A., Ghoshal, S.: Managing Across Borders—The Transnational Solution. Harvard Business School Press, Boston (2002)

Becker, J., Knackstedt, R.: Construction and application of for data warehousing. In: Uhr, W., Esswein, W., Schopp, E. (eds.) Wirtschaftsinformatik 2/Band II—Medien—Maerkte—Mobilitaet, Heidelberg (2003)

Becker, J., Schuette, R.: Handelsinformationssysteme, 2nd edn. Frankfurt, Redline Wirtschaft (2004)

Becker, J., Schuette, R.: A reference model for retail enterprises. In: Fettke, P., Loos, P. (eds.) Reference Modeling for Business Systems Analysis, pp. 182–205. Hershey, London (2007)

Blechard, M.: Magic quadrant for business process analysis tools, 2H07-1H08. In: The Gartner Group (ed.) Research Publication G00148777, 6 Aug 2007.

Bossidy, L., Charan, R.: Execution: The discipline of getting things done. New York, NY, Crown Business (2002)

BPM-D (ed.): BPM-D's Corporate Social Responsibility Initiative supports Jazz Project—Production and Release of Gunnar Mossblad's CD R.S.V.P. Press Release, Philadelphia (2015).

BPM-D, RIFM (ed.): Research Institute for Fragrancy Materials (RIFM) moves the Safety Assessment Process to the Next Performance Level using the BPM-D Framework—"Assessment Factory" will increase Capacity and Throughput by over 300%. Joint BPM-D/RIFM Press Release, Philadelphia/Woodcliff Lake, February 2016

Bradly, A., Gootzit, D.: Who's Who in Enterprise 'Mashup' Technologies. In: Gartner Research, ID Number: G00151351, 9 July 2007

Brynjolfsson, E., McAffee, A.: The Second Machine Age—Work, Progress and Prosperity in a Time of Brilliant Technologies. W.W. Norton, New York, London (2014)

Bullinger, H.J., Scheer, A.W.: Service Engineering—Entwicklung und Gestaltung innovativer Dienstleistungen. In: Bullinger, H.-J., Scheer, A.W. (eds.) Service Engineering—Service Engineering—Entwicklung und Gestaltung innovativer Dienstleistungen, Berlin/Heidelberg, e.a. (2003a)

Bullinger, H.J., Scheer, A.W. (eds.): Service Engineering—Service Engineering—Entwicklung und Gestaltung innovativer Dienstleistungen, Berlin (2003b)

Cantara, M.: Start up your Business Process Competency Center. In: Documentation of the Gartner Business Process Management Summit, National Harbor 2015.
Carter, S.: The new language of business—SOA & Web 2.0. IBM Press, Upper Saddle River (2007)
Champy, J.: X-Engineering the corporation—Reinventing Your Business in the Digital Age. Warner Business Books, New York (2002)
Cheese, P., Thomas, R.J., Craig, E.: The Talent Powered Organization—Strategies for Globalization, Talent Management and High Performance. Kogan Page, London (2008)
Chow, L., Conner, C., Comes, S., Mei, J.-L., Bullotta, T.: Cloud-enabled ACM for the Age of the Customer. In: Fisher, L. (ed.): Innovation in Adaptive Case Management—Best Practices for Knowledge Workers, pp. 57–76. Lighthouse Point, FL (2016)
Christensen, C., Johnson, M.: Business model innovation. Report to the US Council of Innovation. The Conference Board, 01/2007
Christensen, C.M., Raymour, M.: The Innovator's Solution: Using Good Theory to Solve the Dilemmas of Growth. Harvard Business School Press, Boston (2003)
Collins, J.: Good to great—Why Some Companies Make the Leap... and Others Don't. HarperBusiness, New York (2001)
Curran, T., Keller, G.: SAP R/3 Business Blueprint: Business Engineering mit den R/3-Referenzprozessen. Addison-Wesley, Bonn (1999)
Davenport, T.: Mission Critical—Realizing the Promise of Enterprise Systems. Harvard Business School Press, Boston (2000)
Davenport, T.: The coming commoditization of processes. In: Harvard Business Review, June 2005a, p. 100–108
Davenport, T.: Thinking for a Living—How to Get Better Performance and Results from Knowledge Workers. Harvard Business School Press, Boston (2005b)
Davila, T., Epstein, M.J., Shelton, R.: Making Innovation Work. Upper Saddle River (2006)
de Jong, M., van Dijk, M.: Disruption beliefs: A new approach to business model innovation. In: McKinsey Quarterly, July 2015
De Wilde, L.: Monk. Marlowe, New York (1996)
Elzina, D.J., Gulledge, T.R., Lee, C.Y. (eds.): Business Engineering. Springer, Norwell (1999)
Ewenstein, B., Smith, W., Sologar, A.: Changing Change Management. In: McKinsey Digital, July 2015
Exel, S., Wilms, S.: Change management with ARIS. In: Scheer, A.W., Abolhassan, F., Jost, W., Kirchmer, M. (eds.) Business Process Change Management—ARIS in Practice. pp. 23–48. Berlin, New York, and others (2003)
Fairlie, R.W., Reedy, E.J., Morelix, A., Russel, J.: The Kauffman Indx 2016 for Startup Activity—National Trends, Research Report by the Ewing Marion Kauffman Foundation, August 2016
Fettke, P., Loos, P.: Reference models for retail enterprises. HMD Praxis der Wirtschaftsinformatik. **235**, 15–25 (2004)
Fettke, P., Loos, P.: Perspectives on reference modeling. In: Fettke, P., Loos, P. (eds.) Reference Modeling for Business Systems Analysis, pp. 1–20. Hershey, London (2007a)
Fettke, P., Loos, P. (eds.): Reference Modeling for Business Systems Analysis. Hershey, London (2007b)
Fettke, P., Loos, P.: Classification of reference models: a methodology and its application. Information Systems and E-Business Management. **1**(1), 35–53 (2007c)
Fingar, P.: Extreme Competition—Innovation and the Great 21st Century Business Reformation. Meghan-Kiffer Press, Tampa (2006)
Fisher, L. (ed.): BPMN 2.0 Handbook—Methods, Concepts, Case Studies and Standards in Business Process Modelling Notation (BPMN), 2nd edn. Lighthouse Point, FL (2012).
Fisher, L. (ed.): Intelligent BPM Systems—Impact and Opportunity. Future Strategies, Lighthouse Point (2013)
Fleisch, E., Mattern, F. (eds.): Das Internet der Dinge—Ubiquitous Computing und RFID in der Praxis. Springer, Heidelberg/Berlin (2005)

Fleisch, E., Christ, O., Dierkes, M.: Die betriebswirtschaftliche Vision des Internets der Dinge. In: Fleisch, E., Mattern, F. (eds.) Das Internet der Dinge—Ubiquitous Computing und RFID in der Praxis, pp. 3–37. Heidelberg, Berlin (2005)

Fleischmann, A.: Subject-oriented Business Process Management. White Paper, Muenchen (2007)

Franz, P.: Prioritizing Process Improvements to maximize Business Agility. Accenture Point of View document, London (2011)

Franz, P., Kirchmer, M.: Value-driven Business Process Management—The Value-Switch for Lasting Competitive Advantage. McGraw-Hill, New York, e.a (2012a)

Franz, P., Kirchmer, M.: Value-driven Business Process Management—The Value Switch for Lasting Competitive Advantage. New York (2012b)

Franz, P., Kirchmer, M.: Process Standardization and Harmonization—Enabling Customer Service in a Digital World. BPM-D Whitepaper, Philadelphia/London (2016a)

Franz, P., Kirchmer, M.: Process Standardization and Harmonization—Agile Customer Service in a Digital World. BPM-D Whitepaper, London/Philadelphia (2016b)

Franz, P., Kirchmer, M., Rosemann, M.: Value driven Business Process Management—Which values matter for BPM. Accenture, Queensland University of Technology (QUT) White Paper, London, Philadelphia, Brisbane (2011)

Friedman, T.L.: The World Is Flat—A Brief History of the Twenty-First Century. New York (2005)

George, M.L.: Lean Six Sigma for Service—Conquer Complexity and Achieve Major Cost Reductions in Less than a Year. McGraw-Hill, New York (2003)

George, M.L., Wilson, S.A.: Conquering Complexity in Your Business—How Wal-Mart, Toyota and Other Top Companies Are Breaking Through the Ceiling on Profits and Growth. McGraw-Hill, New York (2004)

George, M., Works, J., Watson-Hemphill, K.: Fast Innovation—Achieving Superior Differentiation, Speed to Market, and Increased Profitability. McGraw-Hill, New York (2005)

Global360 (ed.): www.global360.com (2007)

Gold, M.: Negotiating Change—Jazz Impact—Business Lecture Series. In: http://www.jazz-impact.com/about.shtml (2007)

Greenbaum, J.: SimEnterprise: The video Gamer's guide to SAP's business-process revolution. In SAP Netweaver Magazine, vol. 2 (2006)

Griffin, E.: Why start ups fail, according to their Founders. In: Fortune Magazine, September 25, 2014, online

Hammer, M.: Don't Automate, Obliterate. In: Harvard Business Review, pp. 104–112. July/August 1990

Hammer, M.: The Internet and the Real Economy. Documentation of Sapphire 99. Philadelphia (1999)

Hammer, M.: Six steps to operational innovation. In: Harvard Business School Working Knowledge for Business, hbswk.hbs.edu (2005), 30 Aug 2005

Hammer, M., Champy, J.: Reengineering the Corporation. HarperBusiness, New York (1993)

Hammer, M., Stanton, S.: The Reengineering Revolution. Harper Collins, Glasgow (1995)

Harmon, P.: Business Process Change Management—A Manager's Guide to Improving, Redesigning, and Automating Processes. Morgan Kaufmann, San Francisco (2003)

Harmon, P.: A new type of activity. In: Business Process Trends (ed.) Newsletter, vol. 5, Number 19, 11/2007

Hess, H., Blickle, T.: From Process Efficiency to Organizational Performance. ARIS Platform Expert Paper. Saarbruecken 3/2007

Heuser, L., Alsdorf, C., Woods, D.: International Research Forum 2006—Web 2.0—IT Security—Real World Awareness—IT as a Tool for Growth and Development. New York (2006)

Heuser, L., Alsdorf, C., Woods, D.: Enterprise 2.0, The Service Grid, User-Driven Innovation, Business Model Transformation—International Research Forum 2007. New York (2008)

IDS Scheer AG (ed.): ARIS Design Platform—ARIS Enterprise Architecture Solution. White Paper. Saarbruecken 3/2006

IDS Scheer AG (ed.): ARIS Platform. Product Brochure. Saarbruecken (2007)
Imai, M.: Kaizen—Der Schluessel zum Erfolg der Japaner im Wettbewerb. 8. Auflage, Muenchen (1993)
InsightsSuccess (ed.): BPM-D—Enabling the Next Generation Enterprise. In: IS Top 50 Most Valuable Tech Companies, December 2015
IQPC (ed.): Proceedings of the Business Process Management Summit, Las Vegas 10/2007
Isaacson, W.: Steve Jobs. New York, e.a. (2011)
Johnson, M., Suskewicz, J.: Accelerating Innovation. In: Pantaleo, D., Pal, N.: From Strategy to Execution—Turning Accelerated Global Change into Opportunity, pp. 49–64. Berlin e.a. (2008)
Jost, W.: EDV-gestuetzte CIM Rahmenplanung. Wiesbaden (1993)
Jost, W.: Vom CIO zum CPO. In: Harvard Business Manager, 9/2004
Jost, W., Scheer, A.W.: Business process management: a core task for any company organization. In: Scheer, A.W., Abolhassan, F., Jost, W., Kirchmer, M. (eds.) Business Process Excellence—ARIS in Practice, pp. 33–43. Springer, Berlin (2002)
Kagermann, H., Keller, G.: mySAP.com Industry solutions. London/New York (2000)
Kalakota, R., Robinson, M.: E-Business—Roadmap for Success. Peachpit Press, Berkeley and others (1999)
Kalakota, R., Robinson, M.: M-Business—The Race to Mobility. McGraw-Hill, New York (2002)
Kalakota, R., Robinson, M.: Service Blueprint: A Roadmap for Execution. Addison-Wesley, Boston (2003)
Kaplan, R., Norton, D.: The Balanced Scorecard—Translating Strategy into Action. Harvard Business School Press, Boston (1996)
Kirchmer, M.: Market- and product-oriented definition of business processes. In: Elzina, D.J., Gulledge, T.R., Lee, C.-Y. (eds.) Business Engineering, pp. 131–144. Springer, Norwell (1999a)
Kirchmer, M.: Business Process Oriented Implementation of Standard Software—How to Achieve Competitive Advantage Efficiently and Effectively, 2nd edn. Springer, Berlin, New York and others (1999b)
Kirchmer, M.: e-Business process improvement (eBPI): Building and managing collaborative e-Business scenarios. In: Callaos, N., Loutfi, M., Justan, M. (eds.) Proceedings of the 6th World Multiconference on Systemics, Cybernetics and Informatics, vol. VIII, pp. 387–396. Orlando (2002)
Kirchmer, M.: E-business process networks—successful value chains through standards. Journal of Enterprise Management. 17(1), (2004)
Kirchmer, M.: Business Process Governance: Orchestrating the Management of BPM. Whitepaper, Berwyn, PA (2005a)
Kirchmer, M.: ARIS SmartPath—From process design to execution in mid-market organizations. In: Scheer, A.W., Jost, W., Wagner, K. (eds.) Von Prozessmodellen zu lauffaehigen Anwendungen—ARIS in der Praxis, p. 87–98. Berlin (2005b)
Kirchmer, M.: Knowledge communication empowers SOA for business agility. In: The 11th World Multi-Conference on Systemics, Cybernetics and Informatics, July 8–11, 2007, Orlando, Proceedings, vol. III, pp. 301–307. (2007)
Kirchmer, M.: Process innovation through open BPM. In: Pantaleo, D., Pal, N. (eds.) From Strategy to Execution—Turning Accelerated Global Change into Opportunity, pp. 87–105. Springer, Berlin (2008)
Kirchmer, M.: The Process of Process Management: Delivering the value of Business Process Management. Accenture Point of View Document, Philadelphia (2011a)
Kirchmer, M.: Competitive Advantage is an era of Change: 11 Typical situations where Business Process Management delivers Value. Accenture Point of View Document, Philadelphia (2011b)
Kirchmer, M.: Value-driven Design and Implementation of Business Processes—From Strategy to Execution at Pace with Certainty. In: Proceedings of the Fourth International Symposium on Business Modelling and Software Design, Luxembourg, 24–26 June 2014, pp. 297–392

Kirchmer, M.: The Process of Process Management—Mastering the New Normal in a Digital World. In: Business Modeling and Software Development (BMSD) Proceedings, July 2015

Kirchmer, M.: The Discipline of Value-driven Business Process Management. BPM-D Executive Education Documentation (3 Days). Philadelphia (2015)

Kirchmer, M.: Enabling High Performance through Digitalization—The BPM-Discipline as Value-Switch. In: CIO Review, January 14th, 2016

Kirchmer, M., Enginalev, A.: Internationales informationsmanagement—aufbau von informationssystemen im internationalen verbund. In: Zentes, J., Swoboda, B.: Fallstudien zum Internationalen Management, pp. 717–729. Wiesbaden (2000)

Kirchmer, M., Franz, P.: Targeting Value in a Digital World. BPM-D Whitepaper, Philadelphia, London (2014a)

Kirchmer, M., Franz, P.: Chief Process Officer—The Value Scout. BPM-D Whitepaper, Philadelphia/London (2014b)

Kirchmer, M., Franz, P.: The Process of Process Management—Strategy Execution in a Digital World. BPM-D Whitepaper, Philadelphia, London (2015a)

Kirchmer, M., Franz, P.: The Process of Process Management—Strategy Execution in a Digital World. London, Philadelphia (2015b)

Kirchmer, M., Franz, P.: The Process of Process Management—Strategy Execution in a Digital World. In: BPM-D Whitepaper, Philadelphia, USA; London, UK

Kirchmer, M., Scheer, A.W: Change management—key for business process excellence. In: Scheer, A.W., Abolhassan, F., Jost, W., Kirchmer, M. (eds.): Business Process Change Management—ARIS in Practice, pp. 1–14. Springer, Berlin, New York, and others (2003)

Kirchmer, M., Scheer, A.W.: Business process automation—combining best and next practices. In: Scheer, A.W., Abolhassan, F., Jost, W., Kirchmer, M. (eds.) Business Process Automation—ARIS in Practice, pp. 1–15. Springer, Berlin, New York, and others (2004)

Kirchmer, M., Spanyi, A.: Business Process Governance. Whitepaper, 2nd revised edn. Berwyn (2007)

Kirchmer, M.: Strategy Execution in a Consumer Goods Company: Achieving Immediate Benefits while building Lasting Process Capabilities for our Digital World. In: Proceedings of BPM 2016, Rio de Janeiro, Brazil, September 18–22, 2016

Kirchmer, M., Brown, G., Heinzel, H.: Using SCOR and other reference models for e-business process networks. In: Scheer, A.W., Abolhassan, F., Jost, W., Kirchmer, M. (eds.) Business Process Excellence—ARIS in Practice, p. 45–64. Springer, Berlin, New York, and others (2002)

Kirchmer, M., Gutierrez, F., Laengle, S.: Process Mining for Organizational Agility. Industrial Management January/February 2010

Kirchmer, M., Franz, P., Lotterer, A.: The BPM-Discipline—Getting more value out of Six Sigma and Traditional Process Improvement. BPM-D Whitepaper, Philadelphia, London (2015a)

Kirchmer, M., Franz, P., Rosing, M.v.: The Chief Process Officer: An Emerging Tope Management Role. In: Rosing, M.v., Scheer, A.-W., Scheel, H.v.: The complete Business Process Handbook—Body of Knowledge from Process Modeling to BPM, vol. 1, p. 343–348. Amsterdam, Boston, e.a. (2015b)

Kirchmer, M., Franz, P., von Rosing, H.: The Chief Process Officer: An Emerging Tope Management Role. In: von Rosing, M., Scheer, A.-W., von Scheel, H. (eds.) The complete Business Process Handbook—Body of Knowledge from Process Modeling to BPM, vol. 1, p. 343–348. Amsterdam, Boston, e.a. (2015c)

Kraemer, W., Mueller, M.: Virtuelle corporate university—executive education architecture and knowledge management. In: Scheer, A.-W (ed.) Electronic Business und Knowledge Management—Neue Dimensionen fuer den Unternehmenserfolg, pp. 491–525. Heidelberg (1999)

Kraemer, W., Gallenstein, C., Sprendger, P.: Learning management fuer fuehrungskraefte. In: Industrie Management—Zeitschrift fuer industrielle Geschaeftsprozesse, pp. 55–59. (2001)

Lapkin, A.: The seven fatal mistakes of enterprise architecture. In: Gartner Research publication, ID-Number: G00126144, 2/22/2005

Livingstone, M.: Pop Art—A Continuous History. Thames and Hudson, London (2000)

Lochmaier, L.: Management 2.0 und der intelligente Schwarm. In: manager-magazin.de (2007)

Lueg, R., Malinauskaite, L., Marinova, I.: The vital role of business processes for a business model: the case of a startup company. Problems and Perspectives in Management. **12**(4), 213–220 (2014)

Maggin, D.: The Life and Times of John Birks Gillespie. Harper, New York (2004)

Majchrzak, A., Logan, D., McCurdy, R., Kirchmer, M.: Four keys to managing emergence. In: MIT Sloan Management Review, Winter, 47(2), (2006a)

Majchrzak, A., Logan, D., McCurdy, R., Kirchmer, M.: What business leaders can learn from jazz musicians about emergent processes. In: Scheer, A.W., Kruppke, H., Jost, W., Kindermann, H. (eds.) Agility by ARIS Business Process Management. Berlin, New York, and others (2006b)

Matter, E.: Die technische Basis fuer das Internet der Dinge. In: Fleisch, E., Mattern, F. (eds.) Das Internet der Dinge—Ubiquitous Computing und RFID in der Praxis, pp. 39–66. Springer, Heidelberg/Berlin (2005)

McAffee, A.: Enterprise 2.0: The dawn of emergent collaboration. In: MIT Sloan Management Review, 43(3), Spring (2006)

McDonald, M.P.: Digital Strategy Does Not Equal IT Strategy, Harvard Business Review, November 19, 2012

McGovern, J., Ambler, S.W., Stevens, M.E., Linn, J., Sharan, V., Jo, E.K.: A Practical Guide to Enterprise Architecture. Prentice Hall, Upper Saddle River (2004)

McHugh, P., Merli, G., Wheeler, W.: Beyond Business Process Reengineering—Towards the Holistic Enterprise. Chichester, New York (1995)

McKenzie, M.: Images We Love—Popular Art in America. (2003)

Melenowsky, M. J.: Business Process Management as a Discipline. Gartner Research, 08/2006

Microsoft, Inc. (ed.): http://www.microsoft.com/dynamics/default.mspx, (2007)

Microsoft, Inc. (ed.): Your Business—Connected. BizTalk. In: Microsoft.com (2007)

Natalie, N.: Viewing Ascension Health from A Design Thinking Perspective. In: Journal of organization design, 2013.

Newman, D.: BPM & SOA: Real world stories of business success. In: IQPC (ed.) Proceedings of the Business Process Management Summit, Las Vegas, October 2007

Nixon, N.: Viewing Ascension Health from a Design Thinking Perspective. Journal of organization design (2013)

Nolan, T., Goodstein, L., Pfeiffer, J.W.: Plan or die! 10 Keys to Organizational Success. Pfeiffer, San Diego (1993)

O'Reilly, T: What is Web 2.0—Design Patterns and Business Models for the Next Generation of Software. www.oreilly.com (2005)

O'Rourke, C., Fishman, N., Selkow, W.: Enterprise Architecture using the Zachman Framework. Thomson Course Technology, Boston (2003)

Oleson, J.: Pathways to Agility—Mass Customization in Action. Wiley, New York/Chichester (1998)

Oracle, Inc. (ed.): http://www.oracle.com/applications/e-business-suite.html (2007)

Oracle, Inc. (ed.): http://www.oracle.com/applications/jdedwards-enterprise-one.html (2007)

Oracle, Inc. (ed.): Oracle Fusion—Next Generation Applications. oracle.com (2007)

Osterwalder, A., Pigneur, Y.: Business Model Generation _ A Handbook for Visionaries, Game Changer, and Challengers. Hoboken, NJ, 2010.

Osterwalder, A., Pigneur, Y., Bernarda, Greg., Smith, A.: Value Proposition Design. Hoboken, NJ (2014)

Packowski, J., Gall, J., Baumeister, H.: Enterprise Process and Information Governance—Integration of business process and master data governance as competitive advantage—Study Results, Camelot Whitepaper (2014)

Palmer, N.: Case Management in Industry 4.0: ACM and IoT. In: Fisher, L. (ed.) Innovation in Adaptive Case Management—Best Practices for Knowledge Workers, pp. 17–24. Lighthouse Point, FL (2016)

Pantaleo, D., Pal, N.: From Strategy to Execution—Turning Accelerated Global Change into Opportunity. Springer, Berlin (2008)
Pegasystems (ed.): www.pega.com (2007)
PMOLink (ed.): Project Management Processes—Based on the PMBOK Guide. New Orleans (2004)
Porter, M.: What is strategy? Harvard Bus. Rev. (1996)
Porter, M.: Competitive Strategies: Techniques for Analyzing Industries and Competitors. Free Press, New York (1998). Originally published in 1980
Recker, J., Rosemann, M., van der Aalst, W., Jansen-Vullers, M., Drelling, A.: Configurable reference modeling languages. In: Fettke, P., Loos, P. (eds.) Reference Modeling for Business Systems Analysis, pp. 22–46. Hershey, London (2007)
Reilly, B., Hope-Ross, D., Knight, L.: Marketplaces and process mediation—the missing link. In: Gartner Group (ed.): Research Note 19 September 2000. Rummler, G.; Brache, AL: Improving Performance: Managing the White Space on the Organization Chart. Jossey-Bass (1990)
Robinson, M., Kalakota, R.: Offshore Outsourcing—Business Models, ROI and Best Practices. Mivar Press, Alpharetta (2004)
Runyan, G.: Logistics marketplaces: Shaping the evolution of BtoB commerce. In: The Yankee Group (ed.) BtoB Commerce & Applications Report, 5(13), (2000)
Salesforce.com Inc. (ed.): http://www.salesforce.com/products/ (2015)
SAP: Explore the SAP Portfolio. In: http://go.sap.com/solution.html (2016)
SAP AG (ed.): SAP Info—Quick Guide: SAP NetWeaver—The Power of Lower TCO, p. 40. (2003)
SAP AG (ed.): http://wwwll.sap.com/usa/solutions/business-suite/erp/index.epx (2007)
SAP AG (ed.): http://www.sap.com/usa/solutions/sme/index.epx (2007)
SAP AG (ed.): SAP NetWeaver Helps Put You Ahead of the Curve. In: sap.com (2007)
Schaller, J.: Biography. In: http://www.pinkcowstudio.com/about/bio.html (2008)
Scheer, A.W.: Business Process Engineering—Reference Models of Industrial Enterprises, 2nd edn. Springer, Berlin (1994)
Scheer, A.-W.: Business Process Engineering—Reference Models for Industrial Enterprises, 2nd edn. Springer, Berlin, e.a. (1995)
Scheer, A.W.: ARIS—Business Process Frameworks, 2nd edn. Springer, Berlin, New York, and others (1998)
Scheer, A.W. (ed.): Electronic Business und Knowledge Management—Neue Dimensionen fuer den Unternehmenserfolg. Heidelberg (1999)
Scheer, A.W.: Start-Ups Are Easy, But... Berlin, New York (2001)
Scheer, A.W.: Epilog: Jazz improvisation and management. In: Scheer, A.W., Abolhassan, R., Jost, W., Kirchmer, M. (eds.) Business Process Change Management—ARIS in Practice, pp. 270–286. Berlin, New York, and others (2003)
Scheer, A.-W.: Industry 4.0: From Vision to Implementation. Whitepaper Number 5, August-Wilhelm Scheer Institute for Digital Products and Processes, Scheer GMBH, Saarbruecken, Germany, May 2015
Scheer, A.-W.: Industry 4.0—From Vision to Realization. Scheer Whitepaper 5. Saarbruecken, Germany, May 2015
Scheer, A.W., Habermann, R., Koeppen, A.: Electronic business und knowledge management—Neue Dimensionen fuer den Unternehmenserfolg. In: Scheer, A.-W. (ed.) Electronic Business und Knowledge Management—Neue Dimensionen fuer den Unternehmenserfolg, pp. 3–36. Heidelberg (1999)
Scheer, A.W., Abolhassan, R., Jost, W., Kirchmer, M. (ed.): Business Process Excellence—ARIS in Practice. Berlin, New York, and others (2002)
Scheer, A.W., Abolhassan, R., Jost, W., Kirchmer, M. (eds.): Business Process Change Management—ARIS in Practice, p. 1–14. Berlin, New York, and others (2003)
Scheer, A.W., Abolhassan, R., Jost, W., Kirchmer, M. (eds.): Business Process Automation—ARIS in Practice. Springer, Berlin, New York, and others (2004)

Scheer, A.W., Jost, W., Wagner, K.: Von Prozessmodellen zu lauffaehigen Anwendungen—ARIS in der Praxis. Springer, Berlin, Heidelberg (2005)
Scheer, A.W., Kruppke, H., Jost, W., Kindermann, H.: Agility by ARIS Business Process Management. Springer, Berlin, New York, and others (2006)
Scheer, A.W., Jost, W., Guengoez, O.: A reference model for industrial enterprises. In: Fettke, P., Loos, P. (eds.) Reference Modeling for Business Systems Analysis, pp. 167–181. Hershey, London (2007)
Scheruhn, H.-J., Rosing, Mark v., Fallon, R.L.: Information Modelling and Process Modelling. In: Rosing, Mark v., Scheer, A.-W., Scheel, H. v. (eds.) The Complete Business Process Handbook—Body of Knowledge from Process Modelling to BPM, vol. 1. Amsterdam, Boston, e.a. (2015)
See Wikipedia, 3/2016.
See: www.bpm-d.com (2016)
See: www.signavio.com (2016)
Signavio (ed.): The Business Transformation Platform—Signavio Process Editor. In: http://www.signavio.com/products/business-transformation-platform/
Sinur, J.: Knowledge Workers are the Emergent Heroes of the Digital World. In: Fisher, L. (ed.) Innovation in Adaptive Case Management—Best Practices for Knowledge Workers, pp. 25–38. Lighthouse Point, FL (2016)
Sinur, J., Odell, J., Fingar, P.: Business Process Management—The Next Wave. Meghan-Kiffer Press, Tampa (2013)
Snee, R., Hoerl, R.: Leading Six Sigma—A Step-by-Step Guide Based on Experience with GE and Other Six Sigma Companies. Upper Saddle River, New York, e.a. (2003)
Snowden, D.J., Boone, M.E.: A Leader's Framework for Decision Making. In: Harvard Business Review, pp. 69–77. November 2007
Software AG (ed.): http://www.softwareag.com/corporate/products/default.asp (2015)
Spanyi, A.: Business Process Management is a Team Sport—Play it to Win! Meghan-Kiffer, Tampa (2003)
Spanyi, A.: More for Less—The Power of Process Management. Meghan-Kiffer, Tampa (2006)
Spath, D., Baumeister, M., Barrho, T., Dill, C.: Change management im Wandel. In: Industrie Management—Zeitschrift fuer industrielle Geschaeftsprozesse, 4/2001, pp. 9–13
Stolz, H.: Composite Applications Framework—Designing Cross Solutions. In: SAP AG (ed.): SAP Info—Quick Guide: SAP NetWeaver—The Power of Lower TCO, 4/2003, p. 40
Supply Chain Council (ed): Supply Chain Operations Reference Model—Plan, Source, Make, Deliver, Return. Version 8.0, 2007
Swenson, K.D., von Rosing, M.: Phase 4: What is BPM? In: von Rosing, M., Scheer, A.-W., von Scheel, H. (eds.) The complete Business Process Handbook—Body of Knowledge from Process Modeling to BPM, vol. 1, p. 79–88. Amsterdam, Boston, e.a. (2015)
Troupe, Q.: Miles and Me. Berkley (2000)
Value Chain Group (ed.): Business Transformation Framework. In: www.value-chain.org (2007)
Van Belle, J.: Evaluation of selected enterprise reference models. In: Fettke, P., Loos, P. (eds.) Reference Modeling for Business Systems Analysis, p. 266–286. Hershey (1997)
Wahlster, W., Dengel, A.: Web 3.0:Convergence of Web 2.0 and the Semantic Web. In: Technology Radar Feature Paper, Edition 11/2006, Germany June 2006
Wheatland, T.: Jazz in Business. In: http://www.jazzinbusiness.com/engelse%20versie/indexen.htm (2007)
Widener University, School for Business Administration: Business Process Innovation. At: www.widener.edu 5/2007
Wikipedia (ed.): Blog. In: www.wikipedia.org 12/2007
Wikipedia (ed.): Small and Medium Enterprise. In: wikipedia.org 12/2007
Wikipedia (ed.): Web 2.0. In: www.wikipedia.org 12/2007
Wikipedia (ed.): Business Process Execution Language. In: wikipedia.org 12/2007

Bibliography

Wikipedia (ed.): Web 2.0. In: wikipedia.org, 12/2007
Wikipedia (ed.): Innovation. In: Wikipedia.org (2015)
Williams, L.: E-Markets: How BtoB marketplaces are creating a commerce operating system. In: The Yankee Group (ed.) BtoB Commerce & Applications Report, 5(11), (2000a)
Williams, L.: Corporate-sponsored vs. independent BtoB exchanges: who will win? In: The Yankee Group (ed.) BtoB Commerce & Applications Report, 5(12), (2000b)
Woods, Dan: Enterprise Service Architectures. Beijing/Cambridge/Koeln and others (2003a)
Woods, D.: Packaged Composite Applications. O'Reilly, Beijing/Cambridge/Koeln and others (2003b)
Woods, D., Mattern, T.: Enterprise SOA—Designing IT for Business Innovation. O'Reilly, Beijing/Cambridge (2006)
Zentes, J., Swoboda, B.: Fallstudien zum Internationalen Management. Gabler, Wiesbaden (2000)